ZOOS of the World

JAMES FISHER

ZOOS
of the World

The Story of Animals in Captivity

Nature and Science Library

published for

The American Museum of Natural History

by The Natural History Press / Garden City, New York

The Natural History Press, publishers for The
American Museum of Natural History, is a division
of Doubleday & Company, Inc. The Press is
directed by an editorial board made up of
members of the staff of both the Museum and
Doubleday. The Natural History Press has its
editorial offices at The American Museum of
Natural History, Central Park West at 79th Street,
New York, New York 10024, and its business offices
at 501 Franklin Avenue, Garden City, New York.

First published in the United States of America in 1967 by
The Natural History Press, Garden City, New York
in association with Aldus Books Limited
Library of Congress Catalog Card Number 67-14047
© Aldus Books Limited, London, 1967

Printed in Italy by Arnoldo Mondadori, Verona

Contents

page 10   INTRODUCTION

18   1   ANCIENT ZOOS

44   2   MODERN ZOOS

72   3   ZOOS AND BREEDING

108   4   ZOOS AND SURVIVAL

134   5   ZOOS AND ANIMAL SUPPLY

158   6   ZOO ACCOMMODATIONS AND ARCHITECTURE

184   7   ZOO RISKS AND RESEARCH

206   8   PATHS TO ZOO PROGRESS

236   APPENDIX: LIST OF ZOOS AND AQUARIUMS

246   INDEX

252   CREDITS

Introduction

If we leave out most of the small wayside zoos that have sprung up in North America and Europe in recent years, we can say that there are now almost exactly 500 permanent zoos and aquariums scattered throughout the world. In an average year their turnstiles click a third of a billion times. This does not mean that 333 million different people visit a zoo every year, because a great many clicks represent repeat visits by keen zoo-goers and members of zoo societies; but even if we allow for a high proportion of repeat visits these figures indicate that at least a twentieth of the world's entire population goes to a zoo once at least every year.

There cannot be many other institutions with such a colossal box-office appeal, and there are certainly few whose appeal is as universal. If we look at the latest available figures for world zoo attendances (1963) we find that the eight highest "gates" were in seven different countries. The zoo which estimated most visitors that year was the Parque Zoologico de Chapultepec, in México City, with 5,000,000. Next came the Parque Zoologico de Barcelona, Spain, with 4,742,316. Then followed the Ueno Zoological Gardens in Tokyo; the Peking Zoological Garden in China; the Lincoln Park Zoological Gardens in Chicago; the Giza Zoological Garden in Cairo; the National Zoological Park in Washington D.C.; and the Moscow Zoo—all with more than 3,000,000 visitors. Of the remaining twelve zoos in the top twenty, eight were in the United States, two in Germany, and one each in Japan and Cuba. Two other zoos in the United States, one in Argentina, one in India, and one in South Vietnam also had a 2,000,000 gate or more.

Just why do so many people visit zoos? In some parts of Asia and Latin America, it may be partly because there are not a great many rival attractions such as museums, art galleries, theaters, opera houses, and so on. In places it may be partly because the zoo costs so little. Nobody pays to visit the Mexico City Zoo or those of Havana, Bombay, Chicago (Lincoln Park), St. Louis, Kansas City, Detroit, Memphis, San Francisco, New York (Central Park), or Washington, D.C. The Barcelona Zoo is free to all children under the age of seven, the San Diego Zoo to all under 17, and the Peking Zoo to everyone under the height of one meter, or 39.37 inches; and there are scores of other attractive zoos that offer cheap rates of admission for special categories of people, or on special occasions such as public holidays. But cheapness

Zoos—we learn about them when, as children, we are taken by our parents. Later, as parents, we take our children, and find that we ourselves are still fascinated. Modern posters (above) lure millions into zoos every year. But even in the pre-poster era, the citizens of Berlin flocked into their newly opened zoological gardens (right).

The Frankfurt Zoo employs the giant globe (above) to show visitors where the animals on display come from. It also uses the conventional notice boards attached to the front of each cage (below). All are useful educational aids.

and lack of rival attractions go only a little way toward explaining the immense popularity of zoos. The simple fact is that people all over the world deeply love animals and have an immense curiosity about them; and the ordinary citizen, with no specialized knowledge of animals, may see more different species in a single day at the zoo than he could find by searching the globe for several years. What is more, he can usually see them in the delightful surroundings of well-laid-out gardens. More often than not there are guidebooks or signs that tell something about the habits of each species and what part of the world it comes from, so that the visitor can feed his mind as he feasts his eyes. And if he gets tired, as he may well do when he walks around a large zoo on a hot day, there are invariably pleasant snack bars or restaurants where he can find rest and refreshment.

When we consider how little it costs to visit most zoos, all this sounds like excellent value for money. Indeed it is. Yet, however satisfied the average visitor may be with all he sees, the chances are that he witnesses only a small fraction of the whole life of the zoo. He is like a man looking at an iceberg—impressed with the one-ninth that is visible but scarcely aware of the eight-ninths hidden below the surface.

Now it happens that much of my working life, as well as much of my leisure time, has been intimately tied up with zoos, zoology, and zoologists; I have worked for one of the world's finest zoos, the Zoological Society of London's establishment in Regent's Park; I have been commentator for some 80 or 90 television programs about zoos in Britain, Europe, and America; and I am lucky enough to count zoo men in many parts of the world among my close friends. All this has inevitably made me keenly aware of the eight-ninths of the zoo iceberg that the casual visitor fails to see. So this book will be mainly concerned with the work, organization, purpose, and even the fun that are to be found behind the zoo scenes; and because I am a very small part of the zoo world and the zoo world is a very large part of me, my account will occasionally strike a personal note. And because I happen to be Anglo-Scottish I shall often refer to zoos in the United Kingdom for examples and experiences.

Perhaps one of the biggest surprises behind a zoo is the sheer number and variety of jobs that have to be done to keep it working efficiently. The casual visitor normally sees only a handful of the zoo staff—a man at the entrance gate, a few keepers feeding fish to the seals or meat to the lions, a gardener trimming a hedge or weeding a flower bed, waitresses in the restaurant, and perhaps one or two truck drivers. Yet at least 10 big zoos in Asia, America, and Europe have a permanent staff of well over 200 people. If we take 80 typical major zoos, we find that the average permanent staff is 125. What do all these people do? Again taking the average, we find that 20 are administrators, librarians, and scientists, together with their secretaries and assistants; 46 are animal keepers, including overseers and foremen; 30 are engaged in maintenance, transport, and the upkeep of gardens; and the remaining 29 are engaged in feeding the visitors.

The visitor who enters a zoo may not know it, but he, with his throng of fellow-visitors, is directly responsible for seasonal increases in the zoo personnel. Most of the world's zoos are situated outside the tropics and have their biggest influx of visitors in the summer. At that time of year the visitors eat tons more and drink gallons more than all the animals they come to see; and the zoo's catering staff may well rise from 29 to about 100 in a really busy season. In addition the zoo will need to take on perhaps 10 temporary keepers' assistants to help in the children's zoo or pets' corner, and several extra guards or money-takers at the gate.

Zoos also have flower exhibits; their gardens help to make the setting more attractive for visitors and animals alike. Below: A display of tropical bromeliads—two species of *Aechmen*—in the tropical house at the Chester Zoo.

The very titles of members of the senior staff of a zoo give a clue to the immensely varied work being done. In the London Zoo, which is fairly typical of the world's 20 or 30 greatest collections of animals, there were eight senior members of staff on the scientific side in 1962: a Scientific Director, three Curators (one of mammals, one of birds, and one of fishes, reptiles, and invertebrates), a Veterinary Officer, a Pathologist, a Senior Research Fellow, and a Librarian who also acted as clerk of the zoo's publications. On the animal management side there were five Overseers, three Senior Head Keepers, 15 Head Keepers, and a Hospital Superintendent. The senior administrative staff included a Controller, a Chief Accountant, a Private Secretary, an Architect, an Establishments Officer, an Education Officer, a Catering Manager, a Supplies Officer, a Transport Executive, a Head Gardener, a Gardens Executive, a Clerk of Works, and a Head of the General Department. Zoos in other countries have different titles, but roughly the same jobs.

Most of the titles involved on the scientific and animal management side speak for themselves, though they differ from zoo to zoo, but one or two call for some comment. A big zoo needs a hospital, and therefore a hospital superintendent, just as a big community of human beings does, simply because animals do sometimes fall sick, and their lives—even in terms of money—are worth saving. Then the pathologist's job is to study animals when they are dead, to find out what they died of; sometimes, although not always, his findings may help to prevent the premature death of other animals of the same or related species. The Senior Research Fellow, together with other research workers at the zoo or from learned institutions associated with it, is concerned with animal behavior, disease, nutrition, and a host of other problems. Members of the general public know little about these things unless they read the scientific papers published by one or other of the great zoos. Every top zoo has its own scientific publications, and in the Lon-

Veterinary work in zoos is more diverse than anywhere else. It includes finding ways to clip a giraffe's toenails (above right). Here the problem is being tackled at the Toledo, Ohio zoo. Right: Locating a bone fracture in a white-nosed monkey by means of X-ray photographs, in the London Zoo's hospital.

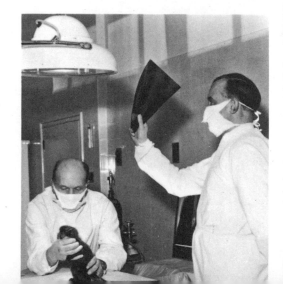

Zoos can play an important role in conserving wild animals by breeding them. The number of African rhinoceroses in the wild is small, and so zoo-born specimens such as this one at the Bristol Zoo are helping the species to survive.

don Zoo, as in many others, the Librarian is a very important member of the publications committee, as well as being in charge of one of the world's most comprehensive zoological libraries.

Occasionally a man may join the animal-management staff of a zoo in some capacity such as an assistant keeper. By sheer aptitude or a kind of green-thumb touch with animals, he may eventually become a curator. But in the great majority of cases, senior members of a zoo's scientific staff have qualified first by zoological or veterinary

Top: The elephant house at Chicago's Brookfield Zoo is specially designed to meet the needs of the elephants, the keepers, and the public. Above: Upkeep of the gardens and paths is a permanent job for a staff of gardeners; the scene here is in the London Zoo.

training at some university and then by years of practical experience with animals. A first-class curator, for example, may be harder to get than a giant panda.

Some of the titles of a zoo's senior administrative staff serve as reminders of the special problems involved in maintaining a large collection of animals. Where creatures as diverse as elephants and hummingbirds, giraffes and snakes, sea lions and parrots all have to be appropriately and comfortably housed, there is an obvious need for an architect and a clerk of works. Where many hundreds of animals and many thousands of people must be fed daily, there is a clear need for specialists in catering, supplies, and transport. Where a zoo covers scores or possibly hundreds of acres of carefully landscaped space, there must be highly skilled gardeners. Where many species of animals are all under the care of a single institution, there are unique opportunities for zoological studies that can only be properly exploited with the help of an experienced education officer.

Other zoo administrators—the Controller, Chief Accountant, Establishments Officer, as the English may call them—do the kinds of work that must be done in any big business enterprise. A big zoo is not only big business, but usually business of a highly complicated kind, having contacts with many lands, many government departments, and a wide range of industries. In one recent year the London Zoo spent about 1½ million dollars, the Moscow Zoo about five million dollars, and the San Diego Zoo about 3¼ million dollars. The average zoo spent about $370,000. A few small private zoos, mostly owned by skilled animal breeders who concentrate on a limited range of animals, manage to run at a profit: but no big general zoo exists anywhere in the world without some form of subsidy. This may come from a national or city government, a charitable institution, wealthy individuals, or any combination of these. No matter how, help must come; gate money often provides a large part of a zoo's income, but never the whole.

This tells us something about the very purpose of zoos. Man began to study animals while he was still living in caves, and he is likely to go on doing so as long as he walks the earth. The essential purpose of a zoo is to provide special opportunities for such study that could not well be provided by any other means. This is commonly considered so important that, once a civilization has reached a certain level of wealth, there is usually some government or ruler, some rich man or institution ready to bear all or part of the cost. To give pleasure and entertainment to the public is an important but secondary aim of zoos. But the fact that people flock to zoos in such vast numbers is clear proof that this aim is understood and achieved.

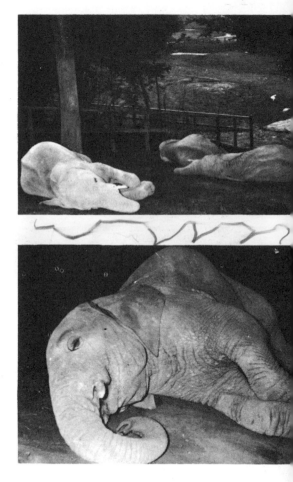

Studies of animals' behavior in captivity have enabled us to discover facts that would otherwise remain unknown. For example, much is now known about the sleeping habits of elephants. They do not sleep soundly on their feet, but lie down for short intervals during the night.

1   Ancient Zoos

A view through the main hall of the cave at Lascaux, France, with one of man's first collections of animals. These paintings were made when man was mainly a hunter, and when a knowledge of wild animals was essential for his survival. Most of the cave paintings of south-western Europe were probably done about 12,000 to 25,000 years ago.

I should like to repeat here a statement made in the Introduction: "Man began to study animals while he was still living in caves, and he is likely to go on doing so as long as he walks the earth. The essential purpose of a zoo is to provide special opportunities for such study that could not well be provided by any other means." That is simply another way of saying that zoology began before zoos and is still the main purpose of zoos.

I have a belief, shared so far by rather few scientists, that people were adequate zoologists about 100,000 years ago. This is because I think that the amazing pictures on the walls of the cave at Lascaux in central France were painted not, as most experts tell us, something like 12,000 to at most 25,000 years ago, but much more like 100,000 years ago.

The animals depicted at Lascaux were painted by people of high talent. The artists were primitive zoologists and no doubt their paintings were highly accurate. And most of the animals as painted could not have existed in that part of France 15,000-25,000 years ago. All the evidence we have from fossils, some of which can be fairly closely dated, indicates that the local fauna of that time consisted of mammoths, woolly rhinoceroses, and a variety of animals that we associate with cold steppe country. It was a time at the close of the last glaciation of the Ice Age, and it was still a period of cold, sub-arctic conditions. The bison painted on the cave walls at Lascaux are wrong for that time, so are the red deer, so is the rhinoceros, and so are the wild horses.

The bison closely resembles the ancient race or species called *Bison priscus*, about which we know a lot from many skulls and other bones that have been fossilized. This animal, with its fine upstanding horns, flourished in a comparatively warm interval between glaciations about 100,000 years ago. The red deer with many-branching antlers, depicted on the walls of Lascaux, are often mistaken for giant deer, or the so-called Irish deer, but they are not. They are red deer belonging to an ancient race of the modern species *Cervus elaphus*, which flourished 100,000 years ago and was notable for its splendid antlers.

One of the finest animal paintings at Lascaux is that of a rhinoceros. This animal, with two horns, is certainly "woolly," or hairy, and all the pundits except the late Professor Zeuner have identified it with the common woolly rhinoceros, a cold-climate animal that did, indeed, live in central France 15,000 years ago and for a

The Lascaux rhinoceros (above) is a variety that is extinct today. It may be the woolly rhinoceros. But some scholars believe that the animal depicted is a Merck's rhinoceros, which died out about 90,000 years ago. A living form closely related to Merck's rhinoceros is the Sumatran rhino (left), now in danger of extinction. The specimen illustrated here is in the zoo at Copenhagen, Denmark.

long time afterwards. But in Zeuner's opinion, and in mine, it is not. It has a completely different figure from the woolly rhinoceros. Zeuner believed it to be an extinct animal called Merck's rhinoceros, which belonged to the same genus as the very rare Sumatran rhinoceros of today. Fossil records show that Merck's rhinoceros probably became extinct not less than 90,000 years ago and that it last existed in considerable numbers in the warm period of 100,000 years ago. It was a woodland species, and not an open-country animal like the woolly rhinoceros.

The horses pictured at Lascaux are wild horses, and there are two races that they could have belonged to. One of these is represented by a relict animal still living today—Przewalski's wild horse, which is a cold-country, open-plains animal. The other possible race is a wild horse called the tarpan, or forest horse. This had a more slender figure than Przewalski's wild horse and different coloring, including a dark line along its back. There seems to me no question but that the Lascaux paintings are of these tarpans; and such forest horses are much more likely to have flourished in central France in the warm period of 100,000 years ago than in the boreal (cool-weather) conditions of 15,000 years ago.

Incidentally, it is interesting that no mammoths are pictured at Lascaux, even though there were certainly some in the area 15,000 years ago. Further, none of the animals shown belongs exclusively to a cold-country

Przewalski's horses are very rare in the wild today. Their last natural home is in the cold grasslands on the border between Mongolia and China. This species survives, however, in several zoos, such as the one at Prague (top). Once, Przewalski's horses roamed the plains of Europe. Another species, the tarpan, lived in its forests. The painting of horses at Lascaux (above) is probably of tarpans.

fauna. There are wolves, it is true, but wolves are not necessarily boreal. There were, and still are today, wolves that lived in comparatively warm woodland regions.

The Beginnings of Domestication

All the evidence of Lascaux, then, leads me to believe that people were taking practical interest in field zoology 100,000 years ago. Indeed, I should not be surprised to discover that they had already made some attempt to domesticate certain animals by then. But I must emphasize that this cannot be proved. There is no certain fossil evidence that people kept wolves as pets 100,000 years ago, although there is every reason to believe that they could have done so.

What we do know beyond all doubt is that domestication began in Paleolithic (Old Stone Age) times, was going quite well in Mesolithic (Middle Stone Age) times, and was flourishing in Neolithic (New Stone Age) times. However, the Paleolithic period spans an immense number of years, and the question is: when, in Paleolithic times, did domestication begin? Archaeologists have found what they believe to be fossilized dog dung in human habitations belonging to the Gravettian culture in Europe. This culture may have begun 60,000 years ago or even earlier, and seems to have continued for at least 25,000 years; and it was the first culture in which we can be sure that the bow and arrow were used. So there are signs that dogs were inmates of human camps between 35,000 and 60,000 years ago.

By Mesolithic times dogs were certainly becoming established as domesticated animals. In fossils found in a bog at Senckenberg, near Frankfurt-am-Main, there are aurochs (ancestral wild ox) bones that were clearly gnawed by domestic dogs that lived about 9000 B.C. The complete skeleton of a dog has also been found in a human camp of perhaps 7500 to 8000 B.C. And in Denmark there is clear evidence that people of the Maglemosian culture had two kinds of domestic dogs between 6500 and 8000 years ago; so by that time there were even distinct breeds of dogs.

There seems little doubt that the dog was the first animal to be domesticated, and indeed its psychology adapted it particularly well to the process. When you capture the puppies of wolves or jackals—and the dogs we know today may be descended from either or a mixture of both—you become a kind of substitute parent to them. They become "imprinted" on you, and treat you as they would treat a leading member of their own clan. All the submissive gestures that they would normally make to the leader of their pack are transferred to you, a human leader. So from wolves and jackals the dog was doubtless domesticated, separately and independently,

A painting from the Tassili region of the Sahara, in southeast Algeria. In this once-fertile land of several thousand years ago lived a population of pastoralists who also hunted. They had domesticated the dog for use in hunting.

by many tribes of the Old Stone Age, Middle Stone Age, and New Stone Age, without much difficulty.

The next successful attempts at domestication almost certainly came a good deal later, and it is less easy to identify the animals concerned. However, geese must have been among the earliest, if only because they are easily caught. Between late July and early September most adult waterfowl in the northern hemisphere molt their primary wing feathers almost simultaneously and become flightless. This molt coincides with the running of their goslings or ducklings, so that when the young become full-winged during the same week, they can all start flying together. During the brief earth-bound period the birds are easy to catch, so once Stone Age hunters reached the stage of making semi-permanent camps they could easily domesticate geese. They could keep the stock going by taking eggs from wild birds' nests and putting them under the tame birds. That way they would get an extra brood, so that they could kill off a few tame birds from time to time without risk of wiping out the whole stock.

If we try to analyze why people began to domesticate animals, we are forced to conclude that there was no single motive, but several. Consider a human family of the Stone Age, having a little surplus of food and generally enjoying life. The children might bring home a wolf puppy, just because they were curious about it or amused by it. It caused no particular trouble to the adults and they probably found it every bit as interesting as the children did—and so, without thinking much about it, fell into the habit of treating it as a member of the family. They soon found that it was useful. It could be trained to obey orders and help with the hunt; it could move faster than any human and help chase swift game animals such as deer into traps or pitfalls; and it was an excellent guard for the encampment. In a case of this sort, the practical advantages of keeping a pup were discovered only after it had been kept for a time; the initial reason for keeping it was plain curiosity.

With geese the chain of circumstances was doubtless similar. Stone Age people probably liked to have geese around simply because geese are nice birds. (If we like them—as many of us do—there is no reason why early men should not have liked them too, for human emotional judgments about animals are extraordinarily persistent.) When ancient people first caught flightless geese, they mostly ate them, of course; but they also kept a few alive near the encampment. This was partly to see if it would prove easier to rear their own geese than to keep catching wild ones, and partly because it was pleasant to have geese nearby. Here the motives were affection and utility, and there was no real conflict be-

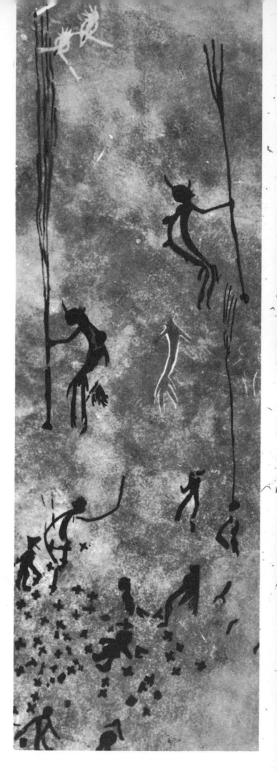

Another rock painting from the Sahara, found at Sefar in the Tassili region, shows hunters carrying trident-like spears, possibly used in catching live birds. Certain species, such as geese, would have been fairly easy to catch and domesticate.

The ancient Egyptians had domesticated the greylag goose. They probably took nestlings, hand-reared and fattened them, and built up a domestic breeding stock. Note the white geese in the lower flock, a variety that the Egyptians valued highly.

Macedonian coin of the fifth century B.C., showing a goose and its egg.

tween them. We still eat many of the animals we like, and are quite content to like both pigs and pork, cattle and beef, sheep and mutton.

Keeping Animals Out of Curiosity

Curiosity and affection doubtless played a part in the domestication of dogs and geese, then; but such feelings were inextricably mixed with the desire for some kind of advantage. Human societies could only begin to assemble anything resembling a zoo when they ceased to be nomadic and had won wealth enough and leisure enough to indulge their curiosity about animals without thought of material reward. Thus we find zoos in existence as soon as we find peoples with cities, kings, and wealth.

Perhaps the first name that springs to mind when thinking of early zoologists is that of King Solomon, a byword for both wisdom and wealth, who ruled from about 974 to 937 B.C. He was, as the Bible tells us, a stock farmer of substance, with great herds of beef cattle and sheep, parks of deer, and fatted fowl. He collected horses from many countries, particularly Egypt, and he had "four thousand stalls for horses and chariots." But more than this, he traded supplies of zoo animals with King Hiram of Tyre: "Once in three years came the navy of Tharshish, bringing gold, and silver, ivory, and apes, and peacocks." Most modern zoologists believe that Solomon's *sukeyim* were indeed peacocks, or possibly guineafowl; but a few feel that the word should be translated as parrots; if they are right, Solomon *may* have been the first man in "Western" culture to show the African gray parrot in his zoo.

Yet zoos, mingled with what we might call the sophisticated domestication of animals, go back many centuries before the time of Solomon. For instance, pigeons (which are not as easily caught as geese) seem to have been domesticated by the civilization of Arpachiya (in what is modern Iraq) around 4500 B.C. The chicken was domesticated by some of the early civilizations of India, like those of Mohenjo-Daro and Harappa, where archaeologists have unearthed figurines of cocks and hens dating from between 3300 and 2500 B.C.

Few early experiments with animals could have been more sophisticated than those which led to the semi-domestication of the elephant; yet these appear to have been successfully carried out in India toward the final flowering of the Mohenjo-Daro civilization, around 2500 B.C. This may seem surprisingly early, but we have to remember that the Mohenjo-Daro of 4,500 years ago was a city-state with a rich governing class. Kings and nobles had the wealth, leisure, and inclination to experiment, and they had no difficulty in recruiting the large staffs needed to work on the semi-domestication and zoo culture of animals.

The earliest known example of true zoo management is to be found in a similar social setting and at about the same time—among the kings of Old-Kingdom Egypt, who ruled from about 2800 to 2250 B.C. The Egyptians of this period did not succeed in domesticating all the animals they experimented with, but they tried almost every one they could catch. Perhaps "domesticate" is

Above: Cattle were brought by slaves for inspection, as we know from the murals of an Egyptian tomb at Thebes, painted about 1400 B.C. Two breeds are shown—a short-horned breed (top panel) and a lyre-horned breed (lower panel). Both developed from the aurochs, or wild ox, *Bos primigenius*.

misleading; "acclimatization" is a better word to describe what they sought to do with many local and exotic mammals and birds. These ancient Egyptians tried to acclimatize hyenas, monkeys, many species of antelope, and at least one species of mongoose.

Fortunately, archaeologists have found at Sakkarah marvelous pictures and written records of the animal acclimatizations of around 2500 B.C. One tomb-picture shows several kinds of antelopes wearing collars, which means that they had either been bred in captivity or kept from an early age as tame animals. We find the addax (a largish antelope with long spiral horns); the ibex (wild goat); two different species of gazelles; and the oryx. There is evidence that these were captured with the help of stockades and lassos. The oryx, a rather large antelope with tall, straight, sharp horns seems to be of the Arabian species. The total world population of this animal is now less than a hundred; and it may be saved from extinction only by the skilled work of zoo keepers in Arabia and Arizona, where small captive breeding herds have been established. It is strange to think that the ancient Egyptians may well have kept in captivity far more of these animals than there now are in the entire world.

Another Egyptian potentate whose meticulous zoo records were found at Sakkarah had 5,358 cattle of at least three different breeds, 1,308 oryxes (perhaps of more than one species), 1,135 gazelles, and 1,244 other antelopes. This means that his zoo or experimental farm, or whatever we care to call it, had more individual animals than any zoo in the twentieth century.

Egyptian rulers of later centuries made many new experiments in animal acclimatization. Thutmose III, who ruled in the fifteenth century B.C., introduced into his temple garden at Karnak new plants, birds, and

Below, far left: Pigeon figurines from Mohenjo-Daro, Indus Valley. Pigeons probably had no economic importance to these people of about 2500 B.C. The birds may have been sacred or merely ornamental. Elephants and bulls were also domesticated at Mohenjo-Daro (below, left and center). As their harness indicates, they were put to work. But the rhinoceros (right) has never been tamed.

mammals from Syria. At about this time we also learn of the acclimatization of lynxes, hares, and wild cats in Egypt. Hatshepsut, stepmother of Thutmose III, was so interested in zoology that she sent collecting expeditions as far afield as "The Land of Punt," most likely what is now called Somaliland. The five-ship expedition to Punt brought back monkeys, greyhounds, leopards (or cheetahs), hundreds of very tall cattle, many species of birds, and—no doubt to the great wonder of Egypt—a giraffe. All these were consigned to the Queen's palace zoo, which must have been very like a modern zoo, except that it housed a larger share of domesticated animals than most zoos of today. Giraffes later became quite fashionable with Egyptian royalty. Around 1250 B.C. Ramesses II had several in his collection, as well as a number of lions and ostriches.

This giraffe, memorialized on the temple of Queen Hatshepsut at Thebes, was probably the first ever seen in Egypt. This queen sponsored a collecting expedition, which brought the giraffe together with a variety of other African animals, including cheetahs.

Many animals reached the Egyptian rulers in the form of tribute. Below: A record of the tribute paid to Ramesses II, who ruled about 1250 B.C., by the Nubians whom he had conquered. Antelopes, monkeys, oxen, cheetahs, a giraffe, and leopard-skins can be seen.

We have seen that the curiosity of the ruling classes inspired the beginnings of zoos in India and Egypt and that they became advanced over 1000 years before Christ. In China, too, the royalty of that age were building up collections of animals, although there we cannot date events as accurately as we can in Egypt. However, we know that the Chinese Empress Tanki, who probably lived about a century after Ramesses II, built a great "house of deer" in marble; and the Emperor Wen Wang, who seems to have reigned before 1000 B.C., established a zoological garden of 1,500 acres, which he named the Ling-Yu, or "Garden of Intelligence." There he exhibited animals collected from all parts of his quite extensive empire. We have no details about the collection except that it included at least three species of deer, a great number of fishes, and "white birds with dazzling plumes." No matter how good or bad a zoo the Ling-Yu may have been, it was certainly an extensive one; and it existed at least 800 years before the Chinese built the Great Wall.

Wen Wang's "Garden of Intelligence" brings us almost up to the time of King Solomon, the great farmer-zoologist of the Old Testament. By then the zoo idea was operating in many of the royal courts of Asia and the Near East. By then, too, the art of writing and keeping records was becoming more widespread; and around many a royal palace there grew up great complexes of temples, libraries, schools, zoological and botanical gardens, and even museums. All kinds of knowledge, including knowledge of animals, could thus be more freely interchanged and handed on to posterity than ever before. Huntsmen, field observers, collectors, breeders, and animal fanciers of every description were all able to add something to the growing body of zoological knowledge.

And what an array of such people we know of between 1000 and 400 B.C. The records that archaeologists have found deal mainly with royalty and nobility, but even within that limited sphere the list is impressive. Semiramis, the almost legendary courtesan of the Assyrian court of the ninth century B.C., was a leopard-fancier. Her son, Ninus, was a lion-fancier. Ashurbanipal, the last important king of Assyria, who died about 625 B.C., inherited a zoological garden and was an expert on lions and camels. Nebuchadnezzar, King of Babylonia in the sixth century B.C., was another lion-fancier.

The Growth of Greek Zoos

Many monarchs and nobles of those times kept animals as part of a general display of pomp and power. Some—especially in Asia Minor—even began to stage animal fights in arenas. But among the ancient Greeks a more studious, inquiring attitude toward animals was developing. From the seventh century B.C. onward the Greeks

Above: Two hares and a gazelle being brought alive into Thebes, perhaps for exhibition in the temple garden of Thutmose III, or perhaps just for eating. Below: Later, in the seventh century B.C., King Ashurbanipal of Assyria caught wild lions (below), then released them to hunt and kill for sport.

began to import and keep tame monkeys. In the following century they experimented with captive francolins (a kind of partridge), acclimatized cranes and purple gallinules, and introduced domestic cats from Africa.

In the fifth century B.C. we find the Greeks with domesticated Egyptian geese and African guineafowl, pigeons, chickens, ducks, and the spectacular Indian peafowl. The last-named proved so popular that the public came from miles around to see them. Not only that, they even paid for the privilege—the earliest instance of zoo gate-money I know of. Also around this time Greek aviaries were showing sparrows, finches, nightingales, blackbirds, jackdaws, crows, magpies, starlings, pheasants, quails, and even hoopoes and flamingos.

There is good reason to believe that by the beginning of the fourth century B.C., if not earlier, a worthwhile collection of animals was to be found in any Greek city-state; and that young intellectuals at the schools were taken around the zoo as part of their general education. This was the atmosphere in which Aristotle (384-322 B.C.) was brought up. Behind him lay the accumulated observations of some 20 generations of animal-lovers throughout the known world; all around him zoology was taken more seriously, probably, than it had ever been taken by any other human society. He was himself a man of towering intelligence and excellent powers of observation; and he was to produce the world's first great encyclopedia of zoology—his *History of Animals*. In it he described about 300 species of vertebrates well enough for modern scholars to identify them. That is about as many species as the average modern zoo contains.

The cat was domesticated by about 1500 B.C. in Egypt, where it gradually became a sacred animal. From Egypt it was brought to Greece. The marble relief (above), found near Athens and dated about 480 B.C., shows men trying to start the age-old quarrel between dog and cat.

Domestic fowl entered Greece from eastern lands, where the cock was regarded as a symbol of health and vigor. This attitude prevailed in Greece and was illustrated on this fifth century B.C. mixing bowl from Athens. Fowl were also kept for food and for cock-fighting.

Nobody can explain away a great man's greatness, nor would one wish to do so: but Aristotle's achievement certainly owed much to the society in which he lived. The Greeks were the first such to accept the desirability of knowledge for its own sake. They were the inventors of philosophy, which means the love of wisdom, and those who love wisdom are ready to share information. That was the very keynote of Greek education. It was the style of the times for one scholar to visit another: upon every visit the resident master gathered his patrons and pupils together and arranged a series of disputations and symposia (the social equivalents of the intellectual cocktail parties of our age). The pupils and privileged people, young and old, gathered around to listen to the words of wisdom while the scholars argued—not just to score debating points, but in a genuine attempt to arrive at the truth.

As a pupil of the great philosopher Plato, Aristotle must have been present at many, many such discussions. In the course of them he was doubtless introduced to almost every aspect of zoology. He also had access to the largest and best libraries the world had yet known. And he was probably the last wise man who, with the help of libraries and many assistant scholars, could embrace what was then the sum total of Western wisdom in the cells of one brain. Whatever anybody knew, he knew. Perhaps even more important, he had the skill and industry to marshal his information and to put it down in writing for the benefit of others.

Aristotle was unquestionably a brilliant pupil and he later became a brilliant teacher. Whether he himself kept a collection of living animals is not certain; but he must have had access to zoos, and he was clearly able to inspire his pupils with his own intense interest in zoology. His most famous pupil was Alexander the Great, who never forgot his old tutor. When Alexander set out on his great eastern campaign, he took collectors with him and sent back information, specimens, and living animals to the master scholar in Greece.

Household pet monkeys or apes were already quite common in Greece in Aristotle's time. Alexander's expeditions now brought back some queer new ones from India. Nobody knows exactly what species they were, but some people suspect that one may have been an orangutan. Talking parrots were known to the Greeks about 17 years before Aristotle was born, from the report of a Greek traveler in Persia. And in 323 B.C., Nearchus, Alexander's lieutenant, brought back from India at least one, and probably two, species of parakeets. Aristotle may not have lived to see them when they reached Greece, for he died in 322 B.C. Alexander himself had died a year earlier.

Part of a Roman mosaic from Pompeii, showing an Indian ring-necked parakeet (which can be identified by its upturned tail feathers and the red ring around its neck) sitting at a bird-bath, and watched by a domestic cat. This mosaic has been transferred to the National Museum, Naples.

The Great Parade

The ancient Greeks reveal a real change in the motives of zoo culture. The earlier potentates of Egypt and Asia had kept animals for royal show first, royal study second: the Greeks kept them for study and experiment first, for show second. After the deaths of Alexander and Aristotle the zoos of the Mediterranean world seem to have reverted quite quickly to "show business" again. But the motive of study still remained and many new species became available for observation.

In the year of his death, Alexander established one of his generals as King Ptolemy I of Egypt, and in the same year the city of Alexandria was founded. It was soon to become the world's greatest center of learning, and the site of the greatest zoo the world had yet known. We know that Ptolemy I founded the zoo, and we know that Seleucus I—another of Alexander's generals, who had become master of a Near East empire—presented him with a Bactrian (two-humped) camel. But it was Ptolemy II, the successor of Ptolemy I, who made the zoo of Alexandria a wonder of the world.

We know little about what the actual zoo was like, for its royal proprietor did not publish a formal annual report of the sort that modern zoos publish. We can only judge what went on in the Ptolemaic zoo by the accounts of great ceremonies when the animals were put on parade. Early in his reign, which began in 285 B.C., Ptolemy II staged an enormous procession on the Feast of Dionysus, and according to the accounts it took all day to pass the city stadium in Alexandria.

Even if there had been no mammals on display, the birds would have presented a spectacular enough sight, for they included eight pairs of ostriches in harness. There were also men carrying cages with parrots and peacocks, guineafowl and pheasants, and what history calls "Ethiopian birds." Since the fauna of Africa probably had some 1,300 different species of birds then, as it does today, we shall never know precisely what these Ethiopian birds were. In addition, the procession included 150 men who carried "trees to which were attached wild animals and birds of all sorts."

The parade of mammals was fantastic. The elephants alone numbered 96, and they drew 24 chariots—four elephants to each chariot. At this period both African and Indian elephants were available, but those in the parade were probably Indian. They may well have been a gift from Seleucus I, for we know he had a great number of them since he once traded some territory to an Indian king in exchange for 500 Indian elephants. Yet the Ptolemies may have done their own elephant-hunting, because it is possible, though not certain, that a race of

The first great animal procession of antiquity was that of Ptolemy II on the feast of Dionysus (see text). Above: Part of a second century B.C. mosaic from Tunisia, showing another Dionysian procession with animals. The mosaic is now in the Museum of Antiquities at El-Djem.

Above: A more modern animal parade. This American poster, advertising Barnum and Bailey's Circus, was printed in the early 1870s. Below: A third century B.C. silver coin, showing four Indian elephants pulling a chariot. It is from the reign of Seleucus I, of Syria.

Indian elephants still survived in Syria as late as 275 B.C.

But for the fact that archaeologists have often established the truthfulness of Egyptian catalogs of goods and chattels, the accounts of that long-ago parade through the streets of Alexandria would sound like a fairy tale. There were 60 pairs of he-goats, each drawing a chariot; there were seven pairs of wild asses in harness; there were 2,400 hounds, 200 Arabian sheep, 100 Ethiopian sheep, 20 Euboean sheep, seven pairs of oryxes, 26 white Indian oxen, and eight Ethiopian oxen. The Indian oxen were probably zebus, a domesticated breed of cattle introduced to the Mediterranean area about two centuries earlier; the Ethiopian oxen may well have descended from a breed that Queen Hatshepsut brought to Egypt over a thousand years before.

The people of Alexandria with a taste for "more exciting" animals were not disappointed. The procession included 24 lions, 14 leopards, 16 "pantheroi" (probably cheetahs), six pairs of one-humped camels, a "white bear," a giraffe, a gigantic snake said to be 45 feet long (most likely a python of something over 30 feet), and, wonder of wonders, a rhinoceros.

Some of these animals must have been novelties to even the most ardent zoo-goers of the time. Lions were nothing new, and indeed they may still have lived wild in parts of Egypt; and cheetahs had been seen in captivity before, though perhaps not long before. But one-humped camels were certainly new, and Ptolemy II may have been the first to introduce them into Egypt. They had, of course, been domesticated for at least 1,000 years in Mesopotamia. The giraffe, too, was a novelty, for it is doubtful whether any other had been seen in Egypt since the time of Ramesses II, ten centuries earlier. We hear of no more giraffes being kept in captivity until the time of Julius Caesar.

The "white bear" was probably not quite the zoological novelty it sounds, since we cannot possibly imagine it to have been a polar bear; more likely it was one of the Syrian race of brown bears, well-known to be more lightly colored than any other race of European and Asiatic brown bears. The rhinoceros was doubtless an African black rhino. Even today this animal is found in the Sudan, and in those days it may well have lived in southern Egypt. Nevertheless, we can only marvel that the people of Ptolemaic times had the necessary technique to capture and transport so bulky and formidable a creature; for we know that almost the only aids to animal transport were sailing vessels, trained elephants, and hand-operated machines such as pulleys and capstans.

The modern value of Ptolemy's collection of animals would be about $280,000, and it probably included more individual animals than any zoo now in existence. In Alexandria, Greek civilization somehow merged with Egyptian tradition; and Greek scholarship, combined with the native Egyptian genius for acclimatizing spectacular animals, gave rise to what must have been the greatest zoo the world had yet known.

Aviary and Arena

When the Ptolemaic zoo was in its heyday, Rome was emerging as a great civilization; the first exotic animals were already being received there as spectacles, and the arena shows were already beginning. The earliest Roman zoos concentrated first on whatever animals were biggest, strangest, and most exciting; but it was not long before they also became interested in the smaller species, a taste they acquired largely from the Greeks. From then on, zoology in Rome moved forward on two quite different levels, culminating on the one hand in excellent private zoos and aviaries, and on the other hand in the bloody spectacles of the Roman arena. Although the two aspects are here dealt with separately, it should be remembered that they existed at the same time, and often only a very short distance apart.

Probably by the second century B.C., and certainly by the first, many wealthy Romans had established small

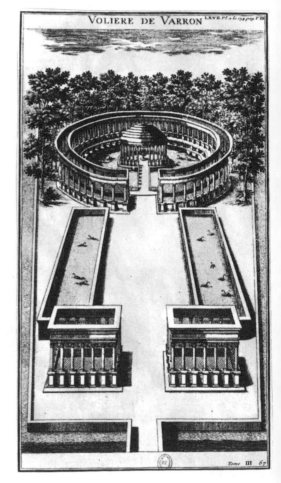

Two nineteenth-century artists' conceptions of Varro's aviary at Monte Cassino, Italy, where it stood during the first century B.C. It had high walls and a roof of netting; the domed pavilion was a dining hall from which guests could watch the birds. The differences in the two drawings are due to the fact that these artists reconstructed the aviary's appearance from details in Varro's diaries.

private zoos in the grounds of their country villas. One of the best was at Casinum (now Monte Cassino) and it belonged to Marcus Terentius Varro, who lived from 116 to 27 B.C. He is the first identifiable person who resembles a Jean Delacour or a Peter Scott of today—at once a scholar and an enthusiast of zoology.

Varro specialized in birds, but he was no sentimentalist about them. Indeed, he was a great poultry farmer, and kept many breeds of chickens, geese, and ducks on a commercial scale. Like most of his friends, he fattened a variety of other birds for the table, including cranes, thrushes, blackbirds, and ortolans. He also kept pigeons, partly for their decorative value, partly for the table, and partly for use as carriers. (The Romans were very fond of keeping pigeons—some estates had lofts or dovecotes with as many as 5,000 birds—and they were among the earliest peoples to use them for pigeon post.) But some of Varro's birds were far more out of the ordinary. They included guineafowl, peafowl—and starlings that had been taught to talk. According to Varro, they talked in Greek as well as Latin—fine scholars, indeed.

In the grounds of his villa Varro built an aviary with one flight cage given entirely to song birds, particularly blackbirds and nightingales. As far as I know, he left no plan or picture of this aviary; but his accounts of it are so detailed that it is possible to make a reliable reconstruction of it, although interpretations differ as to its details. One of the aviaries in the Rome zoo today looks rather like it, although I am not sure whether this is by contrivance or by coincidence.

Varro apparently kept up correspondence and friendship with almost every other man who had a private zoo in Italy at the time. Being a good diarist, he made careful notes of what other people kept, what new acclimatizations they made, what breeding successes they had, and so on. His diaries are as full of fascinating gossip as are the journals of modern avicultural societies; much of the gossip is about his friend Lucius Licinius Lucullus.

Lucullus, a few years younger than Varro, was a poet and an epicure who had a country place at Tusculum, near Rome. Being an epicure, he kept birds partly for the enjoyment of them alive and partly for the enjoyment of them at his table. In those days many Romans were fond of fattening and eating little birds, especially larks and buntings. Lucullus did it more elegantly than most because he had a big dining room that was also an indoor aviary. The birds were allowed to fly about as a pretty sight at meal times, and later some—even the most colorful ones—were eaten. Several modern zoos have claimed the invention of the world's first indoor "walk-through aviary." In fact we may have to go at least as far back as Lucullus for that.

Above: Painting of a blackbird from Pompeii. Blackbirds were often kept in aviaries because of their fine qualities both as songsters and on the dinner table. Below: Thrushes hanging prior to plucking and cooking for a wealthy Roman's banquet.

Part of a lithograph made as a copy of a Roman wall painting. The original painting was in Livia's garden room at Prima Porta, nine miles from Rome. All four walls of this room were decorated with 69 species of birds and a variety of botanical specimens.

At the time of Varro and Lucullus other forward-looking zoo ideas were also taking shape. One was the open-zoo idea, a foreshadowing of modern zoos like that at Whipsnade Park or Woburn in England, Askaniya-Nova in the Ukraine, or the Hagenbeck or Hellabrunn parks in Germany. By Varro's time there were already parks enclosed not as hunting areas but as places where animals were simply kept and observed. And on Varro's own estate there were semi-wild boars and roe, which used to come at the sound of a horn at feeding time.

What we may call the zoological-and-agricultural school of thought continued in Rome for several centuries. Its finest exponent was Pliny the Elder, who was killed in the eruption that buried Pompeii in A.D. 79. He was certainly the greatest recording naturalist since

Aristotle, and two years before his death produced a book of natural history that to this day remains outstanding.

A short while ago I was visiting Pompeii, in Campanian Italy, where I was very interested in the bedroom of a house excavated some ten or fifteen years before. The walls are covered with portraits of a fantastic variety of birds, and the artist who painted them was clearly an ornithologist of the highest caliber. The portraits are so

Above: A mosaic found in a Roman villa near Bône, in Algeria, shows a hunt in the African bush. The object was not to kill the animals, but to force them into nets where they were caught alive, caged, and sent to Rome for the games.
Right: A terracotta shows the scene in the arena at Rome, with a combat between gladiators and lions.

37

exquisitely executed that I am inclined to believe that the house may have been the headquarters of the Campanian ornithological or zoological society. If so, I should think that Pliny, as commander of the fleet at nearby Misenum, was probably the society's president. That room, with its tenderly executed bird paintings, shows that a scholarly and humane attitude to zoology persisted in Italy at least into the first century A.D. Yet just down the road from it was an arena, where bloody shows were going on at the same time. Pliny and his friends must have shared a general knowledge of animals seldom to be equalled and never surpassed until the Renaissance. Yet the majority of Roman emperors and citizens were arena-mad.

If we define menageries as zoos with no detectable scientific purpose, then there were Roman menageries at least as far back as the third century B.C. The first big arena shows were of elephants—usually elephants captured in battle and shown as trophies of victory. By the following century the shows began to center around the *venatio*, the hunting of animals turned into the arena-ring with their hunters. The *aediles*—or officials of the year— used to feel that they could make themselves popular by staging increasingly fantastic shows. Bulls were fought by men (gladiators), and fought other animals; elephants were trained to fight each other; lions and bears also had to do their share of fighting. In 186 B.C. *venationes* of lions and "panthers" (which presumably means either cheetahs or leopards or both) were held as part of a victory celebration. By about 60 B.C. the taste for blood in the arena was such that it became the fashion to put army deserters to the beasts. There were as yet no Christians to fill the role.

It was in this atmosphere that Octavian, soon to be Caesar Augustus, returned to Rome in 29 B.C., shortly after defeating the forces of Anthony and Cleopatra. Caesar Augustus was to build up a zoo perhaps even bigger than that of Ptolemy II, but his purpose was very different from the King of Egypt's. Augustus seems to have tried to see just how many big animals he could lay his hands on for the Roman games. During his rule, which lasted until A.D. 14, he held no fewer than 26 separate *venationes* of "African beasts," and from all accounts about 3,500 animals were killed in the arena. In the first *venatio* he staged, in 29 B.C., hippos and rhinos were killed, along with lions and leopards. In the winter of 20-19 B.C. he received a present of tigers from India, probably the first ever to be seen in Rome: and even these went into the games. In 11 B.C., 600 African beasts were slaughtered on the occasion of the dedication of the Theater of Marcellus. Nine years later 260 lions were killed in the arena and 36 crocodiles in a pool.

Yet in spite of all this wanton slaughter, there was probably still a lively interest in genuine zoology among

Above: A fragment of a white marble slab found at Narbonne, in southern France. It shows a scene from the animal games in the Narbonne amphitheater, in the first century A.D. It is not known whether the bears were trained performers or wild bears in deadly combat with men.

some of the keepers at the zoo of Caesar Augustus. Not all the animals were kept for arena shows, and indeed some of them would scarcely have been suitable. Apart from many small animals, his collection is known to have contained at one time or another huge river tortoises, large snakes—probably including hamadryad cobras and pythons—and a big partridge-like bird that may have been a bustard.

After the time of Caesar Augustus the Imperial zoos of Rome continued to be very big: they had to be, in order to meet the insatiable demands of the arena. They evolved toward mere annexes of the slaughterhouse, until no animal was safe. The climax came when some of the Roman emperors either began to think of themselves as gods or to be told by their friends that they were in fact gods. As gods the emperors came to regard animals as little more than disposable sacrifices. Caligula, who ruled for a mercifully short period, from A.D. 37 to 41, held an inaugural *venatio* of 400 bears and 400 African beasts; he also caused guineafowl, flamingos, peacocks, capercaillie, and pheasants to be sacrificed to his god-head. Claudius, his successor, staged fights between bull and bear, tiger and lion, elephant and African dwarf. In Nero's reign men in boats fought against seals. A century and a half after Nero's time the monstrous Emperor Heliogabalus himself ate flamingo tongues and parrots' brains, served 600 ostrich heads at a banquet, and fed parrots and pheasants to his arena lions.

It would be tedious to continue the story of atrocities

By the early sixth century A.D., the *venatio* had become a sport in Constantinople. The diptych (left) shows the Emperor Anastasius I and, below him, bear-games with vaulting poles and swinging baskets. Above: Mosaic, also from this period, at Constantinople.

any further; but the sorry fact is that it went on and on, with only a few short breaks, almost until the fall of the Roman Empire. The worst of it is that arenas were not confined to the capital. We have already seen that one flourished in Pompeii, very near a place of serious zoological study, in the first century A.D.; and by that time there were similar establishments in many of the towns of Italy. Indeed, arena menageries and amphitheaters for gladiatorial shows spread throughout the imperial provinces. In France alone there were at least 26 of them by the fifth century, and some continued in use for another three hundred years. And when the Empire divided into an eastern and a western section, in the third century, the games began at Constantinople too. There they continued for some 900 years: and the famous menagerie of the Emperor Justinian (A.D. 527 to 565), although probably the best animal collection of the time, was basically a provider of living fodder for the arena.

The Zoo in Decline and Revival

The fall of the Roman Empire brought about a great and long-lasting decline in the number, size, and comprehensiveness of zoos in Europe. The few we know of throughout the darker medieval times were second-rate affairs, most of them in the hands of royalty, some run by the Church, some run by municipal authorities.

The Emperor Charlemagne had three menageries in the eighth century—at Aix-la-Chapelle, Nijmegen, and Ingelheim. In them he kept many exotic birds and mews

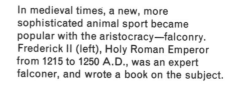

In medieval times, a new, more sophisticated animal sport became popular with the aristocracy—falconry. Frederick II (left), Holy Roman Emperor from 1215 to 1250 A.D., was an expert falconer, and wrote a book on the subject.

of falcons, and occasionally they housed larger animals. In 797 Haroun al Raschid, of *Arabian Nights* fame, sent him monkeys and an elephant; other friendly potentates sent him lions, bears, and camels. Not long after the time of Charlemagne the monks of St. Gallen in Switzerland built a zoo with a rather modern layout of animal houses, keepers' working spaces, and outdoor paddocks, but it seems to have housed only a very limited range of animals. In the twelfth century King Henry I of England developed the small menagerie at Woodstock in Oxfordshire that was probably founded by his father, William the Conqueror. In it Henry had park cattle, lions, leopards, lynxes, camels, and a rare owl.

None of these establishments, probably, could rival the variety of animals kept in the zoos of Greece or Rome or even in the collection of Queen Hatshepsut of ancient Egypt. But there was at least one exception to the general decline of zoos in Europe. The thirteenth-century Holy Roman Emperor Frederick II, the man whose extraordinary abilities earned him the title of *Stupor Mundi* (the Wonder of the World), was a fine naturalist and the author of a classic book on falconry and ornithology, and he liked to study his animals at firsthand. He kept three permanent zoos, at Melfi, Lucera, and Palermo, and on his extensive journeys he was accompanied by a traveling menagerie that included elephants, camels and dromedaries, lions, leopards, cheetahs, and monkeys. In 1235, when Frederick married a sister of England's King Henry III at Worms, this menagerie was fully on show; and some 17 years later, when Henry moved his own Woodstock collection to the Tower of London, it contained several animals his brother-in-law had given him.

There were, of course, other zoos in thirteenth-century Europe—in France, in Florence, in Portugal, and at Nicosia, in Cyprus. There was also quite a big one at Naples, owned by Charles I of Naples and Sicily. But the most extensive zoo we hear of at this time is the one

Above: An illustration from Frederick II's book, showing one incorrect method of carrying a falcon—in this case the goshawk is held too far from the rider's body. Below: Another illustration, showing four peregrines "at hack."

Above: An engraving of the menagerie of the Tower of London as it appeared about the year 1820. Among the first of the European zoos, this collection dates back to the thirteenth century.

Above: Gozzoli, in his fifteenth-century painting of *The Procession of the Magi*, made use of camels (background) and cheetahs (foreground), all of which he could observe in the menagerie of the Medici family at Florence. Dürer's Indian rhinoceros (left) was also based on a zoo specimen, but Dürer worked from a contemporary illustration, not from life.

that Marco Polo saw in Asia when he visited the court of Kublai Khan. It housed elephants, rhinos, hippos, the big cats, bears, many deer, boars, asses, horses, camels, porcupines, monkeys, civets, and many fishes; and the hawks and falcons were so numerous that Kublai is said to have needed 10,000 falconers.

Europe certainly had nothing to rival this collection for a very long time to come. Yet during the fourteenth and fifteenth centuries it showed a steadily increasing interest in zoology; and toward the close of that period it is probably true to say that each of its many monarchies and principalities had at least one menagerie. Some of them were also genuine zoological gardens with charming aviaries, animal houses, and even seal pools. In the Medici-founded zoo at Florence, artists like Gozzoli, Cajano, and Stradan were commissioned to paint the animals. Leonardo da Vinci drew his monkeys, bats, birds, snakes, and lizards in a little zoo in Milan. Albrecht Dürer, a great zoo-goer, drew his famous lion in Ghent in 1521; and his Indian rhinoceros was inspired by a picture made by a Portuguese artist from a living specimen in the Ribeira zoo of Manuel I of Portugal—one of the first rhinos seen in Europe since Roman times.

From the close of the fifteenth century onward, global navigations and explorations, combined with the multiplication of economic and intellectual wealth that came with the Renaissance, speeded up the reviving interest in zoology. Columbus himself brought back the first macaws to Europe, and thereafter a steady stream of new living animals began to flow in. Zoologists began to record the dates of their arrival and to describe them recognizably, as Greek naturalists had recorded and described the animals brought back from Alexander's expeditions.

And explorers did not just discover new zoo animals. In 1519 Hernando Cortés actually discovered a new zoo in México. Montezuma's great menagerie had some splendid aviaries, and those for birds of prey seem to have been better than some we see today. There were so many hawks, falcons, eagles, jaguars, pumas and great snakes that they ate 500 turkeys a day. There was a huge lake, ten waterfowl ponds, paddocks for llamas, vicuñas, deer, and antelope. There was a wonderful collection of colorful Central American birds, ranging from cardinals and quetzals to what stout Cortés described as pheasants (probably tinamous), guans, chachalacas, and quail. There was also a fine assortment of caymans, turtles, iguanas, and rattlesnakes. The whole collection was so big that it had a staff of 300 keepers—far more than most big zoos have today.

Cortés was seeing a fine old zoo of the New World. There were soon to be fine new zoos in the Old World.

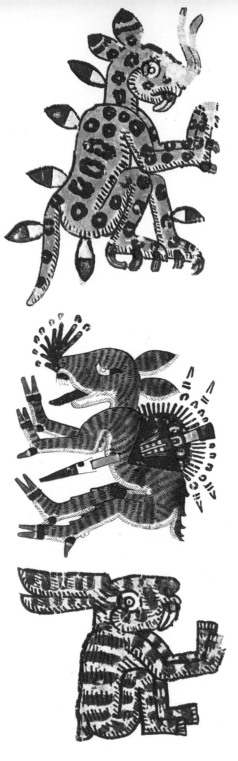

Three Mexican animals, as represented on an Aztec codex. Top: An ocelot, the patron animal of a group of warriors. Its fierceness is implied by the daggers all around it. Middle: A sacrificial deer. Bottom: A rabbit. It was believed that there was a rabbit on the face of the moon.

2 Modern Zoos

The surprisingly modern Aztec zoo that Cortés saw could not have been built up in a few years. We know for certain that at least one other was going strong half a century before the Spanish conquest. However, if we exclude Mexican zoology, we can say that up to the Columbian discoveries the fauna available in captivity for civilized human study was almost exclusively that of Europe, northern Africa, and the continent of Asia.

Until 1492, well over a hundred *families* of birds and mammals alone had never been seen in Europe. When Christopher Columbus brought back the first macaws from the West Indies, he began a process that was eventually to multiply the number of species of vertebrates known to science and available to zoos from three to five times, depending on the class. In addition to the animals of Europe, Asia, and North Africa, those of the Americas, Australia, the Antarctic, Madagascar, and the remainder of Africa gradually became available for zoo culture and acclimatization. The Renaissance, then, ushered in a period of rapid increase in the collection of "novelties." It also ushered in an increase in culture, wealth, and scholarship that enabled the animal novelties ultimately to be absorbed in zoos that outstripped those of Rome in magnificence and those of Greece in scientific merit.

The process by which the zoos of modern times overtook those of antiquity was no sudden one. For instance, I know of no evidence that modern European zoos surpassed the Ptolemaic zoo in the management and breeding of the big cats, or the Greek and Roman zoos in the management of small birds and mammals, until the eighteenth century. And when the influx of new animals first began, there was even some confusion about naming them in such a way as to identify them correctly with their place of origin. Macaws never came from Macao in China, but from Central and South America; Muscovy ducks never came from Moscow, but from Central and South America; turkeys never came from Turkey, but from North and Central America; the guineapig was a domestic animal kept by the Peruvian Incas, and did not originally come from either of the colonial Guineas.

The New World and Australasian novelties did not reach the museums and zoos of the world all at once. Far from it. Not until the nineteenth century were the "hundred families" of birds and mammals of the new continents (and some of their peculiar subfamilies) well

Above: The nineteenth-century German explorers Spix and Martius in the Brazilian rain forest, where they shot many new species. But many explorers brought new species alive to Europe, to the grounds of the chateaus and manors of the aristocracy. Right: Plan of the menagerie of Chantilly, outside Paris, as it was in 1705, after it had been moved from the chateau to the nearby village of Vineuil. (The menagerie is shown in yellowish color.)

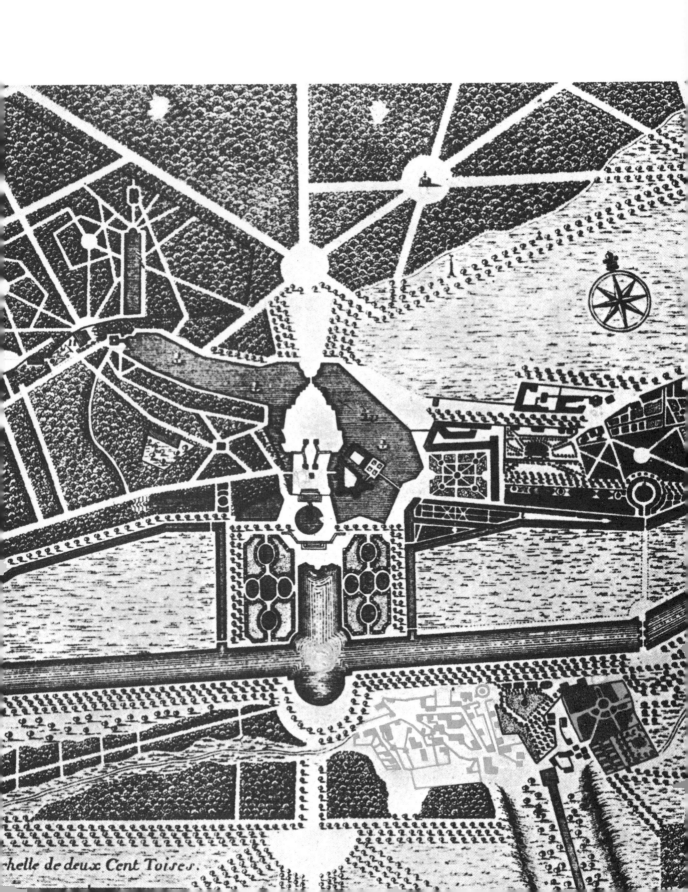

chelle de deux Cent Toises.

represented. During the sixteenth century the menageries of the nobility showed cassowaries, turkeys, macaws, llamas, and guineapigs for the first time. During the seventeenth century they began to show members of the guan-curassow family of South American game birds, South American parrotlets, hummingbirds, cotingas, honeyeaters, tanagers, birds of paradise, and the chimpanzee. As far as I can discover, it was not until the eighteenth century that European zoos first kept penguins, emus, rheas, tinamous, screamers, condors, trumpeters, cockatoos, touracos, the dodo, jacamars, toucans, cardinals, kangaroos, lemurs, South American monkeys (including marmosets), anteaters, sloths, armadillos, pacas, raccoons, and tapirs.

Zoos of the Renaissance

The new animal importations of the sixteenth century became very attractive to the rising class of rich merchants, many of whom must have kept unrecorded bird and mammal "firsts" in their private collections. But we glean most of our information about the introduction of novelties from the major, or "mainstream" zoological gardens of the early Renaissance. Not all of them kept careful records, of course, but we occasionally get a glimpse of how they were run and what animals they had from reports of what they were able to show to visitors. For instance, we learn a little about the only important sixteenth century menagerie in Spain because in 1525 or 1526 its owner, the Duke of Infantando, showed it to Francis I of France, who was then a captive in his country, and of whom a journal was kept.

Between 1530 and 1550 several menageries of considerable size were founded—at Chantilly, Karlsburg, Cairo, Constantinople, Saint-Germain, and Siena. In the second half of the century similar establishments grew up at Ebersdorf, Dresden, Prague, Näugebäu, Elsinore, the Louvre, the Tuileries, Fontainebleau, and in Sweden. Besides these, numerous small menageries and aviaries sprouted in parks and gardens belonging to the chateaus of France and the manors of England. Often they were combined with collections of exotic plants.

The great menagerie of France's Château de Chantilly (which I regard as continuous with its successor at nearby Vineuil) existed from 1530 until August 16, 1792, when it was sacked by French revolutionaries. It seems to have begun, as many early modern zoos did, with domestic animals. The chief inhabitants in its early days were all manner of falconers' hawks and falcons, pigeons, game birds, waterfowl, many fishes, and a few lions and Barbary sheep. The history of the menagerie is very well documented, and we know that it was reconstructed

Four cards from an eighteenth-century French game. They show details of the buildings, waterways, gardens, fountains, and orchards on the Chantilly estate. The central part of the card at bottom left shows the Vineuil menagerie, seen across the canal from the Chantilly gardens (see ground plan, p. 45).

several times, each new plan being more magnificent than its predecessor. At the great reconstruction that began in 1662, we learn that Chantilly was experimenting in the acclimatization of many ducks and waders from Europe, including teal, oystercatchers, redshanks, curlew, and whimbrel; we also learn of the importation of American wood duck, Muscovy duck, and Chinese mandarin duck. In 1671 a second zoological garden was laid out at Vineuil by the famous landscape architect le Nôtre; and 70 years later a large part of the Vineuil animal park was redesigned to illustrate La Fontaine's fables with living material.

The Dukes of Montmorency and their descendants, the Condé princes, who owned Chantilly-Vineuil, may have been largely motivated by prestige and literary considerations; but the scientific impact of their menagerie (or rather, zoo) was great. There, for the first time in Europe, all sorts of zoological curiosities were exhibited, including parrotlets and possibly honeyeaters in 1682, marmosets in 1717, the great anteater in 1778, and (at some less certain date) sloths.

Like Chantilly, the menagerie of Karlsburg, founded in 1538, was moved and reorganized several times in its career; and it has the distinction of being the longest-lived big zoo on record, for it lasted at least as late as 1875. In common with several large zoos of the same vintage (but in sharp contrast with the many small private zoos, which went in mainly for a wide variety of exotic small birds and mammals) it concentrated on "show" animals: birds of prey, monkeys, the horse family, the ox family, elephants, and great cats. Another menagerie with a similar kind of appeal, but in an exaggerated form, was the one established in Dresden by the Elector Augustus I in 1544. This minor king and his successors were great cat, deer, wolf, fox, and bull fanciers, and they revived Roman-style animal fights. The end of the experiment came in 1719. After a series of knock-out contests between tigers, lions, bulls, bears, and boars, Augustus II personally destroyed every survivor with ball shot.

Augustus II cannot even claim the doubtful distinction of being the first man of modern times to commit such an act. In 1570 or 1571, Charles IX of France founded a menagerie at the Louvre in Paris, complete with a charming aviary and an arena for bull fights. His successor, Henry III, improved the original collection—mainly of lions and bears—by introducing camels, monkeys, and parakeets. Then on January 20, 1583, he killed the entire collection with his harquebus, after having dreamed that the animals were going to eat him. The aviary at the Louvre was reconstructed some 30 years later by Louis XIII, a zoologist-monarch who also developed the gar-

dens in the Tuileries and at Fontainebleau that were founded by his father, Henry IV.

The royal collections of animals established in Sweden in 1561 were to have a profound effect on modern zoology. They persisted until the time of Carl von Linné, better known as Linnaeus, two centuries later; and their living material formed the basis for the scientific naming of many animals in the tenth edition of his famous *System of Nature*, published in 1758, now recognized as the basis of modern scientific animal naming.

But of all the zoos and menageries founded in the sixteenth century, none had a more direct link with the zoos of today than those built up by the Holy Roman Emperor Maximilian II, who reigned from 1564 to 1576. There were three of them—at Ebersdorf (1552), Prague (1558), and Näugebäu (1558)—and they all began with the usual big cats, elephants, wild horses, and big ruminants of the deer and cattle families. As time passed, the collections were enriched and enlarged, and in 1736 Näugebäu received many animals from a zoo at Belvédère, on the death of its founder-owner, Prince Eugène of Savoy. Sixteen years later much of the Belvédère-Näugebäu stock found its way to a new zoo at Schönbrunn in Austria. That zoo is still with us and is the oldest surviving real zoo in the world.

The two hundred years that elapsed between the founding of Näugebäu and the founding of Vienna's Schönbrunn marked a great advance in zoos and zoology. Enjoyment of brutal spectacles was on the wane, closer zoological inquisitiveness on the increase; and this showed itself in several ways. Rudolf II, son of Maximilian II, employed such eminent artists as Georg and Jacob Hoefnagel and Roelant Savery to make pictorial records of the animals in the three menageries his father had founded. The great zoo at Versailles, founded by Louis XIII in 1624, was carefully documented at every stage of its history, which lasted until the early years of the French Revolution. Over fifty designers, sculptors, and painters recorded its animals and its architecture, and we know fairly accurately what species it kept and when it kept them. Among species that probably had their first European showing at Versailles were condors, curassows or guans, hummingbirds, jacamars, toucans, contingas, cardinals, tanagers, birds of paradise, lemurs, and American tapirs.

Throughout the seventeenth and early eighteenth cen-

The modern bear pit at Bern, Switzerland, replaces another (left) dating back to the Middle Ages. The style of this structure seems harsh and unsympathetic to the needs of the animals: it is an example of how not to keep bears.

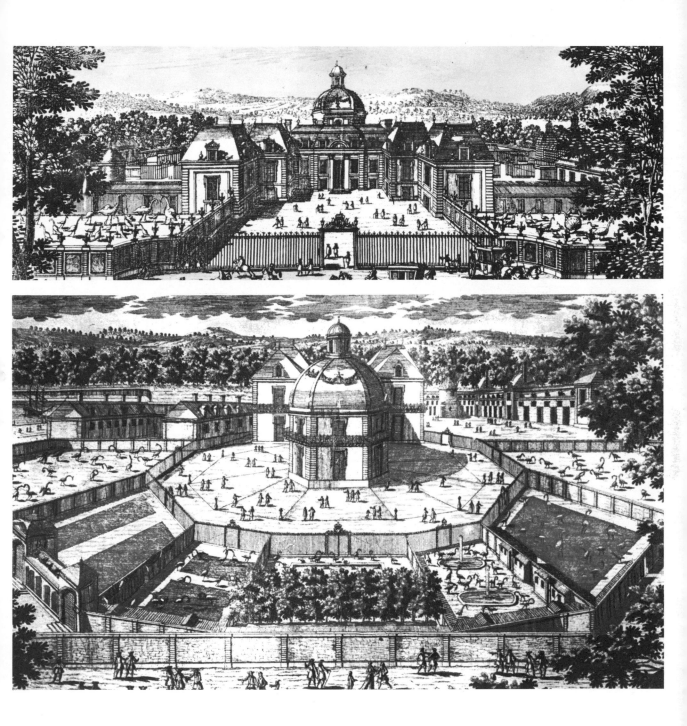

Two views of the Versailles Zoo
at the time of Louis XIV (1643-1715).
Upper: The façade for the two bird
enclosures, in which the artist has
used some imagination, never in
fact existed. Lower: Versailles Zoo
from the rear.

turies new zoos sprang up not only in many parts of Europe, but also in South Africa, Morocco, Egypt, Persia, India, and Russia. They were numerous and they were often very good. And it was in this great world-flowering of zoos that Schönbrunn came into existence.

Above: The Austrian zoo of Belvédère was founded in 1716 by Prince Eugène of Savoy. Despite his personal dislike of Louis XIV, Eugène copied the layout of the Versailles zoo.

Below: Blaauw-Jan, the name of an eighteenth-century zoo in Amsterdam.

The First of Today's Zoos

Schönbrunn, opened in Vienna in 1752, was built by the Holy Roman Emperor Francis I for his wife Maria Theresa, Queen of Hungary and Bohemia and Arch-Duchess of Austria. At its very center he had a lovely pavilion erected where the Queen could breakfast and watch the camels, elephants, and zebras. These were kept in houses with long, tree-lined paths running between them like the spokes of a wheel, through gardens and aviaries. To this day the people of Vienna can see almost exactly the same thing, for the original architecture has been refurbished and modified with such care that even an informed visitor can scarcely notice the changes. The practical and pragmatic Austrians, with their ancient respect for history, have not spirited away Maria Theresa's little present. They have kept the heart of it as a living fossil of past glories; but they have also added many

Above: Schönbrunn Zoo, in Austria, the oldest of the world's zoos that survives to the present day. It was built privately by Francis I for his wife Maria Theresa (below). He began it in 1752, and in 1759 built the rococo pavilion seen above, where he and his wife would breakfast every day during summer.

things to it, among them television links, and one of the finest inland seawater and freshwater aquariums in Europe.

Schönbrunn is a great mainstream zoo today and has been so ever since its foundation. As we saw earlier, some of its original inhabitants in 1752 were animals formerly housed at Belvédère and Näugebäu; others came from a dealer who ran the famous old Blaauw-Jan menagerie in Amsterdam. New stock was soon bought from other dealers in Holland and England; and in 1759 the Emperor's own collector, Nicolas Jacquin, returned from tropical America with many rare plants, birds, and mammals. In the same year Gregor Guglielmi decorated the walls and ceilings of the breakfast pavilion with paintings of some of the zoo's animals. They include many rare species and quite possibly a number of zoo "firsts." Among the birds are American trumpeters, the scarlet ibis, the purple gallinule, guans, curassows, eclectus parrots from Papua, and some interesting species of macaws. Among the African mammals depicted are the mountain zebra, now very rare indeed, and the kaama, or Cape hartebeest, now definitely extinct.

In 1765 Joseph II, the son and successor of Francis I, opened Schönbrunn to the public. For the benefit of the public, the glory of the gardens, and the advancement of science, he sent two collectors, Matthias Leopold Stupicz and Franz Boos, to the Americas. In 1785 they returned with 12 new species of mammals and (it is claimed) 250 new species of birds.

By that time the world's second surviving zoo, that in Madrid (or fourth, if we include the ancient bird collections in St. James's Park and Kew Gardens), had already been in existence for more than a decade; and eight years later, in 1793, the still existing, and still justly famous, zoological collection of the Jardin des Plantes was founded in Paris. No more surviving zoos were established until 1828, but between then and 1865 no fewer than 26 came into being. The modern world has 30 zoos that have passed their hundredth birthday.

An important point about most of these centenarian zoos is that they are modern in more senses than that of mere survival into today's world. This means that their attitude to zoology is essentially scientific, and of this I shall say more later. Many, if not all, of them have also reorganized their layout and architecture from time to time, to keep abreast of new ideas on the care and management of animals. And they are in keeping both with antiquity and with the twentieth century in that they are all zoological *gardens*. All of them were gardens first and are gardens still. Schönbrunn, as we have already seen, was set in a garden of great beauty. Madrid started in a royal garden. The Jardin des Plantes du Musée d'Histoire Naturelle de Paris, as its formal name implies, was originally (indeed, since 1626) a botanic garden. London Zoo is set in a royal park. Dublin Zoo is in the broad expanse of Phoenix Park. Bristol Zoo started on the Clifton Downs, and today it strikes the visitor first of all as a menagerie of plants; Reg Greed, who runs it, employs as many gardeners as zoo keepers on its 12 acres, and it is the prettiest zoo garden that I have seen anywhere in the world. One could continue with this theme of zoos as gardens for a long time without exhausting it; and it is my firm conviction that a zoo with a fine garden is almost invariably a fine zoo.

Perhaps, at first sight, the most surprising thing about the list of centenarian zoos is that it includes only one in the United States. The people of America had the wealth, and the space, to start zoos earlier than they did, but they had to put first things first. As pioneers in a new continent, their first zoological concern was with the preservation of *wild* nature. Federal action was taken early about that. In 1871, only six years after the Civil War ended and only 11 years after the area was first explored, Yellowstone National Park was dedicated to the conservation of wildlife. The importance of that action can be measured by the fact that this great nature pre-

1	Regent's Park, London	England
2	Clifton, Bristol	
3	Belle Vue, Manchester	
4	Woburn, Bedfordshire	
5	Tower of London	
6	St. James's Park, London	
7	Kew, Surrey	
8	Lilford, Northamptonshire	
9	Stuttgart	Germany
10	Berlin, West	
11	Frankfurt-am-Main	
12	Cologne	
13	Dresden	
14	Karlsruhe	
15	Hanover	
16	Hamburg	
17	Schönbrunn	Austria
18	Vienna	
19	Wroclaw	Poland
20	Jardin des Plantes, Paris	France
21	Lyons	
22	Marseilles	
23	Jardin d'Acclimatization	
24	Tours	
25	Madrid	Spain
26	Jerez	
27	Orotava, Canary Islands	
28	Moscow	USSR
29	Leningrad	
30	Copenhagen	Denmark
31	Amsterdam	Netherlands
32	Rotterdam	
33	Rotterdam	
34	The Hague	
35	Antwerp	Belgium
36	Ghent	
37	Brussels	
38	Liège	
39	St. Gallen	Switzerland
40	Bern	
41	Peking	China
42	Trivandrum	India
43	Bombay	
44	Calcutta	
45	Mandalay	Burma
46	Bangkok	Thailand
47	Singapore	Malaysia
48	Saigon	Vietnam
49	Fez	Morocco
50	Central Park, New York	USA
51	Djakarta	Indonesia
52	Melbourne	Australia

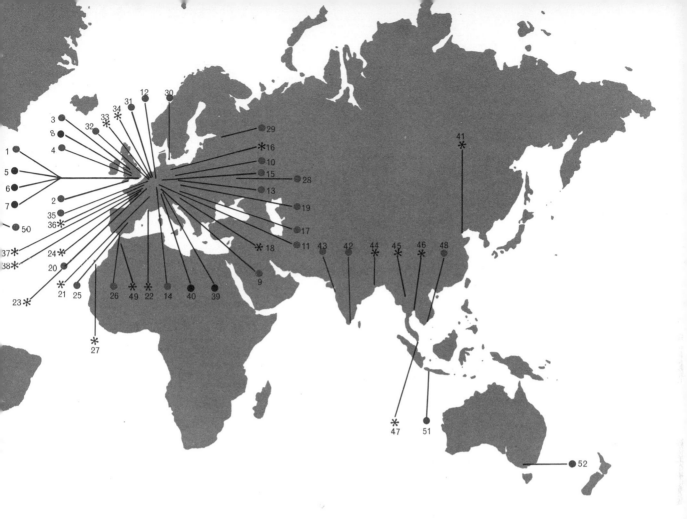

Above: The world's zoos during the last hundred years. Brown dots show major century-old zoos still in existence. Black dots show surviving special or small, semi-private century-old zoos. Black asterisks indicate zoos that have closed down during this period.

Right: The Jardin des Plantes, Paris, as it looks today. Originally founded as a collection of medicinal plants, the zoo was added in 1793. It was at first stocked with animals from the Versailles zoo and from traveling menageries. These latter were suppressed by the government during the nineteenth century.

serve is very much larger than any English county except Yorkshire; and many other areas, though none as big, were soon set aside with the same object. The United States government, then, assumed responsibility for wild nature earlier than that of any other nation.

The zoo movement in America began comparatively late, but when it did start it went well. Of the existing zoos, only that in New York's Central Park was founded before the end of the Civil War—in 1864 to be exact. Buffalo and Chicago (Lincoln Park) were in existence by

America's first zoo, in Central Park, New York, was founded in 1864. Below: (top) An early print showing monkeys, a baboon, and a harpy eagle; (bottom) the original monkey house at the Philadelphia Zoo in 1874, replaced by a small mammal house in 1898.

1870, Philadelphia, Cincinnati, and Baltimore before 1880, Cleveland, the Washington Aquarium, the National Zoological Park (at Washington), and Denver by 1890. By 1900 there were another eight, and by 1937 about 40 more. Today the United States has about 116 zoos—nearly a quarter of the world's total—and some of its finest mainstream zoos, such as St. Louis and San Diego, have built up their stocks and their world-wide reputations entirely in the twentieth century.

Aims of the Modern Zoo

I said earlier that the centenarian zoos were, and are, modern in that their attitude to zoology was, and is, essentially scientific. In that sense one can say that there were modern zoos, especially in France, before the French Revolution, for many of them owed their success as much to truly science-minded thinkers as to the wealth of kings and nobles. In particular, the still-surviving Jardin des Plantes of Paris was actually founded by a scientist. But perhaps the best example of the new style of thinking can be found in London. This is partly because the history of the London Zoo is well documented, partly because London is fairly typical of other early modern zoos, and partly because its initial aims were clearly stated.

The idea of providing London with a zoo came from Sir Thomas Stamford Raffles (1781-1826)—the man who founded Singapore, which to this day has the greatest zoological and general museum in southeast Asia: the Raffles Museum. Raffles appears to have discussed the project as early as 1817 with no less a person than Sir Joseph Banks (1743-1820), who was then president of the Royal Society in London. They seem to have exchanged minutes in writing calling for the establishment in London of "a zoological collection which should interest and amuse the public." As aims go, these were broadly and fairly stated. From all we know of the work and character of both men we can be sure that "interest" meant "interest by making proper scientific arrangements," while "amuse the public" certainly did not mean making a mere picnic-place or circus for them. Raffles and Banks knew that from a good collection of animals, of intrinsic interest, the amusement of the public would flow naturally.

Banks was a pure scientist of the highest caliber, and his wide interests included both plants and animals. He was the man who arranged the famous surveying voyage of H.M.S. *Bounty*, under Captain Bligh; he also inspired the fund-raising and the tradition that later enabled civilian scientists like Charles Darwin and Thomas Henry Huxley to accompany British naval surveying voyages; and, most important, he was president of the learned and influential Royal Society from the age of 32 until his death more than 40 years later. Banks, then, was clearly the right man for Raffles to approach about the founding of a great scientific zoo; but unfortunately he died in 1820 before the project really began to take shape. Raffles himself also died before the Zoological Society of London received its charter, but he lived long

Above (top): Bust of Sir Thomas Stamford Raffles, a founder-member of the Zoological Society of London and its first president. The London Zoo was opened to the public in 1828, and the illustration of it as it then appeared (above) was published in *The Mirror* on September 6, 1828. Since then the zoo has become much larger, and today it covers 36 acres.

enough to become the zoo's real founder and first president.

The world's largest collection of living animals (with the exception of that in West Berlin) owes its existence to a meeting of "friends of a proposed zoological society" held in London on August 22, 1824, under Raffles' chairmanship. Of the 21 members of this unofficial committee almost all were either noble, or wealthy, or both; more important, they were all learned in the pursuit of zoology, and most of them were scientists of distinction. Among them were Sir Humphry Davy, president of the Royal Society, pioneer chemist, and inventor of the miners' safety lamp; Edward Smith Stanley, later 13th Earl of Derby, who founded the first modern private menagerie in England at Knowsley Park and who commissioned Edward Lear to picture many specimens in his collection; Thomas Horsfield, Pennsylvania-born naturalist who had recently published the first scientific descriptions of over 20 new eastern birds; Edward Adolphus Seymour, the 11th Duke of Somerset, a man of great all-round learning who later became president of the Linnean Society of London; William Kirby, eminent pioneer entomologist; and Nicholas Aylward Vigors, an Irish landlord and distinguished ornithologist.

In 1827, soon after Raffles died, the Marquis of Lansdowne became president of the Zoological Society. He was instrumental in obtaining a Royal Charter and the patronage of King William IV, and to this day the monarch of the United Kingdom is patron of the Society.

The Royal Charter stated the aims and objects of the Zoological Society of London in 19 words: "The advancement of zoology and animal physiology, and the introduction of new and curious subjects of the animal kingdom." In fact, the word *zoology* covers everything to do with animals, so three words could have been saved by cutting out the expression "and animal physiology;" but the founding fathers of the London Zoo doubtless retained it to draw attention to the fact that they were especially interested in the study of *living* animals. In the language of 1829 "animal physiology" covered everything to do with them. Then, as now, every mainstream zoo had a group of friends who were waiting for the animals to die so that they could study their anatomy. Indeed it would be wrong if no such use were made of the material. But the founders of the London Zoo rightly emphasized that their main interest was in living animals. The aims set forth in the Royal Charter were therefore expressed as briefly as common sense allowed, and they have never yet been modified by a single amendment.

Nearly all the surviving mainstream zoos of the world were founded with similar aims in mind, even if they

Two lithographs by G. Scharf showing scenes inside the London Zoo in 1835. Top: The monkey house, a constant source of amusement. Right: Two open bird gardens and an enclosed aviary. Even at this date, black swans had been brought across the world from Australia.

do not all have charters that say so. And those aims, however briefly expressed, have wide implications.

The Advancement of Zoology

We shall see in a later chapter that the simple charter expression, "the introduction of new and curious subjects of the animal kingdom," involves the whole immensely complex business of animal supply. We shall also see that "the advancement of zoology" includes dealing with the increasingly difficult problem of animal conservation. If we cannot keep animals alive, we cannot study them. For the moment, however, I should like to keep to the more direct implication of the phrase.

It is an important duty of mainstream zoos to educate, because you cannot "advance zoology and animal physiology" without teaching. Research alone is not enough.

That word "advance" implies both research and teaching. Mainstream zoos are relatively few. Mainstream zoos are those large enough, rich enough and scientific enough significantly to advance the science of zoology. As time goes on, more and more zoos tend to advance to the mainstream class. To specify them precisely is perhaps invidious, but readers of the world list (pages 236-245) can surely identify the outstanding ones.

Now it happens that *Homo sapiens* has an inherent drive to gather all kinds of miscellaneous information — a drive that makes our species more efficient and more likely to survive. This drive includes a great innate curiosity about animals. Zoos are among the many instruments that we have devised for the satisfaction of this drive; and many of them cater to zoological curiosity at all levels, from that of the schoolchild to that of the university professor.

Here I should like to take the London Zoo as a classic example of a satisfier of curiosity. I select it simply because I know it and love it well. As zoology's servant it is special but not unique, for the Bronx, Antwerp, both the Berlin zoos, and a dozen others I could name all serve in similar ways.

Not long ago London Zoo started the XYZ Club — the Exceptional Young Zoologists' Club — whose members pay only a low subscription and have many privileges: special publications, special lectures, and conducted tours with the Society's education officers and curators. Later in life some XYZ members may slip away to botany, some to water-skiing, some to football, some to big business. But even if they do, they may well return to the zoo one day, if only to repay the debt they might think they owe to the Society for encouraging them; and more than one of them may some day be zoo curators or even zoo directors.

However, it has to be remembered that in sophisticated countries the zoo is an aid or ancillary to the general stream of zoological education; it is a "without-which-not," but not perhaps the focal point. The focal point is the good school, under whatever name it may go, or the university; and indeed it is primarily from these sources that Western zoos recruit senior members of their staff, most of whom have a degree either in zoology

Zoos have two main objectives—to educate and to entertain. Above: The "Desert Ark," in Arizona, is a kind of traveling zoo that visits local schools and other organizations in order to promote knowledge of Arizona's wildlife. Left: An early effort at education in a zoo—the first guided bus tour at San Diego Zoo, in 1927.

or in veterinary medicine. Today the mainstream Western zoos are repaying their debt to the schools and universities by offering special services to them. Universities commonly make arrangements for their students to visit the local zoo and study its material at first hand. London Zoo, always advanced in academic know-how, has lately housed two newly-built scientific foundations for comparative animal research, the Wellcome Institute for Comparative Physiology and the Nuffield Institute of Comparative Medicine. From the XYZ Club to these advanced centers of learning, London Zoo thus continues to pursue "the advancement of zoology" at all educational levels.

As for scientific research on animals, its very bedrock is documentation. Zoology is a highly sophisticated science, and nobody can do research properly unless he knows what is already known on his chosen subject. Perhaps the greatest research instrument that the London Zoo possesses is it magnificent library, which includes a comprehensive file of its own records and those of other zoos. Apart from the great copyright libraries, it is the finest zoological book collection in the world, with well over 100,000 volumes; indeed, if we count annual volumes of scientific journals as separate volumes, the total must be thousands more.

Let us imagine a student who wants to read up on a specific problem—for instance, the color vision of the Amphibia, and of the clawed frog in particular. His first task—and it sounds a formidable one—is to compile a list of essential reading. In the library of the Zoological Society of London he could compile his basic bibliography in a few hours at most.

He would begin by going straight to the *Zoological Record*. This is an annual that has been published in parts by the Zoological Society of London since 1864, listing scientific papers published during each year. A substantial part of each volume is devoted to the Amphibia, and under the heading "Amphibia" everything is classified under families. Since the student is obviously interested in clawed frogs, he will certainly know which family they belong to (Pipidae), and a generally used scientific name for them (the genus *Xenopus*). So under the main heading, "Amphibia," in each year's volume,

Above: Television is an effective way of showing zoo animals to millions. Here a young African elephant is being televised at the San Diego Zoo. Right: London Zoo has established an XYZ Club—for "exceptional young zoologists," here seen watching a chimpanzee demonstration supervised by Dr. Desmond Morris (center).

he looks first for the family, "Pipidae," and under that, in alphabetical order, for the generic name "*Xenopus*." There he will find a list of all the scientific papers published on clawed frogs during that year. I say "all," but the *Zoological Record* is compiled by human beings, and occasionally its highly expert compilers miss a few papers. This does not matter so much because any that may be missing will usually be referred to in other papers that the student does find and read.

A researcher who has had some experience in using the *Zoological Record* can sometimes draw up in a morning a whole species bibliography covering the past half century. If the species is one on which an exceptional number of papers have been published it may take him a day to write out all the necessary citation slips. Then, very often, the articles he wants are immediately available on the library shelves.

Once the student gets down to serious reading, he may find that earlier workers he knew nothing about have already done a lot of research on his chosen subject. To start afresh and go over the same well-trodden ground would be as rewarding as reinventing the sewing machine. Yet, unless he is very faint-hearted, the student will not be discouraged, for often his reading also reveals gaps in knowledge that earlier workers had noticed but not filled. He will then redirect his efforts into more worthwhile channels.

When he eventually embarks on his research course, with his planning improved by the study of earlier research literature, the student still finds that zoos in general, and the Zoological Society of London in particular, can help him. Suppose that our student is not a clawed-frog enthusiast but an ibis addict, interested in the breeding habits of the sacred ibis in captivity. Could zoos provide him with some observational material on this bird?

In any good zoo library there will be a file of avicultural journals, including the *Avicultural Magazine* and *Zoologische Garten*. These will help to put him on the track, simply because they give a great deal of information about which birds are to be found in which zoos. One publication of the Zoological Society of London would be of special use. It is the *International Zoo Yearbook*, which has been running since 1959; it gives basic information about what goes on in all the main zoos of the world, and includes information about nearly all the rare and interesting birds and mammals kept in captivity, which birds and animals breed in captivity, and what improvements in zoo techniques have been made. This publication would provide the student with all relevant information in a very short time. He would realize that he should consult Dr. Ernst Lang, Director of the Zoo-

Above (left and right): Josie, a chimpanzee at London Zoo, performing her "burglar act," in which she undoes several locks and bolts before getting to the "loot," which is a bunch of grapes.

logical Gardens in Basel, Switzerland, for Dr. Lang has been breeding ibises of many kinds in captivity for years. The student would also see that as an alternative he might do well to visit the small zoological garden (especially for students and not for the general public) in the University of Tel Aviv, in Israel.

Does zoological research produce quick increases in human wealth? Not to any great extent. Through work in zoos one gets to know things about the management of animals in captivity that may, in some cases, help to improve agriculture; some zoo experiences in the breeding of wild or semi-wild species of cattle may have benefited the beef industry; and a few experimental zoos, like that in Askaniya-Nova in the Soviet Union, still try to develop new kinds of domestic animals. To a certain extent the study of animal diseases in zoos has helped the advance of veterinary science, especially in the field of parasitology, but on the whole I would say that vets put more into zoos than their own science gets out of them. In fact, zoo research is intended essentially to improve the general *background* of knowledge; and only in rather exceptional circumstances does it yield immediate dividends by increasing agricultural profit or by alleviating the sufferings of human beings or domesticated animals. In the long run, background knowledge can be of more use than knowledge derived from short-term (or foreground) research.

"Interest and Amuse the Public"

There is nothing in the London Zoo's charter about interesting and amusing the public, but we have seen that Raffles and Banks had that aim well in mind when the London Zoo was still no more than an idea. What is more, the charter itself implicitly includes this aim (in Raffles' and Banks' sense of "interest" and "amuse") under the phrase "the advancement of zoology." The advancement of zoology is clearly served when the public is genuinely interested and innocently amused by a fine collection of animals. A housewife says: "It's a lovely day! Let's take the family to the zoo and see the monkeys; they're such fun!" They gape at the monkeys and the violet-colored bottoms of the mandrills, and say, "How extraordinary!" They admire the pheasants and waterfowl, and say, "Aren't they pretty!" They express their appreciation of the zoo in terms of entertainment value; but even if they do not realize it, they are satisfying a basic thirst for knowledge, and they go home a little better informed about the animal world than when they set out.

So the mainstream zoos frankly, and quite properly, go in for entertainment. But entertainment is not regarded as a primary duty. Rather it is a valuable by-

Below: (left): Winnie, London Zoo chimpanzee, demonstrates her problem-solving abilities with the "chimpomat," a coin-in-the-slot machine; (right) Daisy, another London performer.

product of good zoo-management—one that is thoroughly appreciated by the public and is also in the best interests of the animals. A good zoo does not provide entertainments that are unsuitable for animals or contrary to their natural dignity. In the United States, St. Louis, Detroit, and San Diego zoos are well known for their fine animal shows of the proper kind.

For many years the London Zoo has staged daily tea parties for young chimpanzees. Adults as well as children enjoy watching, and the parties are a valuable form of occupational therapy for the chimps. Without the parties the mammal department would have to design other

Sea lions, like chimpanzees, have high intelligence and respond well to training. Here, in San Diego's sea lion pool, over a thousand spectators at a time can watch the performance of these aquatic mammals.

forms of therapeutic activity. Indeed, others have already been designed, and the public finds them equally entertaining. Desmond Morris, the mammal curator, has devised some interesting slot-machine tricks for chimps to do. Some involve the solving of certain choice problems, while others test the animals' ability to aim straight and knock down grapes that are lined up like targets in a baseball-pitching gallery. Both make it possible to test the chimps' capacity to learn, and when a chimp succeeds in solving a problem or knocking down a grape it automatically gets a token reward. If the animal fails, there is no punishment; there is simply no reward.

Slot machine "chimpomat" experiments, as they are called, were first pioneered in the Yerkes Laboratories of Primate Biology in Florida. Morris, who developed them in London, also spent many, many hours watching chimps paint—after he provided them with materials of all kinds. These experiments not only gave the chimps plenty of agreeable things to do; their results, it is believed, have already taught us something about the very origins of human art.

Many zoos, as well as many good circuses, put on highly entertaining sea lion acts. Any act in which sea lions do swimming and balancing tricks, or play an appropriate melody on horns and so on, keeps the performers happy and provides them with a substitute for their natural wild hunting drive.

There is an extremely beautiful old zoo, the Wilhelma Botanical and Zoological Garden in Stuttgart, which puts on a combined chimpanzee and sea lion act. The chimp is a tame and particularly intelligent youngish female, and she has been taken on the staff of the sea lion and elephant seal department. (There is no fear of her causing a labor dispute, because she has been made an honorary member of the Keepers' Union.) Every day during the summer it is she who dishes out the fish. First she throws them very neatly for the Californian sea lions to catch; then she walks calmly up to the gargantuan elephant seal, which must by now weigh every bit of three tons, and posts fresh cod and whiting into his great slit of a mouth. Finally she pretends to make a big fuss about washing her hands in clean water before going back to the ape house.

It is all a put-up job between her and the keeper, of course; and her air of enormous reluctance has been carefully rehearsed. She loves the job, loves the public, quite understands their applause, and claps back whenever they clap. Everyone enjoys it—the chimp, her public, and the sea lions and seals as well, for they do not seem to mind who feeds them as long as they are fed. The spectacle is funny and the visitors laugh; but they do not laugh at the chimp. Her dignity is not the

Top: A young elephant splashing in the bathing pool at London Zoo's new elephant and rhinoceros house. This provides entertainment for the visitors and keeps the elephants healthy. Above: An elephant in the more spacious bath at the London Zoo in 1832.

Feeding-time for the animals is entertainment-time for the visitors, and this has been true through the centuries. Above: A tea party for two young chimpanzees and three young orangutans at the Bronz Zoo in 1911. Left (above): A different kind of entertainment is a ride on the elephant; the scene here is London Zoo in 1905. Left (below): Feeding the lions at London Zoo in 1871.

Top: Many children fear snakes, and a survey has shown that their fear is greatest at around six years of age. Above: Some pythons used to be force-fed, as seen in this picture taken in the 1930s at the San Diego Zoo.

Right: Young apes share the dislike of snakes found in young humans: Top to bottom: A young chimpanzee is seen investigating a clockwork "snake," then picking it up by its tail, swinging it round, and striking it against the wall.

same as human dignity, and her job certainly does not outrage it. Animal tricks become open to criticism only when the animals are being misapplied; then they are an affront to human dignity as well as to the dignity of the animals.

Occupational therapy for animals is a continuous study at all mainstream zoos. One simple method is to employ tameable or domesticable animals in the style to which their species is accustomed. Nearly all zoos therefore provide camel rides, pony rides, donkey rides, and rides in carts drawn not only by ponies and donkeys but even by zebras and elephants. Elephant rides are becoming less common; they are good for the elephants, but there is occasionally some slight risk to the public. Even a docile and well-trained cow elephant may on rare occasions cause trouble when she is in some discomfort that her keeper, just that once, has not recognized.

There is also a perfectly proper tendency to make the animals' feeding time as spectacular and interesting as possible. This is, of course, old stuff, and involves public delight at the sea lion pond, a mixture of delight and horror at the large-cat house, and curiously conflicting attitudes in some other places. The average member of the public, I suspect, is not at all keen on watching the vultures being fed; and I very much doubt if zoos would get a crowd nowadays to watch the boa constrictors being fed on live rabbits or white rats, as they were in the old days. The tendency today is to feed all reptiles on dead food.

There is a curious hierarchy of public like and dislike of animals, which actually changes with age. Not long ago, on one of his television programs for the London Zoo, Desmond Morris asked young visitors to write to him and name the animal they liked best and the animal they disliked most. He took postcards at random from 100 boys and 100 girls of each age from four to fourteen and made a top-ten list of both likes and dislikes.

As a zoologist, I have *interests* rather than likes or dislikes, and I found his list rather surprising. The top-ten likes came in this order: monkey and chimpanzee, equal (13%), horse (9%), bush baby and giant panda (8%), bear, presumably including polar bear (7%), elephant, presumably both kinds (6%), lion (4.5%), dog (4%), giraffe (3%). Two animals on this list call for some comment. Only one giant panda has been kept in any British zoo since 1945, just because they are hard to get, yet the giant panda is nearly the most popular animal. Dogs are not usually shown in British zoos—and the London Zoo has none except dingos—yet they, too, figure on the list.

The top-ten dislikes, starting with the most hated, were snake, spider, lion, rat, crocodile, skunk, gorilla, hippopotamus, rhinoceros, and tiger. Snakes had a score of 28%, spiders a score of 10%, and all the rest, only mildly disliked, had a score of 5% or under.

The lion was in a very odd position. Its 4.5% "like" score came entirely from the over-sevens; its 5% "dislike" score came from younger boys and girls, who evidently found it more frightening. Elephants and giraffes were very popular with the under-sevens, less so with older children. Snakes, it seems, are at once a subject of horror and of fascination at all ages, and this attitude is one that men share with the gorilla, the chimpanzee, and the orangutan. The ancestors of these animals, in common with our own, lived with snakes in the wild, where you had better hate snakes *and* watch them, because they are dangerous. So the hatred of snakes that *Homo sapiens* shares with the anthropoid apes may well be a very ancient drive that has helped all of us to survive. At least a few children still dislike gorillas, but I think this will change now that gorillas are being bred in captivity and babies can be seen in some enlightened zoos like Basel.

Zoo Critics and Top Zoo Men

There are a few people who would argue that because snakes, crocodiles, and spiders are disliked, zoos should close down their reptile and insect houses. This is a naïve and negligible argument, since the first duty of a zoo is the advancement of zoology—a duty to which the entertainment of the public must take second place.

But apart from this somewhat unsophisticated point of view, there is another school of thought, strongly held if not widely shared, which says that animals should not be kept in zoos at all. In the English-speaking press particularly, there are periodic outbreaks of letters saying that zoos are outdated, and cruel, that the animals must be miserable pacing up and down in their narrow cages, and so on. I do not suggest for a moment that the holders of these views are ignorant or sentimental or stupid. They are often sensible and educated people, and most of them feel strongly against zoos basically because of the confinement issue.

Today, probably, no zoo authority would admit to confining any animals more than is necessary. But it must be remembered that this is a lesson they have only lately learned. In the last century, and even into this, most zoo people did not scruple to confine almost any kind of animal in general-purpose, small, barred cages. If certain animals did not "do," or "work out"—that is, if they did not thrive and breed—it was just too bad; other species were promptly tried instead. At that time, also, there were strong protests from libertarian-minded people; and they doubtless did a very good job in helping zoos to decide that things needed reforming.

Above: The sad state of a chimpanzee kept in solitary confinement in a small, bare, stone cell. Right: Two further examples of bad housing conditions for animals. Top: "Polito's Royal Menagerie" in the Strand, London, in the nineteenth century. Bottom: A traveling menagerie at England's Yarmouth Sands, on August Bank Holiday in 1891.

The huge Scripps Aviary at San Diego Zoo. Here, visitors stroll through the spacious cage along a winding path amid the rich subtropical vegetation. Birds of many species, including the Andean condor with its 10-foot wing-span, sail around at their ease in the space overhead.

The fact is that sweeping reforms have now been made, and I am sure that much of the anti-zoo feeling of today comes from middle-aged or elderly people who still retain unpleasant memories of the crude zoos of their childhood. If only these people could be persuaded to visit a really well-appointed modern zoo, I am confident that most of their prejudices would disappear.

However, it is true that certain families of animals—notably the birds of prey—still tend to be kept in unsuitable cages, in which they can never fully indulge their natural wild drives. In the case of birds of prey, it is almost impossible for zoos to solve this problem completely. No zoo can ever provide a bird of prey with an enclosure large enough to allow it to soar on rising thermals of air to a height of 2,000 feet, as it would when hunting prey in the wild. Here zoos have to take a decision: are they to hold all or only some birds of prey in captivity and frustrate their natural drive to soar; are they to keep none at all; or are there any satisfactory compromise solutions? Today many zoos have decided to keep only a few selected birds of prey, and most of the old cages, in which eagles and huge soarers could hardly stretch their wings, have disappeared. Many such dreary aviaries have been superseded by large flight cages. One of the finest is at San Diego, where they have simply built a dome 150 feet long and about 80 feet high over a large natural canyon. In this, Andean condors—almost the largest birds of prey—fly freely up and down, and glide, even if they cannot soar; they have also bred there.

Even in this modern reform it may well be that the protests of the anti-zoo critics have played some part. So while it is true that ill-informed pressures can be a nuisance to zoo people, it is also true that justifiable pressures help to keep zoo men on their toes.

Anti-zoo feeling is declining as zoos become increasingly humane and efficient; and the zoos of the world have never been more numerous or more popular than they are today. If the world remains peaceful, there are even better prospects of the tender management of animals in captivity. I would emphasize the word "tender." My most vivid impression of a really good zoo, when I visit it for the first time, is that the people in charge are tender, not only in the management of the animals, but also in the way they court and cater for the public and the way they care about the landscape and the flowers.

And when I find a good zoo, I nearly always find a top man in charge, a presiding genius and a "go-getter." There are exceptions, of course. It is difficult to say who is the presiding genius of the London Zoo among all its talented directorate and staff; London relies essentially on a big committee structure, yet it is unquestionably an excellent zoo. Another zoo of the same caliber, which I will not name, has its presiding genius; from him, I have no doubt, stems its near-perfection, but from him, too, stem certain administrative problems because, being a true genius, he finds it hard to delegate responsibility even to responsible people.

The perfect top zoo man is a paragon. He must have an all-round knowledge of zoology and a specialist's knowledge in certain fields; the knack of getting on well with all kinds of people; the ability to drive his staff, and the humility to be driven by them when they are right; and he must have that almost indefinable quality of tenderness. He is indeed a paragon, but he does exist. And when you find him, he will be in a good zoo set in a fine garden.

Above: A spacious gibbon house at Zürich Zoo contains ropes and poles on which the apes can swing.

Below: The trend towards better animal accommodation in zoos is exemplified by the polar bear enclosures at San Diego Zoo, with its artificial Arctic vista.

3 Zoos and Breeding

If animals breed well in zoos, it means that the zoos suit the animals, or the animals suit the zoos, or both.

Many eminent zoologists have said that the breeding of animals in captivity is the measure of good zoo management. I do not believe it is the only yardstick, but I agree that it is probably the most important one. In fact, my own personal list of the best-run zoos in the world would very nearly coincide with a list of zoos drawn up in order of their breeding successes. Fifteen zoos I know of breed at least a quarter of all their mammal and bird species every year, and the species they keep include some that cannot breed yearly. All these zoos are among the world's top twenty by any sensible standards of judgment, and are zoos that suit the animals they have chosen to keep.

I say "the animals they have chosen to keep." Choice is important, because some animal families naturally acclimatize well in zoos and easily produce zoo stock; others have been acclimatized only after a long period of trial and error; others can as yet scarcely be acclimatized at all as breeders.

In the first category are the large cats. Lions and tigers have bred with ease for many generations in the traveling cages of circus menageries and in the ancient—though I must say rather elegant—accommodation provided for them in such zoos as Dublin and Bristol. Lions do not seem to mind what we now regard as rather grim Victorian bar architecture in their living quarters, and indeed old-style menageries can even breed hybrids between lions and tigers. Animals that are so unexacting in their breeding demands do well in almost any zoo.

Certain families of animals in the middle category are so difficult to acclimatize that they should be entrusted only to specialists. These include some of the Australian marsupials, most of which are best dealt with by Australian zoos. A good example is the koala; this peculiar tree-dweller can thrive and breed only if it can eat the leaves of certain species of eucalyptus trees at exactly the right stage of leaf-growth. The Australian government will not allow koalas out of Australia except to two zoos—those at San Diego and San Francisco—where they know there is the right eucalyptus range to satisfy the animals.

Finally there are some species that have languished in menageries for so many decades, or even centuries,

In the zoological park at Askaniya-Nova, in the Ukraine, southwest Russia, scientists are conducting a series of breeding experiments on a large scale, with the aim of producing new hybrid deer and antelope suitable for domestication. Above: Vladimir Treus, the park's director, with one of a herd of Askaniya hybrid deer.

Another purpose of breeding in zoos is the re-creation of extinct species. The Munich Zoo has been especially concerned with this. Top: A herd of bred-back "aurochs," the ancestral species of our domestic cattle, that became extinct in 1627. Above: Heinz Heck, the director of Munich Zoo, with a bred-back tarpan, that died out more recently in 1876.

that it is time to think whether they should ever be kept in zoos at all. These we shall meet later.

Once a zoo has chosen wisely what animals it intends to keep, there are two main factors that will affect the general breeding performance: the provision of good living quarters, and meticulous attention to diet. Over the years zoo managers have learned more and more about the proper housing of animals, and have vastly improved ventilation and hygienic conditions, including the prevention of diseases, and the use of antibiotics and vermicides (worm-destroyers). This has probably been the most important single factor to improve the breeding performance, for bad housing and disease inhibit not only animals' lives but also their reproduction; an unhealthy, unfit animal may survive, but it is less likely to breed than a healthy one.

Next in importance come improvements in animal nutrition, including provision of the all-important vitamins and trace elements—the tiny quantities of certain rare chemical materials essential to the physiological processes. At a recent meeting I attended, Sir Solly Zuckerman (the Honorary Secretary of the Zoological Society of London, and one of the greatest living experts on the zoo management of Primates) recounted that a fine breeding stock of one of the common baboons persisted for many years and then suddenly dried up. It just didn't breed any more. Although the zoo had given enormous attention to the diet of these animals, an essential B vitamin had somehow been dropped out of their food. As soon as it was replaced, the stock began breeding again. So it is clear that vitamins—and the science of trace elements—in nutrition must be understood by every proprietor of a breeding stock of captive animals. So must the proper use of new antibiotics, fungicides, and other infection treatments.

But success in breeding animals in captivity does not rest on the one simple formula of good housing, proper feeding, and modern medication. It is a highly complicated business, demanding study and observation, experience and practice, patience and common sense; and it still depends largely on how readily various orders, families, and individual species of animals lend themselves to acclimatization. Each order, each family, sets its own special problems. It would need many volumes to cover the whole animal kingdom, but in one chapter we can at least see what has been attempted and what has been achieved within a few selected groups.

The Parrots

A good starting point is the parrot family. Parrots, lories, lorikeets, cockatoos, macaws, conures, parakeets,

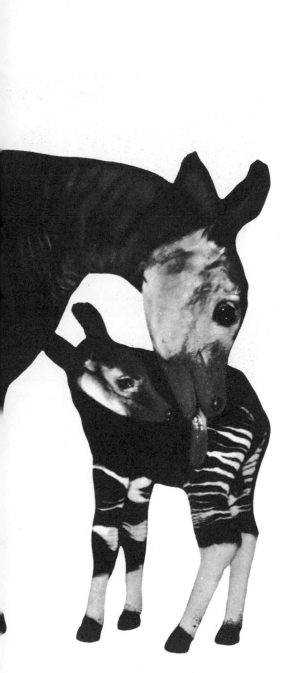

The okapi, discovered at the beginning of the present century in the Congo, remains one of the world's least known large mammals. The few zoos that have specimens are trying to breed them. Above: Bristol Zoo's female okapi with her son, born in 1963; unfortunately this youngster survived only a few months.

lovebirds, and budgerigars have been popular in captivity ever since zoos began, and have always been fascinating to aviculturists, and to individuals who like to have them as pets. But it must be said at once that the keeping of a talking parrot as a pet is no contribution to the breeding potential of parrots in captivity. There are hundreds of thousands of living parrots with no breeding potential at all—often, though not always, because they are without a mate. Zoos must take some share of the blame. So gaudy a show do parrots make that many zoos, including some of the best, have been tempted to keep them in large numbers and in great variety, not mainly for breeding or scientific study but for public amusement. The London Zoo's parrot house has, in my opinion, too many parrots housed in conditions in which they are unlikely to breed; and in fact only a very few of them do so. Even West Berlin Zoo, with its beautiful, brand-new bird accommodation, does not, I think, have enough external aviaries specifically for breeding parrots, although it houses over 50 species and at least 200 individuals.

It is fair to say that practically no owners of pet parrots, and only a few zoos, are in the major league of parrot-breeding. The main history of the parrot family as breeders in captivity centers around private parrot-aviculturists, or psittacologists. One of the greatest of all was the 12th Duke of Bedford. As Lord Tavistock, before he succeeded to the dukedom, he built up part of his father's estate at Woburn, in Bedfordshire, into an enormous private parrot aviary. The cages were very large, built over living vegetation (some of it did not live long), and copiously provided with nesting boxes, since nearly all parrots are hole-nesting birds. Only privileged members of the public were admitted, and some of the birds were allowed to fly around and to breed in semi-liberty. Lord Tavistock got far better breeding results than most other people because of the privacy and size of his collection, and its spacious accommodations.

What degree of success has been achieved in breeding the parrot family? According to the latest reliable count, there are at present 317 living species of parrots. Nineteen others have become extinct only since 1600; five of them died out in zoos. Of the total of 336, I can find records

Poor zoo conditions sometimes make breeding impossible. This was especially true in the past. Above left: The "Parrot Walk" in London Zoo in 1872 may have delighted the public, but each bird lived chained to its perch. Left: London Zoo's indoor parrot house today, where both sexes are housed together in cages.

of 232 having been exhibited in zoos at some time or another. Only 127, as far as I can discover, are known beyond doubt to have fully bred—that is, reared young to their full fledging—in captivity. So breeding successes are limited to 38 per cent of all the parrot species, and the figure would be far lower if regular zoo records alone had been relied on. This figure takes into account the whole of recorded aviculture.

Considering the ancient popularity of the parrot family among private aviculturists and zoos, the record is not impressive. One reason is that the family includes many subfamilies and tribes, some of which breed freely in captivity while others do not respond well even to the best management.

Among the easiest of the parrots to breed is the budgerigar, one of the very few newly domesticated birds of the last hundred years. Even in its wild form it never reached aviculture outside Australia until 1840, and all its present-day color phases and varieties have been produced by artificial selection in less than a century. There are now thousands and thousands of budgerigar fanciers in North America, Britain, Western Europe, and Japan, and many of them get good breeding results without elaborate aviaries. The minimum size for cages is about 64 cubic feet. Most breeders use an outdoor flight with an indoor shelter. The indoor shelter can be climate-controlled in winter, but budgies are fairly hardy, so it never has to be tropically heated. The birds do best of all when they are provided with a biggish indoor flight and an outdoor flight where they can enjoy themselves whenever it is sunny. They can have their nest boxes in the outdoor flight in summer, for breeding purposes.

With budgies as common in captivity as they now are, escapes are everyday events. When budgies escape in England, they may fly about for anything up to a few months, and then they are either recaptured or eaten by a predator, or they die in the winter. But in Florida the climate is almost identical with that of the homeland of the budgerigar in Australia. Escaped budgies have survived and bred in Florida, behaving as members of the local bird community, and it is estimated that there are now about 10,000 of them in one area of the state. The Florida birds, incidentally, are tending to revert to the green color of the original wild budgerigar, which obviously has some selective advantage over the other color forms that have been bred in captivity.

The budgerigar is the commonest of all the grass parakeets of Australia, and in its native territory it still assembles in flocks of up to a million. But certain other kinds of Australian grass parakeets are now rare in the wild. Some of these also breed rather freely in captivity

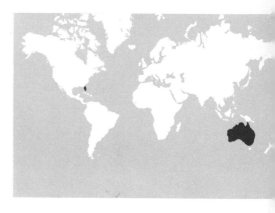

Budgerigars are native to Australia. They have been taken all over the world by man, but have managed to establish themselves in Florida, where they are currently on the increase.

Top right: Budgerigar feeding its young. Prolific breeders, budgerigars may produce up to a dozen young in a season. However, they dislike interruptions and readily desert nest and eggs. Right: Some color varieties produced by breeding: the commonest colors are green, blue, and yellow, but gray and "slate" varieties have also been bred.

Above: The extinct West Indian macaw *Ara martinicus*. It was described by Père Bouton, who made an expedition to Martinique in 1635.

Below: Distribution of the parrot family today. This group includes the macaws of South America, the lories of Australia, the kea of New Zealand, and a variety of parrots from Africa.

when they are looked after properly in quiet surroundings and given large cages with plenty of cover.

Many of the medium-sized and smaller cockatoos are very good breeders in captivity, and whole breeding groups can be run together, almost like budgerigars. The Amazon parrots, much favored as talking birds, will also breed in captivity; but they need a rather large space and good accommodation, and they must be much isolated, pair by pair.

Far more difficult to breed are the great macaws, even though some of them have been in aviculture for many years. The West Indian forms are now extinct, and we know much of what we do know about them because they were exhibited in menageries of the seventeenth century nobles and painted by good resident artists. The big macaws of the *Ara* genus are now all Central and South American birds. Perhaps the most typical is the blue-and-yellow species, which has been exhibited in European zoos for centuries, all too often chained and set on a perch, just being colorful and amusing the public. Arthur Prestwich, secretary and treasurer of Britain's Avicultural Society and a world authority on the history of parrot breeding, shows that this bird was not bred in captivity until 1818, in France; the second success was in Czechoslovakia, around 1901, and the third and fourth successes were in Germany and Australia in 1931. Even today the breeding rate of these birds in captivity remains lamentably low.

Still more surprising is the record of *Ara chloroptera*. It is one of many birds for which no two people seem to use the same vernacular name. Some people call it the red-blue-and-green macaw, others the red-and-green macaw, and yet others the green-winged macaw, which I think will do. We know this bird has been in aviculture in Europe since about 1590, because around that date a certain Lady Arabella Stuart had her portrait painted holding one. Yet as far as I can discover it was not bred in captivity (except for a few hybrids with other species) until 1962, when it bred in both the Tel Aviv zoo and J. S. Rigge's private aviary in Cumberland, England. The record of a very old zoo favorite, the scarlet macaw, or red-and-blue macaw, is little better, for it did not breed in captivity until 1916. Either these are very difficult birds, or else people had not really tried to breed them, but just keep them in cages. There are also a few macaws that have never been bred and reared in captivity at all up to the time of writing, primarily because they are so rarely kept. These include Cassin's macaw and the Brazilian green macaw.

In a big family like the parrots, it is not surprising that there are certain groups that are seldom imported—even these days—into aviculture, and have not bred much because they have not been available. Among the very charming little lorikeets, for instance, is a genus called *Vini*. There are members of the genus in Indonesia and New Guinea, but it flourishes mostly on remote Pacific islands, with several different species. Some of these are rare in the whole of aviculture and have never, as far as I know, been in zoos at all. This is true of Kuhl's lory, first successfully bred in America in 1934 and now being bred in Australia. It is also true of the Papuan lorikeet, which has bred only once in captivity, in Scotland in 1910. The Tahiti blue lory, too, has never been in a mainstream zoo, and was fully reared only by the 12th Duke of Bedford (when he was Lord Tavistock, in 1937). There are also two or three other lories with similar records. So here we have a whole group of birds about which no one except a few private aviculturists knows very much. On the other hand, the brush-tongued lorikeets are now being developed as "good doers," or "adjusters," in captivity. These birds actually chew up flowers and brush out the nectar with their tongues. They are not particularly difficult to feed in captivity because the nectar element in their vegetarian diet can be simulated with honey, glucose, and other foods.

To sum up, the general breeding record for the parrot family is not impressive; but the aviculturists have adopted the parrots into captivity more sensibly than most zoos. It is true that zoos have some obligation to entertain the public, even though this is not their first concern; but it is possible for parrots to provide a public spectacle that is good zoo culture too. Imagine a dozen big macaws flying free around a zoo. The thing is possible, and a few zoos have done it. There is a charming little zoo at Bourton-on-the-Water in Gloucestershire, England, for instance, where the proprietor has four species of macaws in complete liberty, including the greatest of all, the hyacinthine macaw. They fly free-winged about the village, and some species are now beginning to breed.

A free colony of quaker parakeets can also provide a great deal of public interest. The quaker parakeet is allied to the small macaws but has rather different habits. It comes from the southern part of South America, and is one of the very few parrots that builds a nest in the open. This is a communal or social nest, which all the birds take part in building; when it is complete, each bird has its own separate entrance in what looks like a big cartload of sticks up a tree. Such nests were built in freedom in England's Whipsnade Zoological Park before World War II, and similar colonies have been established in other zoos. This is the sort of bird for zoos to have, in my opinion, rather than ranks of tethered macaws living long but barren and noisy lives in crowded rows.

Above: Blue-and-yellow macaws have rarely bred in zoos. One of the few occasions was in 1958, when a pair at Chessington Zoo, England, hatched out a chick after 28 days incubation. Below: Rainbow lorikeets at Currumbin Bird Sanctuary in Australia, feeding at a dish of honey. Unlike the macaw, this is an easy parrot to keep and breed.

A tree shrew. These long-nosed shrewlike animals are now regarded as primates—the order of animals that includes man. They are thus of great scientific interest, but little is known of them, chiefly because they were very difficult to breed. Progress in this line is, however, being made in some German zoos.

The Primates

The order of the Primates is a large and very varied one, including (in ascending evolutionary order) tree shrews, lemurs, monkeys and apes. As zoo mammals, the Primates are in a rather similar position to those famous zoo birds, the parrots. Some of them have been acclimatized since the times of ancient Egypt, Greece, and Rome; yet only in certain far-seeing zoos and private collections have they ever been truly fostered as breeding animals. A few species, it is true, have bred freely for centuries, but only 43 per cent of all species are so far known to have bred in captivity. This compares fairly closely with the figure of 38 per cent for parrots, and the similar situation appears to have arisen for similar reasons. First, the animals have been imported primarily for show or as pets, without much regard to fostering their reproductive potential; secondly, the order includes several groups of "bad doers" that nobody has really

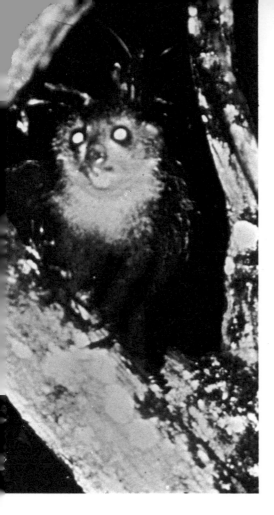

The aye-aye (above), an extremely rare lower primate, lives in the forests of Madagascar, where this photograph was taken. This species has never bred in captivity. Ring-tailed lemurs (below) can be bred in good environments; they are frequently kept by zoos and make attractive and amusing pets.

troubled to tackle, except for a few recent specialists.

Tree shrews have been accepted in the order of Primates only in the present century. It was not realized until then that they are not insectivores but omnivores, closely resembling what the ancestors of the most advanced of the order may have looked like some 70 million years ago. Tree shrews come exclusively from the mainland and archipelago of southeast Asia. They have only recently been tackled as zoo animals, and of the 31 species now known only three have been kept in zoos. Of those three, two have been successfully reared, the first in 1958 and the second in 1960, both in Germany. The German zoo keepers and animal breeders were the first to make the breakthrough in housing and in diet. They found that tree shrews do quite well in small cages provided they have a lot of cover—little branches and things to hide in—and holes to breed in. The Germans had some trouble at first with the tree shrews' diet, which must be very mixed, but they have overcome this problem and have now established a stock.

The true lemurs, the next most primitive of the living Primates, consist of three families of animals that are found nowhere except in Madagascar and the Comoro Islands between Madagascar and Africa. Although Madagascar (now the Malagasy Republic) is only about 240 miles from mainland Africa, the separation is a rather old one, dating back to early in the age of mammals. For some 30 or 40 million years the mammals of Madagascar have followed their own lines of evolution, and the lemurs have evolved in all sorts of queer directions. Fossil evidence shows that one enormous super-lemur evolved, the size of an anthropoid ape. This died out only in the last million years or so. There are among living lemurs small, delicate, squirrel-like forms; slightly gibbon-like forms like the almost tailless indri and the tailed sifakas; curious nocturnal forms like the aye-aye; and average sized monkey-like forms such as the common lemurs.

Except for the genus *Lemur* itself, the zoo breeding record of the Madagascan group of lemurs is bad, probably due to our inexperience in feeding them. Of the four species of the indri family, only two have ever been kept in zoos and only one has bred, at the Malagasy Republic's own zoo at Tananarive, in 1954. The aye-aye, which is now so rare as to be in danger of extinction, was first exhibited just over a century ago but has never bred in captivity. One lived in the London Zoo for 19 years but never had a mate; another lived unmated in Amsterdam for 23 years. In fact, none of the more peculiar lemurs are so far being bred except in very specialized research institutions and in the zoo at Tananarive.

However, the zoo record of the 14 species of the common lemur family is very much better. Eleven have at some time or other been in zoo culture, eight have bred, and some of the commonest have been breeding in captivity for over a century.

There are certain lemur families (though not true lemurs) outside Madagascar. They include the nocturnal lorises of southern India and Ceylon, and closely related groups in the south and west of Africa, such as the potto and the galagos, or bush babies. The Asian slow and slender lorises, the potto, and three species of bush babies have bred in captivity. The lesser bush baby was first zoo-bred over a century ago, and there are now several captive colonies existing. Bush babies are popular household pets, though delicate and inclined to suffer from respiratory trouble. They need so much attention (including frequent meals of live mealworms) that private culture should only be conducted by those who are really dedicated and intend to stay so.

Higher in the evolutionary scale than the lemurs are tarsiers—small, rat-tailed, boggle-eyed, big-eared, nocturnal animals held to be very close to an ancestor of the higher monkeys, apes, and man. They come from Malaysia, Indonesia, and the Philippines. Of the three species, only the Philippine tarsier has ever been shown in zoos, and that only since World War II. Although one has lived for over 11 years at Philadelphia, the species is exceptionally hard to keep. Like most nocturnal animals, tarsiers are hard to study in the wild, and little is known about their natural food; but because of their evolutionary interest, zoologists are naturally anxious to study them. Many people think that the sensible thing would be to acclimatize them near their natural range, such as in the zoo at Manila in the Philippines.

The highest suborder of Primates, the Anthropoidea, embraces all the monkeys and apes, including those of the New World. It also includes extinct ape-men (or men-apes) and men. Some monkeys and apes have been collected as pets, menagerie exhibits, and status symbols since the early civilizations, of both the Old World and the New; but comparatively few have ever bred freely in captivity and some not at all.

All the Old World monkeys belong to a superfamily

The Philippine tarsier has never thrived in captivity and very few zoos have ever kept one for long. This specimen was photographed at the Philadelphia Zoo. This primate is nocturnal, the size of a small rat, and it not only climbs trees, but on the ground jumps like a frog.

known as the Cercopithecoids. It contains two main living groups: 37 species of Cercopithecines—macaques, baboons, and guenons (the most familiar kinds of monkey)—and 28 of Colobines, which are rather connoisseurs' monkeys, and in many ways the most beautiful. Every single one of the 37 Cercopithecines has now bred in captivity. The last two known to have done so (for we cannot be absolutely certain that they did not breed earlier in some zoo that failed to keep records) are the rare Allen's swamp monkey and the patas monkey. Both of these bred in American zoos in the 1950s.

The 28 Colobines have been a much less "zoo-able" group. Only 15 have been acclimatized, and only seven have bred in zoos. Successes include several of the 18 langurs, leaf monkeys, and lutongs of Asia, and one of the five guerezas, Africa's own special Colobines. The 13 Colobines that have not yet been acclimatized have obviously had no chance of breeding in captivity. Some of the others have had very little chance, simply because they are so rare in zoos. Of the two species of snub-nosed monkeys from China, only one has reached a Western zoo—in 1939—and it did not breed. The extraordinary proboscis monkey of Borneo has only occasionally been kept in zoos during the last 70 years; and it is possible that the only specimens in captivity as late as 1962 were three in San Diego and two in Surabaja, in Indonesia, where this species has bred.

Success among the five African guerezas has been limited to one species (the white-tailed guereza, which first bred in the Bronx and San Diego zoos in 1952). These are difficult animals to keep in captivity, and still more difficult to breed; but some races of the very beautiful guerezas are known to have only tiny world populations, and all are of special interest to students of animal behavior. So a number of zoos are now trying to build up breeding stocks. Some of the high-class monkey "hotels" that the foremost European and American zoos have lately built are already accommodating these forest monkeys in air-conditioned, humidity-controlled apartments in which they flourish. In Europe guerezas can be admired at Antwerp, Paris, Frankfurt-am-Main, London, Naples, West Berlin, and Basel, and in the United States at the zoos in Colorado Springs, the Bronx, San Diego, and Cleveland.

Most of the New World monkeys (or "mini-monkeys," as I should like to call them) are bad doers in captivity, or have until recently been so. They include the marmosets and the uakaris, the titis and the squirrel monkey (the pint-sized, delicate little supersonic monkey of the Central and South American jungles), the spider monkeys and capuchins (the organ-grinder's monkeys), and the biggest of all American monkeys, the great howler

Top: A pair of black-and-white colobus monkeys at the San Diego Zoo. This Old World monkey from Africa is a leaf-eater; it has occasionally bred in zoos. Above: A pair of spider monkeys, as illustrated in Brehm's *Tierleben*. This New World monkey rarely breeds in zoos.

The gibbon enclosure at Hanover Zoo. It is a good example of how these apes are best kept—on islands with trees, ropes, and poles to provide plenty of scope for exercise.

monkeys, which reach a weight of 20 lbs. They are all very athletic forest animals; and some of them, including the capuchins, spider monkeys, and howlers, have prehensile tails that serve as a fifth limb, an adaptation not found among any of the Old World monkeys.

All told, the New World monkeys (superfamily Ceboidea) include about 75 species. Fifty-two have been kept in captivity at one time or another, though some only rarely and some only recently; of that total I can find records of only 23 that have bred, more than half of them only in the last 30 years. The best doers are the capuchins, some of which entered menageries in early post-Columbian times. All four species have bred in captivity, and one—the tufted (or weeper) capuchin—has done so for many years.

The highest superfamily of the Primates—the Hominoids—embraces two families: the Pongids, or anthropoid apes; and the Hominids, or man and some of his extinct ancestors. The anthropoid apes consist of two subfamilies: the seven lesser anthropoid apes (gibbons and siamang); and the three (or four) great apes (chimpanzees, gorilla, and orangutan).

In the old days there were thought to be far more than seven species of gibbons, because most of them have several different color phases; to make things more complicated, some species also change their colors with age. All but one of the seven species now recognized have been kept in captivity, and four have bred. But breeding in full captivity is very recent; the first record was around 1925. It is only in the past few years that gibbons have been housed properly, which is probably why they are only now beginning to breed. Since they do not cross water gaps, they are very suitable for exhibition on small zoo islands, with plenty of dead trees, swings, and other things from which they can hang. The daring young gibbon on the flying trapeze is now a feature of nearly every zoo, and while he swings through the air with the greatest of ease, he emits the most remarkable noises. The howls of the siamang gibbons in West Germany's Frankfurt zoo can be heard from the other end of the town when they are really in form in the early morning. The gibbons, tailless like all the Hominoids, have particularly long arms. They swing through the air primarily with the use of their arms, using their legs largely as balancing organs as they hurl themselves from branch to branch.

The great apes are three—the chimpanzee, the gorilla, and the orangutan. If we want to, we can divide the chimpanzees into two species. A disputation is now in full blast between systematists who regard the chimpanzee as one species, and those who would separate the pigmy chimpanzee that lives on the left bank of the Congo River from all the others. Now the Congo River is broad, and chimpanzees do not normally swim. I will not say they cannot swim, because a few have been known to swim; but they certainly do not *like* to swim. Anyway, the water barrier of the Congo River seems to have been quite enough to separate the two populations of chimpanzees for thousands of years. Because the pigmy chimp, or bonobo, on the left bank of the Congo grows to a smaller size than the chimps on the right bank, and has certain other distinguishing features, including the making of very different noises, many people accept it as a different species, and not just as a well-marked race of the common chimpanzee. On the whole, I should prefer to regard the bonobo as a well-marked race; but I admit that the case is a borderline one.

Whether two species or one, the chimp has long been known to zoology and has a long history in captivity. In

The bonobo, or pigmy chimpanzee, that lives on the left bank of the Congo River, is rarely seen in captivity, but there are specimens in the zoos at Antwerp, Frankfurt, and San Diego. The first success in breeding this ape came at the Frankfurt Zoo, where the specimen above was photographed.

about 500 B.C. one of the greatest and most daring of the Carthaginians, Hanno the Navigator, voyaged down the west coast of Africa, probably as far as what we now call Liberia. When he got safely back to Carthage, he recorded that he had met big wild men along the coast. A Greek script that is supposed to be a translation of his account calls them gorillas. In A.D. 1847 this name was applied to the newly-discovered (or rediscovered) true gorilla, so many people have come to believe that Hanno saw true gorillas. It is not impossible that he did; but judging from the present northern limits of gorilla distribution—about a thousand miles farther south than Hanno appears to have gone—it is much more likely that the animals he saw were chimpanzees. Male chimps can indeed be very big and resemble wild men. A full-grown male averages about 110 pounds, but big ones have exceeded 180 pounds. There are reports of other travelers of antiquity who may have seen or heard of chimps, but there is no evidence that any ever came into captivity in ancient Egypt, Greece, or Rome.

The first evidence of the entry of the chimpanzee into the zoo world dates from about 1640. In that year one of the Dutch princes of Orange, Frederick Henry of Nassau, had in his castle menagerie at Honsholredijk in Holland an animal which has often been described as an orangutan but is almost certain to have been a chimp from Angola. Apart from this, the earliest record of a chimpanzee in a Western zoo seems to date from October 11, 1835, when one arrived at the London Zoo. It died, almost at once, on March 25, 1836. Another, for which the Zoological Society of London paid £300 (roughly equivalent in purchasing power to $8500 today), was received on May 10, 1845. It died on December 29 of the same year.

Early chimpanzees in the Age of Modern Zoos were short-lived. Hindsight now tells us that even the best menagerie of over a century ago was unhygienic and totally unsuited to the management of great apes. But what were the officers of the Zoological Society of London to do? They were charged by their Royal Charter to introduce "new and curious subjects of the animal king-

Chimpanzees have excited man's curiosity ever since they first became well known, in the seventeenth century. The tendency has usually been to make the animal appear more human than it really is. This attitude can be seen in the drawing (left) that was made in 1800 and was based on an earlier version of 1699. The artist has shown him incorrectly standing erect and dressed in a garland of leaves for the sake of modesty.

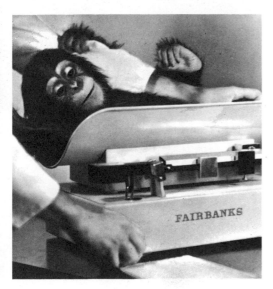

dom." They had to pay fantastic sums for apes of whose expectation of life (in the environment designed for them by guesswork) they knew little and nearly everybody else knew nothing. The London Zoo did its best; most zoos did their best; but the commonest and most available of the great apes was brought in large numbers to Europe and North America for nearly a century before an average chimp in an average zoo lived long enough to provide more than a nine-days', or at most a nine-months', wonder.

Before chimps could survive, let alone breed in captivity, great advances had to be made in the accommodations provided for them and in the amount of individual care given to them. The breakthrough did not come until 1915, when the first pair (or at least the first pair to be recorded in a scientific publication) bred in captivity on the private estate of the late Señora Rosalia Abreu, at the Quinta Palatino in Havana, Cuba. The famous Abreu colony of chimpanzees and other Primates was tended, managed, and housed in a style far beyond its time, with a humanity appropriate to a colony of humans. By 1930, no fewer than seven young chimps had been safely reared at the Quinta Palatino. Meanwhile the first zoo breedings had also been recorded, at the Bronx Zoo in New York in 1920 and at the Berlin Zoo in 1921.

Although Señora Abreu was undoubtedly the pioneer, many mainstream zoos were making big efforts to improve their Primate accommodation between 40 and 50 years ago. Some monkey houses of the early 1920s were probably better designed and better ventilated than ever before. Great hopes were centered, for instance, on London Zoo's great new monkey house of 1927. But when it first opened it did not at once bring about the hoped-for improvement in Primate longevity and breeding. The date of building was too early for a good air-conditioning plant; and glass windows were not placed in front of the apes until later, when it was realized (as it should have been in 1927) that Hominoids are more susceptible to human respiratory diseases than are other monkeys. Conditions at the back of the house were not spacious, and it was not easy to prepare food in com-

Top left: Two chimpanzees photographed at the pioneering ape colony of Señora Abreu, in Havana. She was among the first to conduct experiments with captive apes, testing their intelligence and ability to perform various tasks. Left: A young chimpanzee being weighed at the Yale Laboratories, where Professor Yerkes continued research into the development of apes and reared a large number of chimpanzees.

pletely hygienic circumstances. Nevertheless, the London Zoo and many others were at least moving in the right direction.

In 1931 Señora Abreu's collection was presented to the Yale Laboratories (now the Yerkes Institute) of Primate Biology, directed by the great pioneer of Primate psychology, Dr. Robert M. Yerkes. The Yale group had already reared a young chimp at their new station at Orange Park in Florida a year earlier. In the next five years, from 1931 to 1936, they reared another 15, including the first recorded twins and the first second-generation baby. Meanwhile another zoo birth had taken place; London Zoo's famous Jubilee, the rage of the royal jubilee year, was born to Boo-boo in February 1935. But it took two decades for the best zoos to catch up with the Havana and Florida successes. The fine zoo at San Diego did well with the breeding of chimps in the 1940s and had second-generation babies in the 1950s.

By about 1960, many big zoos had built beautifully designed ape houses—clean, airy establishments of hospital or expensive hotel standards. These houses are air-conditioned and designed to keep out diseases. Some are equipped with model kitchens of their own, and the one at West Berlin even has a bathroom and shower department. No member of the staff of an ape house is normally allowed to remain at work if suffering from any human virus infection. If, in an emergency, he has to work, he must wear a mask.

These new standards have now earned dividends. Baby chimps were reared in at least 21 zoos in 1961, 19 in 1962, 17 in 1963, and 27 in 1964. I say "at least" as these figures are only for zoos that sent their records for inclusion in the *International Zoo Yearbook*. In any one year in the 1960s there may well have been 30 zoos in which at least one chimp was bred in captivity.

The gorilla, greatest of the great apes, has on the whole been spared the nineteenth-century "Babylonian captivity" that the chimpanzee suffered, mainly because it entered the zoo world considerably later, when zoo men had begun to understand the exacting requirements of captive apes.

I have already said that the gorilla was not named and described for science until 1847. In fact Savage and Wyman, the two men who named it, made their original description only from skulls. At that time the exploration of the great central African jungle had only just begun; and it was not until about 1880 that the major museums first stocked up with gorilla skins and skeletons. So variable are gorillas, and so name-mad were some mammalogists of the period, that a dozen or more species and races were named and described during the next 30 years, sometimes from a single specimen. In fact there is only one species of gorilla with, as far as most people now admit, only two clearly-marked races — the lowland race and the rarer, more restricted mountain race. The mountain race lives from Lake Kivu and Lake Edward in the eastern Congo to the extreme southwest of Uganda. The total population, spread among about 60 small groups, is probably no more than 15,000 and possibly as low as 5,000, and conservationists have long been worried about its survival prospects. The lowland race, centered far to the west, on the Cameroons, is in some regions quite abundant, and still thought to be in no danger of extinction.

So little was known of the species in 1855 that an animal in Wombwell's menagerie in England was thought to be a queer sort of chimpanzee until identified by a well-trained zoologist as a female gorilla — the first ever proved to be in captivity outside the Congo and Cameroon forests. Since then nearly every individual gorilla exhibited has been logged by zoo scholars and, allowing for some that may have gone to wayside menageries or to private homes as pets, I think the list is probably within 10 per cent of the truth. The second captive seems to have survived (in England) for only seven months. The third, a young male recorded in 1876, visited first Hamburg, then London for a few weeks, and finally Berlin, where it died after five months. There were perhaps five others in France, Berlin, and London before the close of the nineteenth century, and in 1897 Breslau, now Wroclaw (Poland), bought a gorilla that was the first to survive in captivity for several years.

Above left: The interior of the fine modern ape-house and kitchen at the West Berlin Zoo. This zoo houses its large collection of apes with great care, in ultra-hygienic conditions. Left: Inside the apes' kitchen, where balanced diets for each animal are prepared in hotel-like conditions. The kitchen, as well as the apes, is on view to the public.

In the present century an average of scarcely one gorilla a year reached European and American zoos up to World War II; and only two of these were mountain gorillas. After the war many more gorillas left Africa, sometimes masquerading as chimps because of the export regulations introduced by most gorilla countries. Bernhard Grzimek, director of West Germany Frankfurt Zoo, corresponded with every zoo director he knew and discovered that 35 males and 21 females (nearly all lowland gorillas) were in captivity in 1954. Owing to

Bamboo, Philadelphia Zoo's famous gorilla. A lowland male, he died in 1961, after living in the zoo for 33½ years, thus setting a longevity record for his species. Good zoo conditions and a strong physical constitution together brought about this remarkable life span for a captive gorilla.

better housing conditions and new veterinary improvements, most of them fared much better than gorillas had fared before the war. Most still survive, for a considerable proportion of all gorillas now in captivity have been captive for 10 years or more.

In mid-1965 there were 219 lowland gorillas in 71 zoos and 13 mountain gorillas in six zoos. Not unnaturally, therefore, the few breeding successes to date have been with the lowland race. The first successful birth was at the Columbus Zoo in Ohio on December 22, 1956, the second and third both at Basel, in 1959 and 1961, the fourth and fifth at Washington in 1961 and 1964, the sixth at Basel in 1964, and the seventh through ninth at Dallas, San Diego, and Frankfurt-am-Main in 1965. Of the three Basel babies, all born to the same parents, the first was hand-reared by Mrs. Lang, the zoo director's wife, and the others were reared by their mother.

The rise of the zoo gorilla as a happy hominoid has depended on a stock of good, adaptable, tame, and acclimatized animals. Nearly all the present zoo gorillas have been imported as young ones; and the new technique is to handle them frequently and continuously in a parental way, giving them plenty of opportunities for mental occupation and play. Most top zoos now do this very well; Ernst Lang and his wife and their staff at Basel do it marvelously. I remember calling on the Langs when Goma, the first of the Basel gorilla babies, wearing a diaper, was living in their house. She had a set of little boxes, graded in size, to fit the one inside the other; they were primarily for her amusement, but also so that the Langs could see if she would play the same way as a human child. They did a great deal of observational work on her solution of such problems as might be offered to a human baby of equivalent age. Goma crawled about the Langs' drawing-room at teatime just as a human baby might have done. She investigated everything; and she had come to terms with the family dog in much the same way as many young children do. Goma also used to go out for walks with Mrs. Lang—in her carriage, of course. She has now settled down to what should be a valuable future in the ape house.

The breeding potential of the lowland gorilla is excellent. Although there have been only nine successful births up to the time of writing, the present zoo stock of well over 200 includes a majority of strong adolescents, growing well and doubtless with far fewer mental problems than their predecessors. So far no highland gorillas have been bred in captivity, although two have been born at an accommodation camp in the Congo to females already pregnant when captured in the wild. However, there is every reason to expect that the highland

Ernst Lang, director of the Basel Zoo, with Goma, the first gorilla infant born in captivity in Europe. This baby, a female, was rejected by her mother, but was saved by Dr. Lang and his wife, who reared her with great care in their own home. Two more babies born at the Basel Zoo were reared by their mother.

gorilla will also soon be bred in captivity; adult stock has only just reached the right age as I write.

The orangutan, the great ape of the Malay archipelago, has been kept in captivity for longer than the gorilla. The people of what we now call Indonesia and Malaysia may well have kept orangs as household pets more than a thousand years ago. It is nearly two centuries since the

Painting by the Dutch artist Haag, of William V's pet orangutan (see text).

first (certain) one of modern historical times arrived in Europe (in 1776), to be housed in the private zoo of William V, Prince of Orange, at The Hague. Orangs were imported into Europe throughout the nineteenth century but, like the early chimps, their lot in captivity was a sad one, and continued to be so into the present century. Even in the well-run London Zoo, the average length of life in captivity of 30 orangs kept between 1904 and 1956 was under four years. It must be remembered, however, that quite a lot of them were ailing when they arrived, having formerly been the pets of inexperienced people.

Zoo breeding success came earlier with orangs than with gorillas. The first orang to be bred and born entirely in captivity was at the Berlin Zoo (now the West Berlin Zoo) on January 12, 1928. In the same year two others were born, one at Nuremberg in Germany and one at Philadelphia. By 1964 at least 39 zoos had reared orangs, and those with especially good records include Berlin and Philadelphia, where the famous Guarina, now at least 35 years old, gave birth to her ninth baby in 1955. So the captive breeding record of orangs is so far much better than that of gorillas; but there is another and more worrying side to the orang story, which I shall deal with in the next chapter.

Pheasants and Waterfowl

Even the past century of scientific and tender care in highly efficient zoos and private aviaries did not succeed in getting half the parrots or half the Primates to breed in captivity. However, certain substantial groups of animals can be happily accommodated in captivity and will thrive. These include the pheasants (the tribe Phasianini) and the swans, ducks, and geese (the family Anatidae). These groups are, as it were, pre-adapted to zoo life; and the great majority of species in both will breed if properly handled by experienced people.

The tribe Phasianini comprises the pheasants, fowl, and peafowl. The domestic fowl is the most abundant bird in the world, and there are about as many chickens living on our planet now as there are humans. Descended from the Indian jungle fowl, the chicken has been in domestication for some 5,000 years; and in recent decades it has become, probably, the most abundant single source of high-class protein in man's diet. Another member of the same tribe, the peafowl, has been in aviculture for at least 3,000 years and, like the domestic fowl, almost certainly began its career as one of man's familiars in India. The common pheasant was first acclimatized over 2,000 years ago at the eastern end of the Mediterranean.

It has thus been known for many centuries that some

The most abundant bird in the world, thanks to man's intervention, is the domestic fowl, a prolific breeder. Above: A flock of Light Sussex hens on a Canadian poultry farm.

The San Diego Zoo has installed modern incubators and breeding facilities in order to breed rare and exotic birds. Top: An incubator, with thermostatically controlled heating and ventilation. Above: Swinhoe's pheasants bred at San Diego. This species is a native of Formosa where it is nearly extinct.

members of the pheasant tribe are easy to keep. We now know that there are in fact 48 living species belonging to the tribe. In spite of the fact that several of them are not at all common, every one of them, except the rare Rothschild's peacock pheasant, had reached some aviary outside its native area by 1950. When Jean Delacour published his *Pheasants of the World* in 1951, he could report that only seven were not known to have reared young in aviculture, and of those, two—the Congo peacock and Hume's bar-tailed pheasant—bred successfully after the book was published.

The world headquarters of the pheasant tribe seems to be in southeast Asia; and exactly half the 48 species were first brought into captivity in the quarter-century 1857 to 1882 during the great days of the opening-up of the forests of southeastern Asia and Formosa. That heyday of pheasant importation coincided with the rise of many private avicultural estates and zoos run by people with knowledge and skill. Not surprisingly, the pheasant tribe breeds best still in private estates and small specialist zoos. There are over a dozen semi-private or private places in North America that do extremely well in breeding exotic pheasants, at least three highly skillful establishments in England, and several in France, Germany, Japan, and Belgium, all of which have long histories of pheasant culture. Zoos with fine recent pheasant-breeding records include Arnhem and Rotterdam (Holland), Antwerp (Belgium), Barcelona (Spain), San Diego (California), and Tama Zoo in Tokyo. London, Prague, Paignton (England), and Sofia (Bulgaria) run them close.

The story of the swans, geese, and ducks follows a pattern similar to that of the pheasants. The number of full species of the family Anatidae now living is 146. Less than a century ago there were 150, but four have become extinct; two of them were at one time introduced into captivity but neither bred. The proportion of known species in aviculture has always been high, but now it is truly remarkable: of the 146 living species all but 4 are now usually being kept somewhere in captivity or semi-captivity. The proportion of successful breeders, also always high, is now equally remarkable. Only 26 of all the 146 living species have failed to rear young in aviaries.

The only four species not yet kept in captivity are the torrent duck of the fast Andean rivers, the Brazilian merganser, the Chinese merganser, and the blue-billed duck of Australia. Some of these may prove difficult—particularly the torrent duck, which will probably need to be kept near a waterfall. But none of them should be beyond the wit of the present formidable experts to manage. Within the next few decades at most, I feel sure they will also achieve success with the 26 species still to breed.

Top: Some of the breeding pens at the Ornamental Pheasant Trust in Norfolk, the largest collection of game birds in the world, where nearly 300 young birds of eighteen different kinds were reared in 1964. Above: Day-old Californian quail in an electric brooder at the Pheasant Trust. Note the size of pocket watch for comparison.

The glorious suitability of wildfowl for culture is best illustrated by the fact that a wildfowl collection invariably acts as a magnet for wild species. The history of wildfowl culture has its ancient roots as much in ornamental parks as in zoos; and the magnet principle certainly operates strongly in St. James's Park, London. The Park has been an aviary, or rather a wildfowl ranch,

since before the London Zoo was in existence—at least since Charles II's restoration in 1660. It has been a preserve for wild animals and game since Henry VIII made the Westminster parklands such in 1536. Here anybody can see what happens when someone starts a culture of exotic waterfowl with pinioned birds such as Cape shelducks from South Africa, mandarin ducks from Asia, and wood ducks from the Americas. These resident exotic wildfowl attract wild birds very much, because they are fed, and the ornamental wildfowl lake soon collects a large group of local "panhandlers" that attach themselves and may even settle down to breed. The

Above: The lake in St. James's Park, London, which acts as a magnet to large numbers of wild ducks that come, especially in the winter, to enjoy free handouts from the public. Below: A pair of red-crested pochard on the lake, the oldest surviving wildfowl collection.

common mallard has, of course, nested in St. James's Park for many years; nearly every year, just after the breeding season, London papers publish pictures of mallard ducks leading broods of ducklings past the sentries on duty outside Buckingham Palace. But the present breeding stock of red-crested pochards in inner London may be of wild origin, and if so it is the only colony in the British Isles. Scaup are now regular visitors at St. James's Park, where they show signs of coming earlier and staying later year by year; elsewhere they are quite erratic, but they are increasingly loyal to inner London.

In the United States, the Philadelphia Zoo has the finest collection of swans, geese and ducks; and the Salt Lake City Zoo is building up a good collection of exotic wildfowl. But the greatest collection of wildfowl anywhere is at Slimbridge in Gloucestershire, England. Never before in the history of aviculture has there been so complete a living collection of a large family of birds. At any recent moment at least 120 of the 146 known species of the Anatids could be found there. Like every good waterfowl garden, it attracts birds that were never "planted." At the time of writing I am on the finance committee of the Wildfowl Trust that runs Slimbridge, and I sometimes worry about how much it costs to feed about 1,500 "free-loading" wild ducks; but they look pretty and improve Britain's wild stock.

Among those panhandlers at Slimbridge the most extraordinary species have appeared. The first record in the British Isles of a wild American ring-billed duck was made there by Peter Scott, painting one day at the window of the studio of his house just opposite the best pond at Slimbridge. The ringbill had crossed the Atlantic, as American ducks occasionally do when blown by a gale, had managed to survive and had naturally been attracted to the nearest group of ducks that looked as if they were on to something good. All ducks are on to something good at Slimbridge; so it isn't really amazing that a duck, never proved to have been seen wild in Britain before, should have turned up outside Peter Scott's own window. The fact is that a wildfowl collection often becomes a menagerie where the borderline between wild and captive grows increasingly vague.

The Bovoids

The superfamily of the Bovoids consists of two families: the Antilocaprid, with a single living member (the pronghorn); and the Bovids, with about 110 living species of cattle, antelopes, gazelles, and goats. From a zoo's point of view the Bovoids are the mammalian counterpart of the pheasants and waterfowl among the birds. They have produced seven domestic or near-domestic

The same story is repeated on San Diego's five waterfowl pools (above), where feeding time causes a congested scramble of wild teal, pintail, scaup, red-head, and mallard ducks, as well as a permanent population of clipped ducks and geese.

species (Indian buffalo, domestic cattle, gayal, yak, banteng, goat, and sheep) and quite a number of sub-domesticated antelopes; and they have a general zoo-suitability second to no other large group of mammals.

The single Antilocaprid—the pronghorn, or American "antelope"—has been in captivity for many years, although it did not breed in captivity until the present century. It now breeds regularly in about four North American zoos. The main Bovid family has zoo figures too "round" to seem true, though they are accurate to the best of my knowledge and research. Of the 110 living species, exactly 100 have been kept in captivity and exactly 80 have bred.

Like wildfowl, Bovids respond very well to semi-wild conditions. Well selected, they make magnificent zoo shows, and there are fine collections in every principal European country and in the United States. Some main-stream zoos go in for specialization among the Bovids. South Africa's Pretoria Zoo specializes in breeding rare African antelopes; West Berlin and Munich are particu-

Below: An adult doe pronghorn antelope with a sub-adult in front of her. This species is the sole representative of the Bovoids that sheds its horns every year, in the same way as deer (which are not Bovoids) do. Both male and female pronghorns have horns.

larly good with buffaloes and bison; many North American zoos, including the Catskill Game Farm in New York State, breed rarities. The Naples Zoo, which has a quarantine station for possible cattle-disease carriers coming into Europe and consequently handles material for many other zoos, usually has a good general collection.

Monotremes and Marsupials

The fine zoos now experimenting with Bovoids, including the difficult dik-diks and duikers, are treading paths of zoo culture pioneered in Old Kingdom Egypt, 5,000 years ago. Not so the monotreme and marsupial fanciers. To zoology, let alone to zoo culture, these are relatively new animals. For instance, perhaps the most familiar of the monotremes is the platypus, or duckbill, yet it was finally proved to be an egg-laying animal only 80 years ago.

Australia, the heartland of these two most primitive orders of mammals, is in the forefront of their accli-

Two representatives of the Bovid family of the Bovoids. Left: A springbok, photographed in its natural habitat in South Africa. Above: An Ankole bull, a large, domesticated Bovid, is kept by the pastoral tribes of Central Africa.

matization. The best breeders are the great zoos in Adelaide and Melbourne; hard on their heels comes Sydney. Outside Australia, there are consistent breedings in San Diego, Wellington, Bristol, Antwerp, and Amsterdam, but the Australians are far ahead. There each great zoo may breed up to nine species a year, and all three are experimenting with many rare species newly in captivity.

As long ago as 1910 the Australian naturalist Harry Burrell showed that to manage the platypus in captivity one must simulate the natural environment in which it normally breeds. This animal spends nearly all its life in the water of Australia's slow rivers, breeding in burrows that it excavates in the muddy banks. Burrell built a pioneer platypusary for it; but he found its food requirements almost impossible to satisfy, for it needs prodigious quantities of crustaceans, insects, and worms (or their food equivalents) that are extremely difficult and expensive to provide. Later an effective platypusary on Burrell's plan was built in the state of Victoria, at Healesville, where there is a semi-natural establishment known as the Sir Colin Mackenzie Sanctuary for Native Fauna. There Robert Eadie kept a platypus alive for over four years; and in 1944 David Fleay, then director of Healesville, managed to breed the platypus for the first—and so far the only—time in captivity. Not long after, New York's Bronx zoo made a platypusary. Fleay himself came over to give them expert advice, and the staff were very ingenious in contriving diet; but somehow the platypuses would never breed.

The only other family of monotremes, the egg-laying mammals, consists of the two echidnas, or spiny anteaters, of Australia and New Guinea. The Australian echidna first arrived in Europe in 1845, where it survived for only four days in the London Zoo. However, in 1953 one died in the Philadelphia Zoo at the age of at least 49 years, 5 months, and 15 days. But there has been no similar improvement in the animal's captive breeding records. The Australian species produced a young one in captivity only once, in Berlin in 1908, and it lived for less than four months. The New Guinea echidna has twice lived for over 30 years in zoos, but never bred.

Although both monotremes and marsupials suckle their young, neither has a placenta; that is, they have no apparatus for nourishing the embryo in the mother's womb, apart from the material of the egg. A monotreme lays and hatches its eggs. In the marsupials, the eggs hatch within the mother and the young emerge at a very lowly stage. A young kangaroo when born is only about an inch long, struggles its way by instinct up a path up its mother's belly into her pouch where it attaches itself to one of her teats, with which its mouth almost

Above: The director of the Healesville Sanctuary, Victoria, Australia, standing outside the platypusary. Here the first platypuses, or duckbills, bred in captivity. Right: (upper) A pair of platypuses in the display tank; (lower) a platypus swimming underwater.

Above: An echidna, at the San Diego Zoo. Although sometimes long-lived in zoos, this species has bred only once. It is an egg-laying marsupial that carries the eggs in its pouch and suckles the young when they are hatched.

fuses for some time. There it gets all its nourishment, and grows. Technically speaking, it has its main development outside the mother, in a pouch that is a peculiarly marsupial adaptation.

There are eight families of marsupials, two found only in the Americas, the rest found only in Australia and New Guinea. This is a relict distribution typical of a very old and primitive order of animals, of which but remnants survive. The higher mammals, found all over the world, are more highly adapted, later supplanters; the surviving marsupials, it is generally thought, represent what the mammal stock of the world was like about 150 million years ago.

The culture of marsupials has always been rather difficult and has only lately been tackled thoroughly by zoos. The number of species so far admitted to zoo culture is less than half the total, and the number that has bred in captivity is perhaps a quarter of it. At this early stage of acclimatization, only a few families do well. For instance, there are 11 different genera of the American opossums, and some of them have many species; yet I can find records of only six that have been kept, and only four that have bred, in captivity. However, the common opossum, which in spite of being a primitive marsupial is one of the most successful wild animals of North America, can do quite well in captivity.

Among the Australian marsupials there are many wonderful examples of adaptive convergence; in other words, many of these non-placental mammals, in the course of their evolution, have come to resemble (at least superficially) various placental mammals. The very small pouched mice, for instance, look like placental mice and occupy much the same place in nature as mice or jerboas do in other parts of the world. There are five accepted genera of this particular subfamily of the marsupials, but only two have been kept in captivity and only one has bred. In the next subfamily (the Dasyurines), there are two genera: the dasyures, or native cats, which are certainly rather cat-like and which have bred in captivity; and a queer, sinister animal, the Tasmanian devil, which is often kept in zoos but which seems to have been bred only once, 50 years ago, in Australia.

The marsupial wolf, or thylacine, of Tasmania occupies the same place in nature as a wolf or a dog, and

Left: Representatives of two of the eight living families of marsupials. Above: An opossum at the Philadelphia Zoo. This species is the only North American marsupial and is a member of the family Didelphidae. Below: An Australian tree kangaroo (family Macropodidae) in the San Diego Zoo.

looks very much like a dog. This extremely rare animal, which lives in the almost impenetrable forests of north-west Tasmania, may be on the verge of extinction. It has occasionally been kept in captivity—one came to the London Zoo as early as 1850—but it has never yet been bred. The marsupial banded anteater, extraordinarily like a placental anteater to look at, has never been kept in captivity at all; neither has the marsupial mole, which looks like, and burrows like, a placental mole and belongs to a full family all on its own.

Almost equally unsuccessful in captivity is a whole family of funny little Australian bush animals called the

Below: Another family of marsupials, the Dasyuridae, contains the Tasmanian devil. This small, bearlike animal is a flesh eater. The specimen shown here is in the San Diego Zoo.

Above: Female greater glider with her young on her back. This animal, also known as the "black flying opossum," inhabits the tall trees in mountainous country in Australia and feeds on eucalyptus and other leaves and blossoms. Right: The spotted cuscus, a slow-moving forest creature of Australia and New Guinea. Both glider and cuscus are nocturnal marsupials and have never bred in captivity.

bandicoots, which have rather pig-like snouts. Of the five genera of this family, only two or three have been kept in captivity, and none has bred. The family of the phalangers are beautiful little animals, some of which glide with membranes between their fore and hind-limbs, just as do flying squirrels. A number of these have been in captivity, and some—like the flying opossum—have been favorite pets in Australian households for years. Yet only one or two species can be bred fairly easily.

The well-known and favorite koala has bred in captivity not only in Australia but also in two zoos outside— San Diego and San Francisco. As explained early in this chapter, the Australian government allows koala stock to go to those two non-Australian zoos. They are so far the only ones that can supply the koala with the large variety of eucalyptus leaves that it needs.

The best doers of all zoo marsupials are the many members of the kangaroo family, Australia's counterparts of the deer and antelopes. At least 11 of the 14 genera have entered zoo culture, and nine of them have bred. All the full kangaroos, including the giant red and great grey species, are in the genus *Macropus*; the genus *Protemnodon* embraces the bigger and more common wallabies, including Bennett's wallaby. At least one species of each of these genera has an established colony that has been breeding continuously since 1959 in the following zoos outside Australia: Amsterdam, Antwerp, East Berlin, West Berlin, Frankfurt, Strasbourg, San Diego, Buffalo—and probably a few more. In England's Whipsnade and Woburn Parks, Bennett's wallabies have been breeding steadily for over a third of a century. There, as in many places in America, they are free and at liberty around the parks.

But zoos still have a long way to go with acclimatizing the marsupials as a whole; and since quite a number of wild marsupials are in danger of extinction, the mainstream establishments—and those of Australia in particular—are giving great attention to the breeding problem.

Care and Common Sense

The techniques of breeding and rearing animals in captivity are manifold and, as we have seen, each group of higher vertebrates presents its own problems. There are countless individual problems of housing, nutrition, psychology, cover, and even architecture and engineering. But above all there is always need for consummate care and common sense; and these qualities are just as much in demand for animals that have good and long-established zoo breeding records as for those that are new to zoo breeding.

It is now almost a routine matter for mainstream zoos

Success in breeding giraffes depends on attention to simple details, such as the provision of a soft, nonslip floor surface. Top: A new-born reticulated giraffe at the London Zoo, 22 minutes after birth, when it had not yet stood up. Above: The same animal 50 minutes after birth, trying to rise onto all fours.

to breed hippopotamuses, giraffes, elephants, some rhinoceroses, and other heavy animals; but care must always be taken to see that the female parent has adequate accommodation and adequate isolation at the time of birth. As far as possible, too, zoos must simulate the conditions in which the animals would give birth to young in the wild. For instance, success with giraffes depends on such simple technicalities as having a house with a nonslip floor. One or two giraffe calves have been lost in zoos (although not lately, I am glad to say) by doing the splits and straining themselves as they tried to take their first tottering stand on a slippery floor. In nature, of course, they would be born on a grassy veld, and would not slip. At the time of birth, the floor must also be made a bit soft so that the female giraffe will not drop her calf where it might be damaged; and a keeper should be available in case of emergency.

Hippopotamuses are born in water, and in good hippo pools there has seldom been any difficulty about a normal birth. For years, however, zoos believed that the rare pigmy hippopotamus, now confined to the rivers of Liberia and in possible danger of extinction, would be difficult to breed. The first captive rearing took place at the New York Zoological Park in 1919, and the great establishment at the Bronx has reared a dozen since then. With the zoos at West Berlin, Basel and Washington they have now proved that the pigmy hippo is no more trouble than the common hippopotamus. By common sense and careful management they have contributed not only to zoo technique but also to the survival possibilities of an endangered species.

If birds are to be bred successfully, they must be given the right kinds of nest boxes, holes, or bushes to nest under; they must also have the right cover and the right nest material. And sometimes the zoo man must resort to hand-rearing. In the case of wildfowl, he often has to take the eggs laid by the wild captive parent and hatch them under bantams or silkies (a small, soft-plumaged breed of fowl).

Occasionally, the hand-rearing technique permits a higher output of captive stock than might come naturally. By taking offspring from parents, curators may give them the opportunity of laying more eggs or giving birth to more young than they would in the wild. San Diego zoo has had this experience with the great Andean condor, one of the largest birds of prey. In the wild, this bird breeds only once every two years, simply because the young—there is only one at a time—takes so long to rear in the nest. The San Diego men were able to hand-rear the young after a certain stage and so allow the parents to lay eggs and hatch them annually, thereby increasing the output over that of nature. A similar advantage may also be possible by the hand-rearing of anthropoid apes. But these are special cases. Although zoo breeding has been transformed in the last century, zoos are still struggling to catch up with nature, let alone outstrip it. Successful zoo breeding proves to the zoo man and to the public that zoos are keeping the sort of animals they should keep. It is also an important form of insurance against the total extinction of many species that are now so rare in the wild.

This problem is so grave, and at the same time so interesting, that I do not hesitate to devote the whole of the next chapter to it.

In the pigmy hippo pools and on the flats at the Basel Zoo, great success has been achieved in breeding this rare and endangered species. Below: A female pigmy hippopotamus walks around one of the pools with her offspring.

Right: A five-week-old famale Andean condor, at the San Diego Zoo. Here, a single pair of these giant birds of prey produced nine offspring between 1942 and 1952, nesting on a cliffside ledge in the zoo's huge aviary, which is 160 feet long, 60 feet wide, and 110 feet high, and contains 60-foot trees.

4 Zoos and Survival

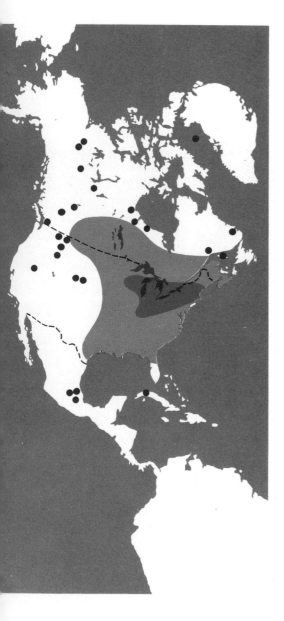

Above: Map of North America showing the distribution early in the nineteenth century of the now-extinct passenger pigeon. The area shown in deep red was its principal nesting area; in the surrounding area (light red) the bird was fairly common; dots represent isolated occurrences.

Since about A.D. 1600, 94 species of birds and about 36 species of mammals have vanished from the face of the earth. All species of animals may have a limited natural life of at most a few million years before they die out or evolve into two or more other species; but it seems likely that in the past few hundred years, man's intensified exploitation of the planet has increased the natural rate of extinction of higher animals by at least three times.

Out of every 20 higher vertebrates extinguished since 1600, an informed guess is that three were rendered extinct by the introduction of alien predators (cats, rats, mongooses) to their range; another two or three by the introduction of better-adapted competitors (particularly on islands); another four by hunting and collecting; and at least another four by the destruction of their habitat. Only six or seven, probably, have become extinct by inevitable natural process.

What have the zoos to do with this situation? How far have they contributed to it, and how far are they able to remedy it? I think it is fair to say that no post-Renaissance zoo would knowingly have contributed to the extinction of any species; yet there are certainly cases where zoos could have done more than they did to prevent extinction, if only they had realized the danger in time.

The saddest example is that of the passenger pigeon, once the most abundant bird in North America. Alexander Wilson, the great American ornithologist, observed enormous flocks of passenger pigeons around 1806. Flying at between 40 and 60 miles an hour, some took four hours to go by. Wilson calculated that one flock was something like 240 miles long and consisted of over 2,000 million pigeons. A. W. Schorger, who has made a scholarly study of the passenger pigeon's status and examined most contemporary reports of such great flocks, believes that up to about the middle of the nineteenth century the species had a total population of 3,000 to 5,000 million. In Schorger's estimation these made up perhaps one-third of the total individual land birds of North America at that time.

When the passenger pigeon was in its heyday of fantastic abundance it was kept and bred in zoos. It seems to have first bred in captivity in the London Zoo in 1832, and at much the same time at Knowsley Park, also in England. Later it again bred in the London Zoo and quite frequently in North American collections. In

Left: A pair of passenger pigeons, painted by John James Audubon, the artist-ornithologist (1780-1851). Above: Two methods of obtaining pigeons. Upper: Shooting them in Iowa in 1867. Lower: One method of netting, used in New England, in which the birds settled on the ground to be caught in the baited net.

Audubon painted this Carolina parakeet, the only species of the parrot family that lived in the United States in his day. This bird ate a lot of fruit and grain, and was consequently slaughtered by farmers, becoming extinct by about 1920.

the early 1890s a tremendous and sudden collapse overtook the wild population: and for the next 10 years enlightened zoologists in America suspected that the species might be on the way out. But in the early years of the present century American zoos did not pay enough attention to the plight of the passenger pigeon, and did not concentrate on breeding it. In fact the last known bird of all—itself bred in captivity—died in the Cincinnati Zoo on September 1, 1914.

In the same zoo, and in the same month, the last known Carolina parakeet died. A report of a wild survivor seen in 1920 is not universally accepted. This miniature macaw, restricted to marshy woodland in the southeastern United States, was always a far rarer bird than the passenger pigeon; but it was again a bird that had proved its ability to breed in captivity. The first certain breeding records were in France, on two different private estates in 1877, and the species also bred in Vienna in 1879. There are several records from the United States, some of which may be true but only one of which can be checked—at Philadelphia Zoo in 1885, less than 30 years before the species fell into extinction. One factor that contributed to the decline of the Carolina parakeet was that many nestlings were captured in the wild, tamed, and kept as private pets; and talking parrots in small cages seldom reproduce themselves. Hindsight is all too easy: but one cannot escape the feeling that by 1885 the Philadelphia people ought to have known a bit more about the dangerous status of this bird and tried to build up a population. There is no doubt that, given the will, any good zoo or private aviculturist could have done so. Many species of parrots at present in real danger of extinction would doubtless respond to more active culture in captivity, as some "Survival Service" species are now doing in the hands of good Australian aviculturists.

Quite a number of other animals, now extinct, have been kept in zoos, including that most classic of all bygones, the dodo. This extraordinary flightless bird was descended from some unknown ancestor that must have colonized the Indian Ocean island of Mauritius in the last 20 million years—for it is doubtful whether Mauritius, a volcanic island, is older than that. Two neighboring islands of roughly equal age, Rodriguez and Réunion, also had flightless dodo-like birds, the solitaires. All these large birds were extinguished in the seventeenth and eighteenth centuries by colonist hunters.

Before it died out, the Mauritian dodo was exported live to Europe on a number of occasions. We suspect that around 1600 the Portuguese brought a young male to Europe which eventually reached Prague, where it served as a model for the well-known artist Hoefnagel.

the DoDo & Given ...... by C. Edwards ...... F.R.S. AD. 1759.

It seems likely that in 1626 there was a considerable importation of dodos, both male and female, although nobody seems to have kept a pair, except possibly at The Hague. At that date, or soon afterwards, a living male dodo was painted by the famous Dutch animal painter de Hondecoeter, and also by another artist, Adrian van de Venne, probably in Amsterdam; Goeimare painted another in 1627, and Savery painted several more. In 1628 one bird was sent to England, where it probably became the original of several English pictures of the species. During the next four decades several other dodos were kept in captivity—in Vienna, Antwerp, Japan, and elsewhere—but we know of no attempt to breed them. The last living dodos were seen in Mauritius in 1681.

Reproduction of a painting, by Roelant Savery, said to have been based on a living specimen of a dodo. A female is shown, surrounded by other birds—including two macaws and the now-extinct red rail.

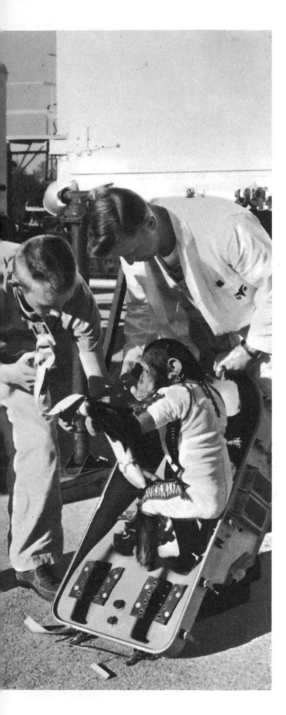

Chimpanzees were used early in the United States space program as substitutes for man. Here is Ham with the capsule in which he made a 16-minute space flight. He performed a variety of tasks and showed that the capsule's environmental and recovery systems were safe for man.

Although some animals have become extinct after having been kept and even bred in early zoos, this was not always the fault of the zoos. It may be that in a few cases they could have made more strenuous efforts to ensure survival, but in general there were two more potent reasons for their failure. First, although the care and maintenance systems of these zoos were often as good as any of the time, they were not good enough to keep a breeding stock going. Secondly, and probably more importantly, the zoos sometimes did not have enough information about the wild state of the species to realize that they were handling something that should have been on the danger list. Nowadays, it is probable that they would be better informed.

The global danger list is in fact a rather belated modern conception. Today, the Survival Service Commission (of the International Union for Conservation of Nature and Natural Resources) keeps intelligence on all species that are in danger of following the dodo, the passenger pigeon, the Carolina parakeet, and many others into oblivion. On its books are about 120 mammals and 200 birds. No animal is taken off the Survival Service's "red list" and given a green sheet until the Service is confident that, though formerly rare, it is now in no need of special attention.

In this chapter we shall see many instances of what zoos can do, and have done, to save animals from extinction once they are known to be in danger. But it is fair, first, to ask if we can blame zoos for over-demanding rare animals for their collections, and so helping to put them *on* the danger list. If we can so blame them, we must have them share that blame with dealers in living animals, and with the dealers' other customers—the pet trade, the drug trade, medical research laboratories, space research institutions, and the like.

All these other customers, I should say at once, demand common animals far more than rare ones. The pet trade, for instance, concentrates heavily on such semi-domesticated animals as budgerigars and hamsters; while the drug trade and medical research institutions make big demands on common monkeys, such as rhesus macaques and savanna monkeys. Yet these customers do also go in for rare animals. The pet trade calls for certain "survival animals" simply because prestige-pet keepers like very rare animals; even if it is totally illegal to obtain them, these people still continue to demand them. Medical research and space research institutions are at present taking an inordinate number of orangutans and chimpanzees. For such institutions these anthropoid apes have the advantage of being physiologically closer to humans than are the lower Primates. But the vital work for human health that is done with them will inevitably run itself into a dead-end if controls on ape imports are not enforced. Old-established zoos (see Chap. 2) are now breeding so many animals themselves that they are able to get some new stock by mutual barter and exchange; but certain species are reluctant to breed in captivity, and in addition large numbers of new zoos are springing up, all of which are in the market for rare animals.

Mainstream zoos are now making vigorous efforts to control their own part in the rarity trade. In June 1964 representatives of the main zoos of the world, the I.U.C.N. Survival Service Commission, other conservation organizations, and the top international dealers all met together in London and decided that it was now time to form a self-regulative union to control their own demands for rare animals. No organization has actually been set up at the time of writing, but we can expect results soon. The top zoo people and the top dealers are well aware of the parable of the goose and the golden eggs. They are themselves thoughtful conservationists, and are not likely to await public pressure to do the right thing. Indeed, many of them are in advance of their own governments in pressing for stricter animal export and import laws.

Pressure on One Wild Species

The case of the orangutan illustrates all the complexities of human pressure on the wild animals of our planet.

In prehistoric and early historic times the orang was widely distributed over the mainland and great islands of southeast Asia. We know from fossil and other evidence that its range once extended westward into India. It also lived from Malaya to China as far north as Peking; and it was found in the great islands of Sumatra, Java, Borneo, and Celebes. It now has only a restricted range in Borneo, and a more restricted one in Sumatra; and there is no evidence of its continued wild existence anywhere else on earth.

The latest estimates of the world population of the orang may be no more than guesses, but they are educated guesses made by the resident naturalists best qual-

Above: orang-utan eating a durian fruit. Never abundant, orangs were fairly common in some regions in the past (pale red on map at right), but today they are found only in a few small areas (dark red). Fossil orangs have been found at sites marked with black asterisks; teeth were on sale in bazaars at places with red asterisks.

ified to make them, including Tom and Barbara Harrisson. Harrison (formerly Curator of the Museum at Sarawak) is an expert on Bornean, Indonesian, and Malaysian fauna. His wife, as keen a field observer as he, is an experienced nurse for young orangs. The Harrissons believed not long ago that the total wild population of orangs was less than 5,000: about 2,000 in North Borneo (now known as Sabah); about 700 in Sarawak, the largest Malaysian province of Borneo; about 1,000 in Indonesian Borneo (one of the areas from which we have least information); and about 1,000 in the island of Sumatra, where numbers seem to be decreasing more rapidly than elsewhere. Since this estimate was made, the population has undoubtedly become further reduced.

Barbara Harrisson has written a book on the orang in which she gives her opinion that in the early centuries of the Christian era the orang population was at least half a million. A thousand years ago there were still more apes than men in Borneo, she writes, but today the island's few thousand orangs coexist with about three million humans. The rapid upsurge of human population in Indonesia and Malaysia, accompanied as it was by the felling of large areas of forest, may have been the original cause of the decline of the orangutan. But it is not the main cause of the continuing depopulation today. The reason, undoubtedly, is the animal trade.

One method of catching orangs for the trade that has been employed in the present century was to "beat" a large family group into an area of the forest, and then fell the trees around it until the orangs could be forced out and run into stockades. This was done only with considerable labor. Quite a bit of the apes' habitat was, of course, destroyed but only a few orangs were killed in the process.

The more usual collecting method is certainly worse. Individual hunters simply shoot females carrying babies, in order to get the babies; often they hit the baby instead of the adult female. Barbara Harrisson thinks that for every baby they finally get for the trade, they kill two females and another baby. For each baby that comes into the trade by this method, four orangs are thus removed from the wild population. What is more, of that four the chances are that three are females, because two are certainly mothers and one of the two babies is likely to be a female. Three potential mothers of further young ones are thus removed from the wild population just to get one baby.

The hunter who has captured the baby takes it to the nearest townlet and sells it for a rather small sum. Then it passes through several hands until it reaches a big dealer. If he is an Indonesian he is quite likely to sell it locally as a household pet. There is an immense trade in

Above (left and right): Two infant orangutans photographed in 1963 in Singapore, where they were awaiting shipment, probably to a zoo in Europe or America. Their capture, export, and import are all illegal.

To help orangutans survive, a national park has been set aside for them at Bako, a peninsula in the north of Sarawak. Here young orangutans—confiscated by the government—are caged, cared for, and studied, until they are old enough to live at liberty in the park.

such status-symbol pets among the newly propertied and moneyed classes of Indonesia, especially the officers in the army. The Indonesian government has legislated against the practice, but the law is not yet vigorously enforced. All young orangs that become household pets are effectively removed from the dwindling population whatever happens, because there is no practical possibility of their breeding in captivity. We do not know what percentage of the total take of orangs stays in Indonesian Borneo and Sumatra in this way, but we believe it to be large.

Besides these pets, a very large number are exported from Indonesia to Malaysia by dealers. The importation of orangs into Malaysia is illegal, but even in these politically troubled times it is extensively done by smuggling; and the center of the smuggling, until lately, has been Singapore. Early in 1964 the Survival Service Commission set up an Orang Utan Recovery Service—OURS— in Singapore, under Barbara Harrisson. Smuggled orangs

Two adult orangutans, Adriaan and Tineke, with the infant Ernst, born at the Rotterdam Zoo in 1951. This zoo has a fine reputation for breeding orangutans, but in 1964-65 a disease outbreak severely depleted the population.

In good conditions, orangutans may live many years in captivity. Below: Two orangs at New York's Bronx Zoo. Andy, the male (left), arrived in June 1947; Sandra (right) even earlier, in October 1938.

discovered in Singapore should now find their way straight to OURS, which knows how to treat them.

There is, so far, no intention of restoring these animals (mostly human-reared) to the wild when they reach maturity. But they can become breeding stock. What has been arranged is this: certain zoos that have proved themselves capable of breeding orangs—there are under 40 of them—are chosen by the Survival Service Commission to be the recipients of the animals that OURS discovers. These can be sent to them by the finest air transportation. In exchange for this, and without strings, the Service gets donations to its orang fund from the zoos. In a sense the Survival Service Commission is acting as a dealer, but it does so only with the object of discouraging the trade.

Already, as a consequence of the setting up of OURS, there are signs that the smugglers' trade is now moving to Bangkok, to become a problem to the Thai government and another headache for the Survival Service. Although export regulations are better enforced in Malaysian Borneo than in Indonesian Borneo, there is still some smuggling from that area; but the Harrissons, and the governments they advise, think they may soon be able to stop this at the source. Meanwhile, the drain on the wild orangutan population is still disturbingly high. A whole group of orangs has been exported through Honolulu eastward across the Pacific; no fewer than 84 reached American medical laboratories in the last four months of 1963. The trouble was that although export from Indonesia and Malaysia and import into Hawaii were illegal, the United States has not strictly enforced its own regulations against illegal imports. By the time this book is published there will certainly be new importation laws in several countries, and possibly better enforcement measures too; but as late as 1965, eight orangs reached Holland in spite of both Indonesian and Malaysian export prohibition. An attempt to export more than 20 young animals from Indonesia was stopped by the national conservation authority.

What is the outlook for orangs in captivity? *The International Zoo Yearbook* showed a total of 349 orangs in 107 zoos in mid-1965, and since then the zoo population must have risen. With the 84 that somehow got through to American medical research institutions in 1963 and a considerable number in laboratories elsewhere or in zoos not reporting to the *Yearbook*, the total captive population was carefully estimated as just over 500 in November 1964. This is perhaps over ten per cent of the world's entire stock; and not many more than 50 of the captive animals are in organizations capable of breeding them. It is clear that, among the large number at present in captivity, relatively few represent any reproduction potential whatever; for far too many zoos exhibit only a single specimen. All conservationists and progressive zoo men now want to see orangs kept only by zoos with modern hotel-like ape houses, which can really breed them.

Among the zoos that have bred orangs at least for the second time during or since 1960 are Frankfurt, Rotterdam, Detroit, Philadelphia (which, as we saw in Chapter 3, has a particularly fine record), Sydney, West Berlin and Colorado Springs. Upon zoos like these, which give their great apes as much individual attention as an honored guest at a good inn, the whole future of the orangutan species may well depend. Zoos that do not measure up to these standards, and yet plan to show lone adult orangs, should think again.

Animals Saved by Zoos

The case of the orang is a paradoxical one. The demands of captors, zoos among them, have doubtless contributed to its rarity in the wild; yet the future restoration of the

Ever since the white man reached Hawaii, the number of Hawaiian geese, or nenes, has declined. Just in time, however, man intervened, and nenes were captured and bred. At Pohakuloa, in Hawaii, the birds were later released (as seen in the photograph below).

Woodcut of a nene, after a drawing of
one of the original geese that the Earl
of Derby obtained from Hawaii for his
menagerie at Knowsley Park, England. The
picture comes from an illustrated book
on captive birds, published in 1851.

population may depend upon the animal's fortune in the very captivity that helped to make it rare. There are a few other examples of dangerous over-demand by captors: but on the whole zoos have done little to make rare species rarer still; and in some notable instances they carry credit for the contrary. I can think of many examples in which zoos or zoo-minded private landowners have materially contributed to the recovery of a rare species; sometimes, indeed, they have quite certainly saved an animal from extinction. The story of the Hawaiian goose, or nene, is an excellent example.

When the Polynesians first came to Hawaii, sometime between the fifth and ninth centuries A.D., they seem to have fallen into an easy relationship with its striking and unique native fauna. Although they took many skins of several very pretty birds to weave into the great feather cloaks of their kings, there is no evidence that these colonists ever put a bird in danger of extinction. They led their quiet and uncrowded lives all over the archipelago without really upsetting nature at all. Paul H. Baldwin, a great scholar of Hawaii, believes that among the birds the Polynesians lived happily upon and with were the little Hawaiian geese—birds in the same genus as the brant and barnacle geese but brownish rather than blackish in color, and with neck feathers arranged in a different pattern from other members of the genus *Branta*. There is no doubt that the Polynesians hunted the nenes in the craters of Mauna Loa and other volcanos—where they lived during their flightless state of molt, when they had their goslings. But Baldwin thinks that the Hawaiian geese maintained a steady population of at least 25,000 until white men came to the islands.

The fauna of the Hawaiian islands has been peculiarly vulnerable ever since the coming of Western man; there have been more bird extinctions there since then than on any other archipelago in the world. It is hard to say what factors have contributed most to this state of affairs; but among them are the extension of agriculture, accompanied by the felling of forests, and the introduction of alien species. Native birds have also suffered from disturbance by gone-wild pigs and gone-wild dogs, and from hunting (by Westerners, not by Polynesians). Altogether, no fewer than 14 species of birds have been extinguished; and many of those that survive have become so rare as to cause great concern to the Survival Service Commission.

Among those in mortal danger has been the Hawaiian goose. Not much more than a decade ago it was thought by many to be doomed. We have no evidence of any change in the population of the nene before Captain Cook visited Hawaii in 1770, but we are certain that a

In 1851 the Earl of Derby's estate, together with its animals, was sold. Here, in three woodcuts from the *Illustrated London News* advertising the sale, we see (top to bottom) an elk, a gnu, and a Brahmin bull.

slow decline began not long after. By about 1800 this little goose was still living in the lowlands of the island of Hawaii and the neighboring island of Maui, but its numbers were decreasing. Soon after 1850 it became restricted to the wilder parts of high ranges on both islands. By 1900 the state of the nene was very low. It was rare even in mountainous areas of Hawaii, and on Maui it was probably extinct. In the next few years it would almost certainly have died out had it not been for the work of zoos and zoo-minded landowners.

Let us see what was happening to the Hawaiian goose in captivity during its century and more of decline in the wild. The first nenes to reach Europe were sent to Lord Derby's great private menagerie at Knowsley Park in Lancashire, England, in 1823. They happily bred in 1824 and in the following years. They had fully entered aviculture. In 1832 Lady Glengall, who had some connections with Hawaii, presented a pair to the London Zoo. One of these became the type of the species—that is to say, the species was formally described from it.

The birds started breeding in the London Zoo in 1834, and the breeding pair continued to rear young for many years. These were distributed among other zoos and private collections all over Europe. If only the European aviculturists had been aware of the rapidly declining state of the nene in the wild, they might have paid more attention to keeping the captive stock breeding. But apparently they did not realize it. By 1910 there were only a few captive birds left, and they had lost the urge to breed. The stock had not been refreshed by "new blood" from Hawaii for many years, and was by then probably senile. (One male nene reared in Holland in 1898 was transferred to Jean Delacour's collection at Clères in France. When it died or disappeared during the German invasion of 1940, it was the longest-lived waterfowl ever recorded with indisputable documentation.)

The task of saving the Hawaiian goose from the verge of extinction was now taken up in Hawaii itself; and the man who undertook it was Harold C. Shipman, a Hawaiian landowner and aviculturist. In 1918 he started to keep and breed a captive flock of nenes at a place called Keaau, near Hilo. In 1927 the Hawaiian Board of Agriculture and Forestry started a similar venture. During the next 30 years the Shipman farm reared 43 birds, although some of these disappeared during the tidal wave that struck the island in 1946 and others (more valuably) reverted to the wild. The Board of Agriculture built its own flock up to about 42. But for some reason this was broken up in 1935, distributed to private aviculturists, and virtually disappeared. By 1947 it was estimated that there were only 50 nenes left on

Hawaii—wild and captive—and none anywhere else in the world. The time had come for emergency measures.

The Hawaiian Board of Agriculture quickly started a new farm at Pohakuloa, with a couple of pairs of nenes from Shipman, a gander from the Honolulu zoo, and a wild goose caught in 1949. (There were a very few wild birds still existing then.) In April 1950 John Yealland (now Curator of Birds to the London Zoo but then Curator to the Wildfowl Trust) flew from Hawaii to Slimbridge in England with two Shipman birds. Early in 1951 *both* these birds laid eggs! However, a cable and an airplane brought a gander over from Pohakuloa inside a week.

Kamehameha, named after the great Hawaiian king, settled down at once with his geese, Emma and Kaiulani; and nine young were reared from the trio at Slimbridge in the following year. When Kamehameha died in 1963 he was the ancestor of over 230 birds—well over half the world's population of living nenes. Over 170 of Kamehameha's progeny were living in luxurious and fertile captivity in Europe, a round dozen in the continental United States, and 50 returned to the wild in Hawaii. Meanwhile, the breeding stock at Pohakuloa was also building up. By 1962 the total world population of the Hawaiian goose, captive and free, was estimated at approximately 430. The captive stock in Europe has now been spread over about a dozen different menageries, as an insurance against disease or parasites or any other hazards of aviculture. This European stock has its headquarters at Slimbridge, England, the main home of the Wildfowl Trust, with other groups of at least one pair at Peakirk (a satellite of the Trust), Leckford, London, Whipsnade, Antwerp, Basel, West Berlin, Clères, Cologne, Copenhagen, and Rotterdam.

The available figures show that the world population of nenes—around 50 between 1947 and 1951—had doubled by 1957, doubled again by 1959 or 1960, and doubled once again by 1962 or 1963. A doubling every three or four years is geometrical progression indeed! The foresight of all concerned—Shipman, the Hawaiian farming authority, and the Wildfowl Trust—has paid fine dividends.

The captive nenes in Slimbridge and Hawaii essentially constituted a "zoo bank" from which it was eventually possible to recolonize the wild. The zoo bank system was much earlier applied to a great mammal on the verge of extinction in Europe.

Top: Nene-rearing pens at Pohakuloa, Hawaii. In 1950, a nene stock was started at Slimbridge, England. The whole present flock is descended from one male, Kamehameha (far left), and two females, one of which was Kaiulani (near left).

Once upon a time the European bison, or wisent, *Bison bonasus*, was abundant. In Stone Age times this animal—or a larger and probably ancestral race, *Bison bonasus priscus*—was found over most of Europe. By Renaissance times its range had already been restricted, largely by the destruction of forests. (The European bison is very much a forest species, unlike the American bison, which had both a woodland and an open plains race.) By the early years of the nineteenth century the European bison was already rare. Since it was a great beast of some magnificence its status was maintained to some extent by royal and wealthy people who hunted it; but all the same its distribution was of the relict type. There were two populations. One, which we may call the Lithuanian race, had withdrawn from its once wide European range to a mainly Polish headquarters; the other (if it was a separate race, as most experts think it was) had become restricted to the forests of the Caucasus in the southern part of the Soviet Union. Probably the last of the Caucasian race died in the Hamburg Municipal Zoo on February 26, 1925, though the Moscow Zoo may still have specimens. The Lithuanian race has managed to survive only because of tender human culture of semi-wild herds in Poland and because of later culture in the world's top zoos.

It is believed that the herd in Poland had about 300 to 500 individuals in 1803, when it came under the protection of the Tsar of Russia. Unfortunately these animals chose a politically insecure area to live in. Their headquarters was the Bialowieza Forest, which has changed hands many times since 1803, and has been overrun by many armies in wars up to and including the Second World War. In peaceful intervals the forest herd, although free, was under human management, but its numbers fluctuated greatly. Around 1860 the number rose to nearly 1,600; in 1890 it fell to 403; by 1913 it had risen again to 750. Then came the First World War, bringing a sharp decline; and by 1925 the herd was totally exterminated.

At that time, however, there was a stock of about 45 wisents scattered among the parks and zoos of Europe. From this stock efforts were made not only to re-establish the Bialowieza herd but also to build up "insurance" herds in private parks and zoos.

In 1923 the whole problem was considered at an international meeting in Paris, and it was decided to form an international society for the protection of the European bison. One of the society's first jobs was to collect information about bison in zoos and parks everywhere and to start a stud book—a pedigree book of all European bison that were known to be pure bred. There had, of course, been a fair number of experiments in hybrid-

Map (above) shows the former distribution of the European bison, or wisent. A browsing animal, its fate was linked with deforestation. It has avoided extinction only because it has been protected, as in the London Zoo (right).

European bison are still kept in such zoos as Woburn Park, England (above), and also in the fine, natural forest reserve at Bialowieza, Poland (right).

izing, or cross-breeding, European and American bison; and in 1932, when the excellent Polish naturalist Jan Zabínski compiled the first stud book, he found that the 60 or so European bison then in existence were not all pure bred. By 1938, however, there were 97 accepted pure-bred European bison, housed in four Polish parks and eight European zoos.

In 1939 began the great clash of armies that was to go on in Europe for nearly six years. Only one breeding centre—Skansens Zoo in Stockholm—remained outside the conflagration. Yet, although there were losses, the bison were spared much more by the invading and counter-invading armies than they had been in the First World War. In fact by 1947 there were two more pure-bred European bison than in 1938. From then on the population rose steadily and became increasingly widely distributed. In 1955 the total passed the 200 mark for the first time since 1918, largely due to the restoration and build-up of the herd in Bialowieza. In 1963 the total world population was about 550—representing a quin-

The American bison (top) narrowly escaped extermination by white settlers and hunters. It is today being re-established in North America and elsewhere. The specimen shown is in Woburn Park, England. The saiga, a Siberian antelope (above), has been saved from extinction by Russian conservationists, who maintain an island sanctuary in the Aral Sea.

tupling in 15 years, which is very fine for an animal that in nature breeds only every other year, or even every third year. In zoos the natural slowness of breeding has been speeded up by deliberately quick weaning of the young, which enables the cows to breed every year.

Zoo management has saved the European bison from extinction. What is more, the wisent is still a noble wild animal, not just a kind of large pet forever doomed to be kept in small enclosures to be gaped at by zoo visitors. A high proportion of the total population is living semi-wild in parks, including 80 at Bialowieza. Any visitor there can carry himself back to medieval times when the European bison was one of the kings of the wild.

The story of the American bison is somewhat similar to that of the European bison. The American bison was also once one of the monarchs of the wild, roaming North America in herds of millions. It, too, was threatened with extinction, largely by hunters and encroaching settlers. And it, too, was saved through the efforts of conservationists and zoo men. Of course, the American bison never became extinct in the wild, but the population declined to a few hundreds by the end of the nineteenth century. It was definitely near the edge of extinction. Then public-spirited people began to arouse interest in preserving this animal. In the forefront was the American Bison Society, organized at New York's Bronx Zoo in 1905. The Society purchased bison, put them in refuges, bred them at the zoo, and took the lead in demanding protective legislation. As a result of such efforts, the bison herds now roam in safe numbers. Once again, zoo men, working with other interested people, have helped to save a species from extinction.

The history of Père David's deer is an even simpler example of the effectiveness of a zoo-bank in conserving a species. This animal was first described for western science by Père David, a nineteenth-century French Catholic missionary in China. David was a naturalist and explorer as well as priest; he discovered his deer in 1865, when it was confined solely to one imperial hunting park near Peking—occupying an obvious relic of what was probably once a wide distribution. Père David's deer was already a rare animal, and it may well be that it had been preserved up to that time only because the royal court of China kept it for hunting. By 1910, after Père David had obtained several specimens of his deer for Western zoos, the stock near Peking was exterminated altogether as a consequence of the various political troubles in China.

Fortunately, by then there was a big enough stock in European zoos to allow the Duke of Bedford to establish a breeding herd at Woburn Park in England. It is from this little breeding herd, started about 70 years

Père David's deer once survived only in the imperial hunting park of the Chinese emperors in Peking. It had been extinct in the wild for several thousand years. Some were sent to European zoos. Later, when the specimens in China died out, these provided the basis for the Duke of Bedford's herd at Woburn (above) and all now-surviving specimens.

ago, that the whole of the present establishment of the species comes. Woburn Park, climatically and in every other way, seemed to suit the deer as well as their ancient home near Peking; and by 1950 the Woburn stock (practically the whole world population except for a few in other zoos) was about 400. The numbers of this animal—still all in captivity including some reintroduced to the Peking Zoo—are now rather above this figure; and the species owes its life perhaps first to the emperors of China, and more recently to Père David and the tenth Duke of Bedford.

The giant panda was not known outside its native habitat until 1869. It lives in the bamboo thickets of Szechwan, in western China, where it is now protected from hunting. Only a few specimens are in zoos outside China. One such is Chi-chi at London Zoo (above).

Another great discovery of Père David in China is not merely on the Survival Service list; it is the symbol of the World Wildlife Fund—the giant panda. We know little about the past range of this extraordinary bamboo-eating relative of the racoon (as some believe it to be), and not nearly as much as we should like to know about its present range; but it is now apparently confined to the bamboo forests of the mountains of central and western Szechwan, in western China. Contrary to popular belief, there was no evidence of any kind until 1965 that a giant panda had ever been seen in Tibet. It belongs to a different tribe of its family from the little red panda of the Himalayas, which is much commoner and quite frequently shown in zoos.

The giant panda was not much hunted by the Chinese until white hunters (particularly Americans) began penetrating Szechwan and convincing the Chinese that someone attached a value to giant panda skins. Then for a time there was hunting pressure on the animal, which helped to reduce its numbers. It might also be suspected that in the early days (and we must remember that Père David first described the giant panda for science as late as 1869) museums and collectors also contributed to its rarity.

Until central and western Szechwan is more extensively explored by naturalists, we shall continue to know little about the numbers and range of the giant panda. We have no evidence concerning its total numbers; but it has a relatively small range, and does not appear to have a very dense population within that range. We also know that this range may be endangered by changes in agriculture, or indeed by any changes that tend to reduce the foothill bamboo forests. However, the Chinese government does protect the giant panda by game laws, and there is no evidence at present of hunting pressure.

In mid-1965 there was one giant panda in the Moscow Zoo, one in London, a pair in Pyongyang, North Korea, seven in Peking, and at least ten in six other Chinese zoo parks; the species bred in captivity for the first time in Peking in 1963. The fact that Peking has bred the giant panda shows that a zoo-bank of these animals may some day be possible. Personally, I am not deeply worried about the giant panda, though I think it is a symbol for the World Wildlife Fund because it is a rare animal and rather cuddly and cosy.

Endangered African Animals

One of the most pressing problems of our time is the depopulation of African animals. Only three human generations ago, a European or an American sportsman could go almost anywhere in Africa and come back with

Four African animals currently in danger of extinction. From top to bottom: White-tailed gnu and bontebok, both South African antelopes saved by thoughtful farmers; and banded duiker and pigmy hippopotamus, both West African forest dwellers.

more hunting trophies than his walls could possibly hold, however large his mansion. All that has changed. Due to over-hunting, poaching, and the competitive grazing of domestic cattle, the ranges of nearly all the African antelopes have been seriously reduced. Not all species have become survival cases, of course, but in most instances their numbers have decreased dramatically. A century or so ago, in the days of Livingstone, Speke, Grant, and Selous, there were herds of game as far as the eye could see across the velds of central and eastern Africa, South Africa, Rhodesia, and Zambia. Today the big herds survive scarcely anywhere outside the great national parks and reserves. Some of these are as big as the states of Massachusetts or New Jersey; and during these days of transition from European to African government most of them continue to be well managed.

Nevertheless, an important minority of African mammals is causing great concern to the Survival Service Commission. Many, but by no means all, of the endangered species threatened are antelopes. Among them are the mountain nyala, the western giant eland, the banded duiker, the giant sable antelope, the scimitar-horned oryx, the addax, the bontebok, Hunter's hartebeest, the white-tailed gnu, the Zanzibar antelope, the royal antelope, the beira antelope, and several rare species of gazelles.

Apart from the antelopes, the list of mammals includes the pigmy chimpanzee on the left bank of the Congo; the mountain race of the gorilla, confined to a narrow area of mountain forest from Uganda into the Kivu area of the Congo; the brown hyena; the south Sahara races of African cheetah; the West African manatee—a most peculiar aquatic animal; the Somali wild ass; the Nubian wild ass; the mountain race of zebra; the white rhinoceros; and perhaps the black rhinoceros.

The files of the Survival Service Commission are full of information on the status of some of these animals, gathered from wardens and biologists all over Africa. Much of this information concerns the animals' manageability in zoos and zoo parks, for the importance of the zoo-bank is well understood.

Let us take the case of the bontebok, a splendid gnu-like antelope with high ascending curved horns, which has always, apparently, been rather rare. When it was

Powdered rhinoceros horn is believed by people in some parts of the world to be a helpful drug. The main sources of supply today are the African game reserves, where poachers are still active, killing rhinos and removing their horns (above). Some of the horns are recovered when poachers are caught (top).

first encountered it seemed to be restricted to the southwest corner of Cape Province, in South Africa. Today it exists in a fully wild state in only one district, around Swellendam; but larger numbers survive in special refuges—in the Bontebok National Park, the de Hoop Game Farm, and some other private farms near Bredasdorp.

A hundred years ago, the total population of the bontebok was alarmingly small; and had it not been for the efforts of private Boer farmers the animal would almost certainly have gone the same way as the quagga, a species of zebra that *did* become extinct in Cape Province around 1878. But about a century ago, the van der Byl, van Breda, Uys, and Albertyn families "farmed" nucleus herds of bonteboks on their private estates. Without their private-enterprise zoo-bank, the bontebok would never have survived until 1931, when the national park was established for it. Even with the farmers' efforts there were only 17 individuals left alive in that year. Then the antelope's fortunes began to improve. By 1935 there were 33, by 1936 there were 57, and by 1938 the total was 69. In 1962—the date of the latest full census available—the figure was 500. It may be some time before the bontebok is taken off the Survival Service's "red list" and given a green sheet; but there is no doubt that its greatly improved chance of survival is due to private zoo-banking.

The case of the white rhinoceros shows as well as any how closely the future of great African animals depends on intelligence and management, in which the zoo-bank may have a part to play. The white, or square-lipped, rhinoceros differs somewhat in its anatomy from other rhinos, and has been put in a different genus from them, *Ceratotherium*. In the old days of animal glory in Africa, it ranged extensively over much of the great open grassland areas from the southern limits of the Sahara right down to South Africa. It is now restricted to four main groups in widely separated areas. In January 1963 there were about 925 white rhinos in southern Africa, 900 in the Congo, 80 in Uganda, and possibly 2,000 in the Sudan. Some people, however, suspect that the Sudan figure may be exaggerated, and that it is doubtful if the total population exceeds 3,000.

The white rhino has been heavily persecuted by men for sport, to some extent for meat, and especially (like all rhinos) for horn for the aphrodisiac trade: many Asians particularly prize powdered rhino horn as a sexual stimulant. It is strongly protected by law over most of its range, and has been so for years, but the difficulty lies in enforcement. Enforcement is best in southern Africa. There the population in the Umfolozi Game Reserve has lately grown to the point where it has stretched the carrying capacity of the land. This herd has formed the basis for an insurance bank, for the white rhino has continued to be very vulnerable in north-central Africa where enforcement of game laws is much more difficult.

The great Umfolozi herd, which numbered 856 in 1963, is the biggest of all. A large-scale operation now in progress is aimed at restocking former white rhino areas (and also some selected zoos) with animals expensively caught in Umfolozi. In this generation a whole new technique of rhino-catching has been developed.

Most operators now catch big wild mammals with the use of drugs. Big game is immobilized with rifle-propelled darts that inject the drug, render the animal temporarily unconscious, and enable it to be manhandled into a truck and taken away, to recover en route. But some of the best hunter-dealers, like Seago, still shun drugs; they use pens, stockades, and very clever lassooing and netting techniques, even with the heaviest animals like rhinoceroses. This method requires whole flotillas of combined jeeps and trucks—expensive equipment.

The cost of moving a white rhino from one range to another, or to a zoo, is many hundreds of dollars, and there can be little reduction for numbers. To a mainstream zoo, however, a white rhino is worth a lot of money. Its importation is not only legitimate but highly desirable as a stock safeguard. No white rhino had ever reached captivity outside Africa before 1950. By 1963 there were 10 males and 12 females in zoos of North America and Europe. By mid-1965 there were 45. Their breeding success remains to be seen, although already by April 1964 a successful birth had been recorded in captivity in Africa, to a female pregnant when caught.

Risks of Zoo-Banking

Zoo-banking, of course, works much better with some families of animals than with others. If a family is known to breed well in captivity, and a species of that family is in danger of extinction, zoos may be more than justified in depleting the wild population of that species still further in an attempt to build up a thriving captive stock. With families that are poor-doers in captivity, the risk may be too great.

A tricky borderline case is the California condor. Most birds of prey are poor breeders in captivity, but the condors are an exception. Four out of the six species in their family have bred in captivity, and we saw in Chapter 3 that in a period in the San Diego Zoo the Andean condors reared more young than they could have in the wild. Now California also has one of the

In some ways, rhinoceroses are safer in zoos than in the African game reserves. The white rhino is the rarer of the two African forms, and is thus in greater need of protection. Above: A white rhinoceros arrives at New York's Bronx Zoo, after traveling from the Umfolozi Reserve in South Africa.

An Audubon engraving of a California condor, a very rare vulture that inhabits a small mountain area in southern California. It nests on ledges like an eagle. Its wingspan of 10 feet makes it one of the world's largest flying birds.

rarest wild birds of prey in the world—the California condor, a cousin of the Andean condor.

The California condor once had a wide range over the southern and western United States and also into Mexico, especially Lower California. Today it lives only in one mountainous area in southern California and careful estimates suggest that there is a total, gradually decreasing world population of only about 50 individuals (1966). For ten years and more there has been a climate of thought among responsible U.S. naturalists that, as an insurance, someone ought to try breeding the California condor in captivity.

In the early 1950s the California State Game Commission authorized the San Diego Zoo to employ a very talented field man, Lewis Wayne Walker, to get some eggs or nestlings, or to trap some young adults, so that the zoo could start a breeding colony. Unfortunately, the trapping efforts did not succeed, and the project has been dropped. But I think the San Diego Zoo should be allowed to take wild California condor eggs and try them under Andean condors. If the experiment were tried, and if it worked, it might provide a valuable "zoo insurance." Admittedly, it is in the sphere of risk: even the most sympathetic naturalists and conservationists are in two minds about it. It is a difficult decision to make, but one that may have to be made, and made soon. If this bird gets rarer, then the risk of cutting down the breeding potential of the wild stock by taking one or two pairs into captivity would be greater than it is today. Meanwhile, an American enterprise proposes to build the new Topatopa dam which, with its construction road, will threaten the main breeding ground of the species.

It is clear that a "survival species" *may* become so rare that an attempt at zoo breeding may not justify the danger of experimenting with the tiny remaining population. I do not think this argument yet applies to the California condor, but I would accept it for the ivory-billed woodpecker. There are two races of this bird, and the combined world population appears to be around twenty. When last surveyed, in 1956, the Cuban form was not believed to number more than twelve or thirteen. The form in the United States, confined to the southeast, may possibly survive in one or more of the Gulf states, although recent reports are conflicting. The task of capturing a breeding pair is almost unplannable; and the task of breeding the species in captivity is surely unmanageable, for woodpeckers are notoriously hard birds to keep in captivity, particularly specialized species such as the ivory-bill. As far as I know, only one of the 209 living species has been captive-bred successfully.

The only chance for this bird is to preserve the large stands of trees in its ancient habitat and hope for the

A pair of Javan rhinoceroses at a mud-hole in their native habitat. This species, which used to occur from Java to Burma, is now reduced to a very few animals in the Udjing Kulong reservation in western Java. Its prospects of survival are very poor.

best. It is idle to think that even the most sophisticated bird-specialist zoo can solve every problem.

Another case where an animal has become so rare that it is doubtful whether zoos can save it comes from southeast Asia. Here the latest information suggests that the Javan rhinoceros may now be entirely confined to the most westerly (and small) peninsula of Java, where it is still under hunting pressure from horn seekers and the army, and has shown no recent sign of breeding. The Javan rhino is officially protected by the Indonesian government, but there is evidence that enforcement is not so good. Indeed, so poor is the outlook that many conservationists believe that, although the world population may now be only between 30 and 50, a last-ditch gamble is justifiable: two pairs, or even three, they think, should be captured from the surviving population and taken to zoos.

There is no Javan rhinoceros now in any zoo, but at least nine have been exhibited outside Java in the past. One lived for about 21 years in Australia's Adelaide Zoo as a great Indian rhinoceros, only to be identified as a Javan when it was dead. Incidentally, the great Indian rhino, which is the only living species in the same genus as the Javan, is perhaps the easiest rhinoceros to breed in captivity. This holds out the hope that zoos may be able to breed Javan rhinos if they can get them. A lot depends on the Indonesian government. I am sure that no mainstream zoo with rhino experience would turn down what might be the chance of its (and the Javan rhino's) lifetime, although the best line on saving the species may still be an effort to save it in its natural habitat.

Zoos and the Future of Conservation

The Survival Service Commission is mainly an intelligence service. It has no executive power to the extent

Above: Map of Saudi Arabia showing the area in which the Arabian oryx occurs. A blue line indicates the route taken by a British expedition in 1962 to capture specimens of this rare species in order to provide a breeding stock.

Below: The expedition brought out three oryxes—two bulls and a cow. These were bound and crated, and sent to Kenya— first to Nairobi, which was too cool, then to warmer Isiolo. Finally they were shipped to North America.

Above: The Arabian oryx breeding pens at Phoenix Zoo, Arizona, where the three specimens caught in 1962 have been housed. They have prospered in captivity, and on October 26, 1963, a male calf (below) was born.

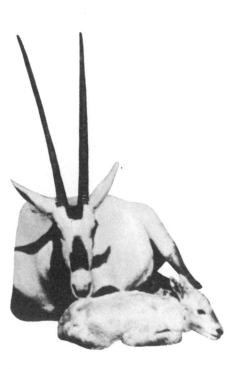

that it can order its own or another's agents into Java to rescue the Javan rhinoceros from poachers. In this case, as in all others, it can only pressurize, advise, commend, write to heads of state and enforcement officers, pull strings, and generally try to get things done. But its first job is to *know*; without knowledge, persuasion and pressure are either impossible or immoral.

By the end of the century the world's human population will probably be twice what it is now. The pressure that this will put on wild nature will be phenomenal and unprecedented. All the implications of this are being resolutely faced by at least a minority of thoughtful people; and the conservation movement is gathering way. But nobody can say that it is yet doing enough. The more pertinent question here is: are zoos doing enough?

In view of the magnitude of the problem it is almost impossible for anyone to do enough, but the zoos are certainly doing more than ever before. The recent conference in London (pp. 150-1) of zoo directors, conservationists, Survival Service, and dealers crystallized and emphasized the emergency role of zoos as reserve banks for certain kinds of rare animals. The zoo-banks that I have mentioned in this chapter are only a small sample of the material that was discussed. We saw in Chapter 3 (pp. 93-4) that most pheasants breed well in captivity, and all over Europe and North America there are now captive breeding stocks of some of the rarest pheasants in the world. The same is true of certain rare wildfowl species. However, zoo-banks are still urgently needed for many rare animals, including some of the anthropoid apes. We can say that they already exist, though only to a limited extent, for the orangutan; but so far only nine lowland gorillas have ever been reared in captivity, while the rarer highland race has not been bred at all. (Two babies have been born to one particular female in semi-captivity in the Congo, but neither of them survived very long.)

The universal zoo-bank is no complete solution to the problem of wildlife conservation, of course, because some of its products (notably, I suspect, anthropoids) may prove unplantable in the wild. But the zoo-bank is at least an insurance against extinction that has been proved to work. Eventually zoos will doubtless succeed in saving quite a lot of species, including some that might otherwise have faded out in the natural course of evolution without the human assistance now so widely offered.

Zoos are still with us for their historical reasons: for the education and entertainment of humans. This is still their primary objective, and must not be lost sight of. But the new facet of the zoo crystal that is now shining brilliantly—the conservation of endangered species—is one that we all can admire.

5 Zoos and Animal Supply

Nobody would expect the animal population of a mainstream zoo to remain static for any considerable length of time; but I suspect that most people are astonished when they discover just how fluid it is. In this, as in most things, London Zoo can be regarded as *fairly* typical; though as it is an exceptionally comprehensive collection, its turnover may be rather more rapid than normal. Still, its figures give a fair glimpse of what the turnover in a mainstream zoo can be.

In the years from 1938 to 1953 London's average stock of mammals, birds, reptiles, and amphibians at the end of each year was 2,953; and in the average year about 54 per cent of the total consisted of new arrivals. Each year London "lost" close to 1,800 animals by gift, sale, return to lenders, exchange with other zoos, and death; each year it gained a similar number by gift, purchase, deposit by lenders, exchange, and birth. If we break down the average yearly intake of new animals, we find that 41 per cent arrive by gift, 24 per cent by purchase, 9 per cent on loan, 12 per cent by exchange with other zoos (or transfer from London's Whipsnade Park), and 14 per cent by birth.

Although London Zoo has not published detailed figures for accessions since 1953, it seems likely that the general outline of the picture has not changed very much. The annual turnover of animals, it is true, has dropped from 54 to 44 per cent. New arrivals could probably be accounted for in much the same way as before, with the exception that the figure for births has risen somewhat. From all this it seems safe to assume that of every 20 animals at present in a good modern zoo, about three have been born there, ten given or lent by private individuals or other zoos, five purchased, and two received in exchange from another zoo or private menagerie.

This does not tell us how many of those 20 were born in the wild and how many reared in captivity, but it gives us at least a clue. If our figures are correct, three were certainly born in captivity; while the 17 received by gift, loan, purchase, and exchange are in some doubt. However, it seems fair to assume that the donors, lenders, sellers, and exchangers had no higher percentage of breeding successes in captivity than did the zoo itself. If that is so, then about 15 of the doubtful 17 were born in the wild and only two in captivity. We cannot regard figures obtained in this way as certainties, but we can regard them as strong probabilities; and they mean that

Even in the 1960s, animal catching
can be a risky and exciting business.
Sequence shows Mike Tsalikis
capturing a large anaconda in Colombia,
using his bare hands. His team helps
him pull the snake out of the water
and stuff it into a sack.

one-quarter (or more) of the animals now in the better zoos are captive-bred, while three-quarters (or less) are not.

If the present quite rapid rate of improvement in zoo breeding continues, a zoo of the year 2000 will be more than half composed of captive-bred stock. Meanwhile, zoos are still heavily dependent on the animal trade, and particularly on that part of it that deals in wild animals. Indeed, the zoos must be the main support of the 150 or so wild-animal dealers of the world, apart from those who specialize in small birds for aviculture or in monkeys and apes for medical research. In the last quarter of a century the London Zoo has spent something over $400,000 on the purchase and inward transport of living animals; New York's Bronx Zoo has spent over $950,000. A fairly large proportion of this money has gone to wild-animal dealers.

In recent years, which have been marked by worldwide inflation, animal prices have soared; at the same time the number of zoos and pet-keepers has multiplied. This means that wild-animal dealers are now operating in a sellers' market in which perhaps up to fifteen million dollars change hands each year. Theirs is a big trade, an interesting one, and one with heavy responsibilities. Much of this chapter reviews briefly how it is conducted.

Collectors, Old Style and New

Collecting exotic wild animals necessarily entails a good deal of travel, often to remote places. In the past such travel was far less common than it is today. Perhaps it was for this reason that the zoo-collector's job became surrounded with all kinds of glamorous associations. Even as recently as a generation ago the public was largely convinced that a great deal of zoo collection was done by daredevil, rip-roaring adventurers. At least, whenever the newspapers wanted to deal with the subject, that was the way they approached it. When I was a young curator at the London Zoo some years ago, a well-known Sunday newspaper wrote to the Society, asking if its curators could supply articles about how the animals were obtained for the zoo. "We want really hot stories, with as much risk to human life and limb as possible," they said. Tangling with snakes, romps with rhinos, the daredevil tiger-trap, how to catch an elephant in seven easy lessons—that was the kind of thing they wanted.

Prominent among those who helped to build up that kind of unsophisticated public image of dangerous wild animals and intrepid collectors was the dealer, writer and movie-maker, Frank Buck. Buck's famous *Bring 'Em Back Alive*, published in 1930, created quite a stir in its day. Written in collaboration with the journalist Edward Anthony, it specialized in sensational adjectives. Here is just a selection of them:

Awe-inspiring (Indian rhinoceros)
Boisterous (mynah)
Cannibal (king cobra)
Demented (tapir)
Destructive (monkey)
Enraged (tiger, water buffalo)
Ferocious (leopard, tiger)
Fiendish (king cobra)
Ill-natured (monkey)
Infuriated (leopard, tiger)
Loathsome (cockroach)
Murderous (crocodile)
Powerful (orangutan)
Ravenous (tiger)
Savage (leopard and others)
Snarling (tiger)
Terrifying (orangutan)
Vicious (crocodile, tiger, and others)

The list of animals that Buck so sensationally describes indicates that he operated in southeast Asia; where he doubtless thought, or liked others to think, nature was red in tooth and claw. Indeed, this energetic collector crossed the Pacific some fifty times, starting his trade shortly before the First World War and continuing until the Second. In the course of his career he imported close to 10,000 mammals and well over 100,000 birds into the United States, and sold them to zoos, circuses, pet shops, and medical research institutions. Almost all the animals he collected were obtained in the wild by people he alluded to as "natives" and purchased by him from middlemen and dealers in Borneo, Java, Sumatra, Malaysia, Burma, India, and Nepal. In his famous book I can remember only one account of a wild capture in which he himself assisted—that of a man-eating tiger in what was then known as Malaya. Among the most thrilling incidents described—all supposedly involving risks to life and limb—are adventures with the man-eating tiger, an orangutan, monkeys, and an escaped lion and king cobra. All these dangerous episodes appear to have been due to imperfectly constructed or imperfectly managed animal accommodations—for which the dealer himself, one would think, was responsible.

Buck was unquestionably a lively dealer and he seems

Above: Frank Buck holding a large land crab, one of the vast number of animals he collected in Malaya in 1941 for the zoos and museums of America and Europe. In fact, Buck was a dealer rather than an intrepid adventurer, but the style of his books earned him a great reputation for courage: Left: He stands watching a full-fed python which has recently swallowed a pig.

to have chalked up some records; he probably imported the first anoa (a small, rare, wild ox), babirusa (a large pig-like mammal), proboscis monkey, and siamang (a big kind of gibbon) ever seen alive in America. But like all animal collectors, he did not always succeed in bringing "'em back alive." The first proboscis monkey in America died on arrival, having lost a baby in transit; and 10 mouse deer had to be destroyed when they arrived at San Francisco, because Buck had forgotten to obtain an import permit for them. A full-grown male orangutan, believed to be of record size, also died in transit. "If enough specimens die en route," wrote Buck (who had imported 52 orangs by 1930), "the collector finds himself 'in the soup.' I ought to know. It's happened to me." Considering the endangered state of the orang in the wild, discussed in Chapter 4, one is tempted to ask who (or what) was really getting "in the soup" at that time.

Frank Buck was as efficient as most dealers of his day. As we shall see, there are some old-established firms with longer experience, and with exceptionally high, and deservedly high, reputations. Buck and many of his contemporaries were heirs to a tradition of collecting that began a century or more ago, though they had doubtless humanized it to some extent and put it on a more business-like footing.

In the early decades of the nineteenth century most dealers and nearly all amateur collectors—there were far more amateurs then than now—had to be almost entirely opportunist, with few rules and little experience to work with. An enterprising person might find himself in the Cameroons in West Africa, or in British Guiana, or in some other tropical area, with very wild country and a lot of interesting wild animals. In those days the normal procedure was for him to set up an establishment close to a port and make it known to all and sundry that he was in the market for any kind of animal that anybody could bring in. This price was given for this animal, that for that, and the other for others. The general technique was to let the native population do their own hunting and to ask few questions about how they did it, as long as they got results. The European collector seldom strayed very far from his beachhead, except for a few special (and usually short) expeditions. The game was to establish yourself as an agent and let people bring material to you. Many dealers in those days got the reputation for being intrepid, rip-roaring adventurers simply by buying animals that other people had caught for them. Beachhead trading may have decreased, but as we shall see later, it is by no means a thing of the past.

However, as time went on, zoo demands became more interesting and more exacting; the beachhead method was not always equal to it, and a few collectors began to equip their own treks. It was at this stage that the large-scale operators first came into existence, including the great European firms, with international links and agents, which still dominate the scene.

The pioneer dealer on the modern scale was William Jamrach, a man of German origin who started business in London in the early 1840s and continued, sometimes in association with his colleague Cross of Liverpool, until 1906. Jamrach was described as "the prince of animal dealers" by many of his satisfied customers. The description is apt, for Jamrach bore a strong resemblance to Prince Albert, consort of Queen Victoria.

If Jamrach was the prince of dealers, Carl Hagenbeck was the king. A German, Hagenbeck began his career at an early age. In 1848 his father, a fishmonger with an interest in animals, established a small dealers' menagerie in Hamburg. In 1859, at the age of 15, Carl Hagenbeck virtually inherited the management of it. Fifty-eight years later, in May 1907, the revolutionary Carl Hagenbeck Tierpark was opened in the Hamburg suburb of Stellingen. Still run by the family, it is among the most trend-setting of all mainstream zoos (see page 164). This was the zoo-building venture of a man who had already risen to heights of international animal dealing that have never been surpassed.

Hagenbeck had agents, travelers, and sub-dealers all over the world, including many of distinction. Lorenzo Cassanova, for instance, was responsible in 1862 for importing the first African elephants into Europe since Roman times; Wilhelm Grieger, in 1901, brought the first Przewalski's horses from Mongolia to captivity in Western Europe (though they had been imported earlier into Russia); Johannsen learned the use of drugs to calm newly captured animals some fifty years before the practice became general; and the able naturalist-explorer Joseph Menges had already been up the White Nile with Gordon before he began his 40 years of collecting for Hagenbeck in 1876. Happily the third generation of the Hagenbeck family continues in the animal trade, just as it does in the business of running a great zoo.

The Ruhes of Alfeld, and later of Hanover, are another three-generation family of German dealers and zoo managers who have built up a century-old tradition of the trustworthy supply of well-cared-for animals. Dealers in this class make it their business to know what zoos want; and when the demand cannot be met by random native collection, they are prepared to man special expeditions to special areas. Their network of agents and collectors, like those of all good modern dealers, cooperates actively with the game wardens and administrators of all the countries in which they operate, sup-

Carl Hagenbeck (right), an early pioneer of animal management, collected his own animals in Africa and Asia, and brought them to Europe with great care. He pioneered the use of moats to surround spacious animal enclosures at his zoological park in Germany. Below (left): Unloading a giraffe with a harness; (right) a drawing of 1870 showing the arrival of a shipment of animals for Hagenbeck's zoo.

porting their game laws and the officers who have to enforce those laws.

The modern, big-scale, conservation-minded dealer of today is indeed a far cry from the amateur, opportunist, beachhead collector of a century ago. But there is still room in the animal trade for the individualist who combines a taste for adventure with a love of, and knowledge of, animals. In the present century the more sophisticated zoos assessed their requirements and realized that their special needs called for special collectors. As a result, a peculiarly twentieth-century vintage of young collector-writers evolved who went, and still go, on expeditions for connoisseurs' pieces in not-very-well-worked territories. Names that immediately spring to mind are Ivan Sanderson before the Second World War, Gerald Durrell and David Attenborough since.

These men, and the Frosts, Shaw Mayers, and Webbs before them, have concentrated mainly on birds and the smaller mammals. Bent on getting species that they knew zoos seldom or never had before and very much wanted to see, they have penetrated much farther into the bush

David Attenborough, well known for his books about expeditions to collect animals, constructs (top) a trap to catch a komodo dragon, on Komodo Island, in Indonesia. Bottom: Success—the eye of a 10-foot specimen stares out from the trap. This giant lizard is found nowhere else.

than most of the old collectors. In fact, these new-style collectors have proved more daredevil than the old, or at least more enterprising. This, I think, is still true even when we allow for the fact that they have had better equipment, including jeeps and motorboats. Yet these men write tenderly and amusingly rather than sensationally. Gerald Durrell's readers, for instance, are not likely to learn much about "Dicing with Death," but they will learn a good deal about such entertaining personalities as the Fon of Bafut. That delightful old rogue is almost worth a place in English literature for the welcoming letter he wrote to Durrell: "Yes, I accept your arrival to Bafut in course of two month stay about your animals and too, I shall be overjoyed to let you be in possession of a house in my compound if you will do well in arrangement of rentages."

The collecting of connoisseurs' pieces—animals of scientific rather than popular interest—is not particularly rewarding financially. Moreover, a private individual with a practical knowledge of animals who wants to go collecting, as Gerald Durrell does, can seldom afford to man a large-scale, superbly equipped expedition. Several recent expeditions have "broken even" only after the publication of books, films, or television programs that are their by-products. In fact, the young man who embarks on a small, specialized collecting trip is well advised to start off with a publisher's contract in his pocket, and the ability to satisfy it by writing a book when he gets back. Even then he would be foolhardy to begin a venture of his own without previous experience. To break into zoo collecting, a man can start by getting himself attached either to zoo expeditions (for many big zoos organize some themselves), or to university expeditions, or to a dealer of good standing and integrity.

Collectors and Conservationists

In a world where the rapid growth of human population is putting ever-increasing pressure on wild life, animal dealers no less than zoos have a moral duty to co-operate to the full with conservationists. One of the finest examples of three-part harmony between conservationists,

Right: On another expedition, to the Guianas in South America, Attenborough caught a black cayman for the London Zoo. Top: A pole is pushed into its lakeside lair and lashed to its back. Bottom (left): The cayman is slowly pulled out; (right): It is being towed across the lake.

dealers, and zoos has emerged in their approach to the white rhino problem.

We saw in the previous chapter (p. 128) that there are around 3,000 white (or square-lipped) rhinoceroses still living. The great majority of the members of the southern race are in the Umfolozi Game Reserve in Zululand where, after nearly 200 translocations, there were some 750 individuals in January 1965. The two to three thousand members of the northern race live in the Congo, the Sudan, and Uganda, also mainly in reserves.

As early as the mid-1940s it was clear that the growing rhino population of Umfolozi was stretching the carrying capacity of the land; and it was impracticable to expand the reserve because the surrounding area was ecologically unsuitable. At this stage Jack Vincent, then Director of South Africa's National Parks of Natal and Zululand, began to send a few carefully selected white rhinos to zoos. In 1946 a deserted new-born female went to Pretoria. The first of her species kept in captivity, she was safely reared on cow's milk and corn porridge and is still living today. In 1949 the Pretoria Zoo received an orphaned yearling male, and in 1952 an orphaned yearling female. They, too, survive.

Vincent's initiative laid the foundations of what may some day be a useful "insurance" stock of animals in captivity. In 1950 the Game Preservation Department of the Sudan sent a pair of northern white rhinos to the Antwerp Zoo—the first ever to leave Africa. A few years later the white rhinos living under protection in the West Nile area of Uganda were increasing so well that the Game Department licensed the dealer John Seago to collect a small number for other mainstream zoos. As a consequence London received a pair in 1955, Washington received a pair in 1956, and a third pair reached the St. Louis Zoo in 1957. By now there are 45 white rhinos in the zoos of Europe and North America.

John Seago and his partner Anthony Parkinson are Englishmen who operate from Nairobi in Kenya. They work only on orders from zoological gardens and similar institutions or from wild nature reserves; and they are the very antithesis of the old bring-'em-back-alive operators. As Seago himself writes: "The man to whom the supposed glamour of the job is the main appeal may not be at all ideal." But although Seago's team approach their jobs in a quiet and unspectacular way, collecting a white rhino is still a job of some dimensions. Male square-lipped rhinos often weigh three tons and sometimes up to four. Not all of them are captured when adult, but it needs a first-class team of highly experienced field men to catch a white rhino of any age at no risk to human life—and no risk to rhino life.

Seago's field team, heavily motorized, usually includes

Top: The very young female white rhinoceros that was captured by Jack Vincent in the Umfolozi Reserve, Zululand, in 1946, and sent to the Pretoria Zoo (see text). Above: The same animal in 1965, at the Pretoria Zoo.

30 Africans of several different tribes, trained to work well not only with the animals but also with each other. "The degree of nervous tension suffered by newly caught animals is not always appreciated," he writes. "It is here that the quiet, confident stockman is so important." Seago has trained his own men to be quiet and confident, and as a result he has a very low mortality rate among the animals he catches. His team is at once tender and tough; it is in the kind of business where it has to be. Unlike many big-game catchers, Seago does not use drug-darts. His main technique with rhinos and other large ungulates involves the use of stockades or corrals, combined with very clever, very gentle driving. Always he works with the game wardens from whom he gets the license to trap; always he works within the law. As a conservationist he is far ahead of many anti-dealer people I could name.

While the 1955-57 square-lips were being dispatched to Europe and America it was becoming apparent that the wild stock in Uganda's West Nile Reserve was increasing so fast that it—like that of Umfolozi—was in danger of outstripping the carrying capacity of the land. Accordingly a translocation campaign was added to the zoo project conducted by Seago. In March 1961 the Kenya big-game trappers Ken Randall and Pat O'Connel caught ten square-lips in the West Nile Reserve, and released them into the 1,200 square miles of Murchison Falls National Park—part of the former wide range of the species in Uganda. Two adult females died, but the other eight animals survived and settled down well.

The Umfolozi Reserve was the starting point of a very much bigger translocation program. In 1961-62 it was so manifestly unable to support its increasing population of southern square-lips that Jack Vincent was entrusted with one of the most massive animal-shifting assignments since the days of ancient Rome. Altogether he and his successors have been responsible for catching over 100 rhinos and sending them to happy homes. The catching was done partly by corraling and partly with the aid of drug-darts. The happy homes included the Kruger National Park (which has had 96), the Matopos National Park and Kyle Game Reserve in Rhodesia, and the Loskop Dam Reserve in the Transvaal—all in areas where the white rhino had earlier become extinct. In addition, four nature reserves in the Republic of South Africa became permanent reception centers. Zoos also had a share of the Umfolozi rhinos. In 1962-63 no fewer than 20 white rhinos (including 9 pairs) reached zoos in Europe, North America, and Saudi Arabia; and by mid-1965 the export was up to 45. Incidentally, not one animal was lost in transit, and all survive up to the time of writing.

Top: Seago's wild animal catching team and their equipment—poles with rope lassos and an armored catching truck. Above: A zebra being transferred from the catching truck to a wooden transporting crate.

143

Capturing whales alive is an extremely difficult operation, and techniques have only been developed during the last few years. Above: Two stages in the capture of a pilot whale. Top: the whale has been lassoed in two places and is brought alongside the *Geronimo*, the catching vessel of Marineland of the Pacific. Bottom: Whale is hoisted ashore.

Here I must stress that, with rare animals, zoo-stocking and translocation schemes are justifiable only if there is a valid reason for reducing the wild stock. In all the instances above there *were* valid, and even compelling, reasons; but this is not always so. In 1961 the Congolese authorities gave a permit to a Nairobi dealer to catch eight northern square-lips in the Garamba National Park. Here the ecological justification was not so clear; and after protests from the International Union for Conservation of Nature and some prominent zoo directors, the permit was cancelled.

Transport and Mortality

Whatever the style or place of a collecting expedition, the man who runs it must stay until he has got enough animals to make his trip profitable. Meanwhile the animals must be fed, housed, kept in good condition, and built up into a transportable unit. Much time must be spent in simply building suitable light, escape-proof cages. Often these have to be made on the spot out of local materials. Carpenters have to be found to help. Assistants have to be hired who can keep the animals fed; and—what is very difficult indeed in some places— a pipeline of suitable food has to be arranged. All these chores represent the least glamorous and most humdrum side of the collector's work, but they are of the utmost importance. The great majority of the animals must reach their destination safely. Otherwise it would have been far better—certainly for the animals and more often than not for the collector or dealer as well—to have left them in the wild.

It would be easy to say that the old collectors' caravans from field to menagerie were trains of death while now all is sweetness and light; but this would be a gross oversimplification. In fact, certain wild animals have been transported in health and safety for thousands of years; yet in our own time the trade in tropical birds and tortoises, as conducted by some, has been as ruthless to its stock as profits will stand. On the whole, however, the collecting of animals for zoos has become progressively cleaner and less lethal. Its agents and customers have demanded that lessons should be learned and mistakes not repeated; and those who have not learned have usually lost their trade.

In the early years of modern zoos some rather terrible things happened, even to the well-run London Zoo and its overseas friends and correspondents. In 1833, for instance, the well-known naturalist B. H. Hodgson was resident in Nepal, and sent nearly a hundred exotic pheasants and other birds to the zoo. Most died on the way to, or at, Calcutta. Not one reached the London Zoo alive. Later, when James Thomson, member of a whole family of first-rate London Zoo keepers, was sent to India to bring back the Governor General's collection of Himalayan pheasants, he returned with the collection "considerably diminished in numbers by the difficulties of the voyage." On the other hand John Thomson brought another collection home in 1864 with "very few losses."

With steamships still in their early years, much seems to have depended on the circumstances of the voyage. In 1867 the experienced Clarence Bartlett was not as successful as John Thomson. He got back with only the remains of another Indian collection, "having unfortunately lost many of the animals by death on the passage." In the following year not even A. A. Lecomte—who started as a dealer but was so skillful that the London Zoo took him on as a collector-keeper—could cope with the appalling shipping conditions in the South Atlantic. He was bringing back the first zoo collection from the Falkland Islands, and started out with at least 84 animals. He lost 70 before the ship reached Montevideo in Uruguay, including three of his four southern sea lions. "A passenger having died of yellow fever, the stock of fish laid in to feed these animals was thrown overboard on account of its smell." Lecomte eventually reached London with his collection reduced to eight.

In the twentieth century transportation by ship remained a problem and a perennial source of mortality right up to the days of relatively cheap air freight. It was difficult, for instance, to get some animals to Europe from southeast Asia because they had to come through the Red Sea, where the humidity is very low and the temperature very high. Such a climate is extremely dangerous to animals of humid tropical forests; and even up to the Second World War many of them died simply of heat stroke in dry conditions. It was then almost impossible to produce the right humidity artificially; and for reasons of space animals commonly had to be transported on deck. Hosing and spraying with water often failed to keep them alive.

Nowadays all but the largest zoo animals are usually transported by air. Among the animals that have passed through London Airport in the last decade are an elephant seal, a great anteater, young rhinos, young hippos, young elephants, tapirs, bears, gorillas, giant tortoises, and penguins—not to mention smaller fry such as leeches, bees, and mosquitoes. Several international airports in the United States can record a similar variety.

The air shipment of zoo and other wild animals has made a wonderful difference to transit losses. Monkeys—which, as we saw earlier, go mainly to research institutions—provide an excellent example. In each year of the

Top: A gray seal cow being slipped into London Zoo's seal pond, after being transported from the Orkneys by helicopter, steamer, and train. Below: A consignment of porpoises in transit by air from the Miami Seaquarium to Chicago's Brookfield Zoo, and accompanied by a zoo attendant.

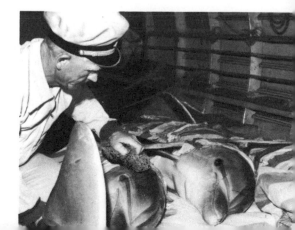

last decade an average of over 65,000 monkeys passed through the center of the Royal Society for the Prevention of Cruelty to Animals at London Airport, though the figure has dropped considerably in the past year or two. At the beginning of the period, transit accommodations had not yet reached today's standards, and the slow propeller airplanes sometimes took up to three days from India. At that stage the monkey mortality rate in transit was around 5 per cent—already a considerable improvement on the sea-travel rate. According to B.O.A.C.'s experienced veterinary consultant (who has personally studied monkey transportation from catching in the Indian jungle to arrival at destination), mortality has fallen to 0.01 per cent since jet freighters came in and reduced the flight time to ten hours. This last mortality figure is insignificant; and similar figures have been proved for practically the whole range of other animals.

But it must be emphasized that these satisfyingly low figures are for the actual air journey only. Serious hazards to animal life exist earlier, at the collecting stage; there we still have little room for complacency. Some enlightened governments, of course, have made strict regulations about the wild-animal trade and strictly enforce them; in India, for example monkeys are very skillfully and humanely netted in the jungles, and only those in good condition and of the right age are retained; the rest are returned to nature. In certain other countries, notably some in Africa, monkeys are still collected cruelly and wastefully, often being bound and hog-tied for some days before reaching an agent's depot. They suffer, in fact, the same unmeasurable (but nevertheless significant) hazards as any smallish animal subject to casual native collection and marketplace or beachhead dealing.

The cost in animal life of getting a healthy animal from the wild into a zoo, a pet shop, or a new wild area is tremendously difficult to calculate. Some dealers, from the way they talk, never lose an animal in collection or transit; and even the most honest and enlightened of them seldom disclose any mortality figures. (Even zoo reports, incidentally, may gloss over the fact that any animal ever dies in a zoo.) Yet collection mortality is the gravest outstanding problem now facing the zoo public and its conscience. A minority of courageous dealers, game park wardens, airline operators, and zoos are at last beginning to face it; and a realistic analysis of collection mortality is now slowly building up.

Such figures as are available vary. Indeed, they vary so widely that it is certain that there is still a really big element in the trade—handling more than half the millions of mammals and birds caught and moved annually—whose standards are far short of the highly professional and experienced top minority. Between field and cus-

The disastrous results of bad handling. A consignment of baboons (above) and vervets (right) was flown to London from Nairobi, Kenya, in October 1961. Of 385 monkeys, 105 were dead on arrival, owing to insufficient ventilation and overcrowding. Even modern jet air transportation must be combined with adequate care for the animals.

tomer, a Kenya firm like Seago's may have a general
mortality rate for all animals of not over 4 per cent, which
is excellent. We have seen, too, that monkey mortality
can be reduced to an insignificant figure with fast jets and
good planning. Mainstream zoos also incur only tiny
field losses on their own collecting expeditions. But many
serious and disinterested men—academic zoologists,
veterinarians, game wardens, and collectors—believe
that some dealers, beachhead operators mostly, work on
50 per cent mortalities; a few, it is believed, can and do

work (at a profit) with mortalities up to 80 or even 90 per cent. Some African mortality figures for recent consignments (quoted by Ian Grimwood, the chief game warden for Kenya) are: large mammals, 84 per cent; lovebirds, 80 per cent; mammals, 58 per cent; savanna monkeys, 22-25 per cent. These figures are intolerable. The fact that the pet trade (especially the trade in small birds), rather than the zoo trade, produces the worst mortalities, is no great comfort to the zoos.

Beachhead dealers still buy thousands of animals that have been captured by up-country tribesmen, and transported in shameful ways—hobbled, hog-tied, foully crated, and inevitably cramped. But few of these animals ever find their way into mainstream zoos. The demands of zoos are now mostly too sophisticated to be satisfied by casual beachhead trade. The Bronx Zoo in New York City, for instance, prides itself on its collection of cotingas (members of the unusually beautiful American bell-bird family); and every now and then it announces the arrival of a new species never before shown in any zoo. Such prizes are usually the result of a special, skilled expedition. Connoisseurs' pieces, often collected under license, are seldom now brought in casually by native collectors; they are especially sought out by highly trained Europeans, caught humanely and brought expeditiously to base.

The real acid-test of a collector's quality is what happens at each end of his operation. The mark of the bad collector is that he doesn't care as long as it pays. He doesn't care where he gets his material; he doesn't care too much what it is; and he doesn't care who buys it. His main concern is that somebody shall pay for it quickly, while it is still more or less alive; after that, as far as he is concerned, it can die tomorrow, because then there will be a demand for more. This, I know, is putting things at their very crudest. It describes only the blackest of the few black sheep in a professional family that has no more than the usual quota. But such bad collectors and collector-dealers do exist, menacing the good name of the profession and troubling the consciences of both zoo critics and zoo-lovers.

In practice zoos now offer only a poor market to the bad collector; more often than not he deals in animals that go very largely to the pet trade. In Western Europe and North America, especially, there is an enormous demand from pet-keepers and small private aviculturists for pretty little finch-like birds of the waxbill family— which do well in small cages and make spectacular shows in small aviaries. Birds of this kind are not very difficult to collect and are easy indeed to sell; so even if his mortality rates are quite high, the man who collects them may still make a fair profit. It is in the pet trade,

An exhibition of cage birds at Olympia, London, in January, 1959, when about 7,000 birds were on display. Exotic cage birds are popular as pets, and there is a large market in them. Although it is illegal to trap resident wild birds, control is often impossible. Many birds are kept purely for showing.

then, rather than in the zoo trade, that there is most justification for anxiety on this issue.

The contrast between the bad collector and the good one is marked by the fact that the latter cares about every aspect of his job. Perhaps most of all he cares about where the animals will go after they leave his hands. The good collector prefers to work to specific orders from customers of high repute. I have in mind a particularly good man in British Guiana and another in India. When they circulate their zoo director friends the message often is: "I am always glad to put on an expedition if you have any special demands." These two particular dealers never go outside the law. What is more, both are very much against tampering at all with endangered species, unless they are specially commissioned by an accredited organization that wants them for purposes of zoo breeding.

The Move Toward a Handlers' Code

Once it is admitted that the trade in wild animals is open to abuses, righteous indignation is not enough. It is more to the point to analyze how, when, and where abuses may arise, and then to see what practical steps can be taken to stop them. Here I should like to sum up the main complications, difficulties, and dangers that arise at seven different stages in getting animals from the wild into zoos.

1. Even before collecting begins, the animals' wild status must be considered. It may be so grave that any collection is a danger to the species' very existence. A particular animal so rare will, of course, have a special sheet in the Red Book of the Survival Service Commission, whose advice, of course, should be sought. This, however, does not *always* mean that collection is unjustifiable. If the species' survival in nature is becoming hopeless—due to ecological disturbance, illegal killing, and so on—it is best at least to try to get zoo breeding stock going.

If the animal is not rare, over-collecting *may* make it so; on the other hand, a big and steady "crop" can sometimes be taken from a wild population without endangering it.

All these things are for field research workers to judge, not zoos or the dealers who serve them.

2. The stage that bristles with most problems is the actual collection of the animal. It is often illegal. If it is legal, certain *methods* of trapping may be illegal; and even some legal methods can be cruel when misapplied. The collection, and collection mortality, of wild animals is the most mysterious part of the animal trade; and badly needs further illumination, for the sake of the

The traffic in live birds is nothing new. Top: In Europe, birds used to be sold in the cities by boys and cripples. Today (above) pet shops offer a wide variety of birds, and anyone with the money can buy, regardless of his knowledge of the problems of bird-keeping.

Ollie, a three-year-old mountain gorilla (above), was photographed in an English pet shop. His asking price was about $8,400. That was in 1964, at which time it was already known that mountain gorillas were very rare. It has since become illegal to import apes into the United Kingdom.

animals and for the betterment of the public image of zoos, the pet trade, and dealers.

In practice, a vast number of newly captured animals, probably the majority, pass through several hands before reaching the exit port or airport. The mortality at this stage is a further mystery. How many die quickly, or disappear as pets within the country of origin, is unknown.

3. Animals that reach the port of embarkation safely must pass inspection under the country's export laws. Not all inspectors are skilled zoologists, however; and many animals whose export is forbidden (usually owing to their rarity) get out under false names.

4. Next comes the journey to the customer country, sometimes *via* a quarantine-clearance country. By air such journeys are now taking place with minimum mortality; by sea the risks are shrinking with the development of air-conditioning. This stage is now probably among the least hazardous.

5. Customer countries have their own import laws, and many now prohibit the importation of rare animals except under license. But again, customs inspectors are not trained zoologists, and the specification of protected animals is often obscure in written laws. Animals may be smuggled through in disguise; indeed, occasionally they are just smuggled, and never seen by customs people at all.

6. The satisfying of quarantine laws is a necessary complication of the animal trade rather than a risk. In Europe, North America, and some other parts of the world these laws are so severe that members of some animal families (notably cattle and antelopes, the dog family, and parrots) have to be quarantined very carefully, and often for a long time. There are special arrangements for zoos. Some have their own approved quarantine quarters, while others pool facilities. Many European zoos import antelopes through a special quarantine islet near Naples (see page 193).

7. Finally, on reaching a zoo, the animals have to be properly housed and acclimatized for exhibition and, it is to be hoped, for successful breeding.

Most thoughtful people connected with the animal trade in any way are well aware of its complexities and its possibilities of abuse. It is not surprising, then, that the whole question of conservation ethics, collection ethics, and the safe transportation of and trade in animals should have been the subject of a recent important symposium. The meeting, held at the London Zoo in June 1964, was sponsored by the International Union for Conservation of Nature, the International Council for Bird Preservation, and the International Union of Directors of Zoological Gardens. It was attended by nearly 40 delegates and more than 40 observers; among whom were zoo men, conservationists, veterinarians, doctors, aviation experts, and dealers from all over the world. The work of this meeting was briefly mentioned in Chapter 4. Here I can think of no better way of conveying its spirit and aims than by quoting two resolutions, both of which were passed without dissent.

The first, proposed by the Director of the New York Zoological Park, reads: "That an international organization of zoological gardens, animal collections and animal traders should be developed through the agency of the I.U.C.N.-Zoo Liaison Committee; that this federation should be formed, among other purposes, for developing a method of distributing certain rare animals for exhibition in co-operation with the I.U.C.N. Survival Service Commission. . . ." The second resolution, proposed by the Director of the Stockholm Zoo, called for "effective governmental control of the importation and transit of rare animals," and the setting up in each country of "an expert committee to advise governments as to the species to which this control should be applied."

What emerged most clearly from the conference was that a code of importation and transit ethics has now arisen. There is general agreement on what safeguards should be employed to get animals safely, comfortably, and humanely through their journeys from the wild to the zoo; and an international handlers' code will soon be written. Its aim will be to make the best methods, now employed by the most enlightened dealers, common throughout the animal trade.

One very important issue concerning the handling of animals remains unresolved: there is no single body that speaks for the conscience of all the zoos of the world. There has always been a certain tension between what I may call the "pure zoos" and the "commercial zoos." The pure zoos are those governed by learned societies, such as the Zoological Society of London, or the Zoological Society of New York, or the Royal Zoological Society of Scotland. Most mainstream zoos fall into this category: but there are others, including many of high integrity, that are owned by companies or by private families who have a history of dealing. This is notably so in Germany, where the great Hagenbeck family of Hamburg has done so much to improve zoos and zoo architecture, and where the Heck family has made Munich's zoo one of the greatest and most beautiful in the world.

Although there is an International Union of Directors of Zoological Gardens, no director who is the proprietor of a commercial zoo, or is himself a dealer, is ever elected to it. Indeed, it is at present almost impossible for anybody to join the I.U.D.Z.G. unless his menagerie is

In 1965 a sailor brought these young chimpanzees to England without an import permit. They were confiscated, and are now in London Zoo.

backed by a society, foundation, or trust—even if he is not a dealer. This means that the I.U.D.Z.G. is not an international association of the zoological gardens of the world, but simply an international association of the *directors* of the "pure zoos." Furthermore, the fact that the directors belong to it does not necessarily commit one of their zoos to anything that they may jointly agree. Thus, although the I.U.D.Z.G. can suggest an international code of zoo management, it cannot impose one.

Trade Among Zoos

In one sense the distinction between pure zoos and commercial zoos is unrealistic. The zoos of the world, whether privately owned or run by societies, are *all* dealers, because they all exchange animals with each other and most sell animals to each other.

Never has there been a better system of trade and exchange between zoos than there is now, intelligently run and with its own journal. All mainstream zoo managers or curators are friends and colleagues, and are in constant touch. Normally the routine purchase or exchange of animals is left entirely to the appropriate animal curator; only if he is going to make a really big purchase or wants a new animal house does he have to put the matter to his committee. A man like John Yealland, the bird curator at the London Zoo, knows everybody in the trade and is friends with them all. In England he knows Terry Jones at the John Lewis Partnership collection at Leckford, one of the finest breeders of waterfowl in the business, and is always in touch with Peter Scott, whom he used to work for at Slimbridge. Overseas he is often in contact with such fine breeders of waterfowl as Jean Delacour's establishment in France, and the Philadelphia Zoo in the United States, as well as with numerous other big zoos and private aviculturists. If a man like Yealland has to replace a stock bird that has unfortunately died at the beginning of the breeding season, it is quite a usual thing for him to make a trans-oceanic telephone call to another zoo, get a quick replacement by air and keep his breeding record intact.

The highly efficient trade among zoos means that in the long run captive stock will replace wild stock. This trend already shows in mainstream zoo statistics. It also shows in private zoo statistics, notably those of specialized aviculturists who breed waterfowl, game birds, and parrots. There are even some animals, including lions, llamas, and certain members of the goat-sheep family, that big zoos tend to over-produce. Some of these find their way to the many small, commercial roadside zoos that have sprung up in the United States,

Jumbo, London Zoo's famous African
elephant, was obtained in 1865 from
the zoo at the Jardin des Plantes, Paris,
in exchange for an Indian rhinoceros,
an early example of trade between zoos.
He became very popular, and there was
a public outcry when, in 1882, he was
sold to a circus in America.

Britain, and parts of continental Europe in recent years. The roadside-zoo movement is one that mainstream zoos deprecate on the whole; but they must recognize that it does exist and that it may as well be run properly and supplied primarily with zoo-bred stock.

As the trade among zoos grows, the run-of-the-mill dealer comes more and more to find his main market among pet-keepers. And frankly this is a bad market (though not in the financial sense) once it extends beyond the familiar domestic and semi-domestic pets, ranging from dogs and cats to canaries and budgerigars. The average keeper of exotic pets learns his job (if he ever learns it) at the expense of animals that are all too easy to buy but none too easy to care for. Zoos know from long and hard experience that it takes a zoo to tend an exotic animal. For this reason it would not be at all easy for just anybody to buy, say, a marmoset from a zoo; it would be far easier for him to give his marmoset to a zoo, and thus admit that he should never have acquired it.

To be successful, a private exotic-pet keeper needs far more time and wealth than most people think; he also needs to have picked up experience by helping another pet keeper before he starts on any scale himself. Furthermore, he should be dedicated to his hobby and determined to become expert with a limited group of animals. With pet keepers of this sort, especially with serious private aviculturists, zoos do a great deal of trading and exchanging.

Animal Prices

The price of a zoo animal, whether common or rare, is usually governed by the guesswork of the dealer who wants to sell it, and the intensity of desire of the zoo that wants to buy it. As a result, some of the more common animals are cheap. Even zoo stand-bys, like lions (unless they belong to interesting races or color varieties), are two for a nickel and almost unmarketable, simply because so many have bred in captivity. Animals in short supply are naturally more expensive.

When there is only one animal in supply and only one customer to demand it a peculiar position arises. Lately there has been only one giant panda in Western Europe—London Zoo's Chi-chi. In the early summer of 1958 Chi-chi was in transit from the Peking Zoo to a zoo in the United States, when suddenly the United States government remembered that she came from Red China and that it was therefore illegal to import her. The dealer, who had been offered a price in the region of $15,000 for her in America, showed her to several continental zoos in Europe and finally let the London Zoo have her in September 1958.

Top: J. E. Edwards, a Londoner, is an exotic pet keeper with wide knowledge of his subject. He specializes in reptiles, including Mississippi alligators, such as the one he is here using during a lecture at the London Zoo. He has built a reptilium for his pets in the basement of his home, where he is seen (above) weighing a snake.

154

Above: Rabion, London Zoo's cheetah.
Cheetahs are becoming scarcer, and so
their value is constantly rising. Right:
Bristol Zoo's pair of white tigers,
Champa and Chameli. White tigers are
extremely rare in nature, and this pair was
especially bred in India, in 1963.
White tigers have ice-blue eyes.

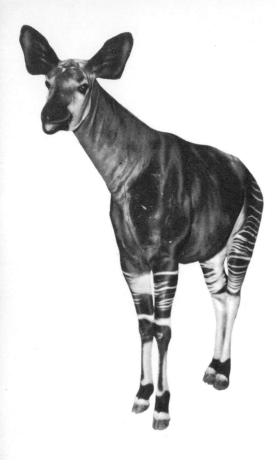

In the late 1930s, when I was on the staff of the Zoological Society of London as an assistant curator, it was my job to do the annual valuation of the animals that was then required by the Society's auditing system. The general brief given to me was to be guided by previous years' valuations; to use my own judgment (for instance, as to whether a particular animal had increased in zoos lately, justifying some marking-down of its value); and to read the dealers' catalogues of the day. I was further told that the value assigned to each animal should reflect the reasonable price of a willing seller to a willing buyer. By working to this brief and questioning curators ("Do you feel giraffes are still around the £750 mark?") I was able to complete the valuation in four or five days. The accountants ran my various items through the adding machine and came up with a total of around £20,000. The Zoological Society of London published a valuation for its stock of animals at Regent's Park and Whipsnade for the last time in 1958. It was then £174,618. Since then the Society has followed the widely adopted practice of considering its animal stock as a "hidden" asset; but from a study of the current value of money and animals, I would guess that it is now worth over £200,000, or $560,000—about ten times the pre-war figure.

Although few mainstream zoos now publish annual valuations of their animals, anyone interested can usually estimate the value of a collection. He knows that over two-thirds of the animals come into the zoo by way of gift or exchange, the rest by purchase. By adding together the annual purchase money of the last fifteen years (for which figures are nearly always published if the zoo is run by a public company or a society), he gets quite close to the total present value.

From a study of the London and Whipsnade accounts emerges an interesting observation: the rise in the value of the average zoo animal. In 1939 the figure was just over $28. It was over $42 by 1944, over $56 by 1946, over $70 by 1949, over $84 by 1956, and over $98 by 1958. I guess from the trend that the average is now over $125. It is true that collections like that of London are improving; but this sensational rise is mainly a reflection of the world's post-war inflation. It also indicates that, with the multiplication of zoos and prestige-pet keepers, the wild animal dealers of the world are now operating in a sellers' market.

The present high average embraces all animals except fishes and invertebrates, including a biggish proportion of cheap small mammals and birds. This means that the top zoo animals—elephants, giraffes, okapis, rhinos, great apes, and so on—are very expensive indeed. Here is a list of current prices of some zoo "stars" in the 1960s: Giant panda: $17,000, great Indian rhinoceros: $8,500,

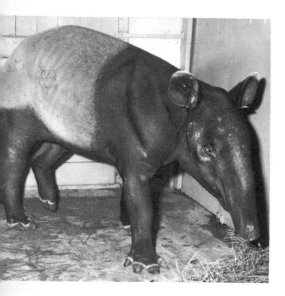

Two very rare and valuable mammals: The okapi (above) of the Congo forest, here seen in the quarantine station at Epulu, Congo; and the Malay tapir of Indonesia (below). This tapir is at the Berlin Zoo.

highland gorilla: $8,500, lowland gorilla: $5,600, giraffe: $5,600, square-lipped (white) rhinoceros: $2,800, African or Indian elephant: $2,800, Siberian tiger: $2,300, African black rhinoceros: $2,000, orangutan: $2,000, blesbok: $2,000, white-tailed gnu: $2,000, clouded leopard: $1,400, cheetah: $1,100, Malay tapir: $900, tiger (common race): $900, hippopotamus: $600, dromedary (pedigree): $600, chimpanzee: $600, quetzal: $300.

This list is based largely on recent price quotations to, or valuations of, mainstream zoos and major dealers. It excludes "values" of such animals as the Sumatran and Javan rhinoceroses or the Arabian oryx, whose sale or purchase either is illegal, or is emphatically discouraged by the International Union for Conservation of Nature and Natural Resources, on the advice of its Survival Service Commission. As circumstances quickly change, nobody should think that these prices necessarily represent *current* market prices, which may well be higher.

Caught and transported with great labor, and often purchased at great expense, animals are eventually "taken on the team" of a zoo. "Beds" must be ready for them, keeper staff alerted, and the catering departments notified. Labels giving their correct names, with maps showing their correct distribution in the wild, must be prepared. The moment each animal arrives, an accession card must be made out for it that will live on in the zoo records, available for research, long after the animal dies. Perhaps most important of all, each animal must have a home where it can thrive and, we hope, breed. Here zoo architecture and engineering play their important part.

The bear pit at Barcelona is a spacious one and houses a number of brown bears. This is a better plan than the one often found, where a single bear is kept in a small pit. Brown bears are easily obtained.

6 Zoo Accommodations and Architecture

Zoos vary so much in size, comprehensiveness, site, and age that it is almost idle to discuss "zoo architecture" in its own right, as if there were established standards of utility and aesthetics by which we may judge it. Yet zoos certainly differ from all other enclosed spaces, and demand their own special architectural approach. They must combine buildings and services designed for the comfort of a wide variety of animals, with buildings and services designed for the pleasure and intellectual profit of human beings. Perhaps the only worth-while test of zoo architecture, layout, and engineering is that they make this combination both efficient and attractive.

To gain some idea of the complexity of the problem, I have checked the statistics of 60 mainstream zoos in 1962. Each of them, on the average, contained about 600 mammals of 120 species, 1,350 birds of 260 species, and 280 reptiles and amphibians of 73 species. In addition, half of them had an aquarium of some sort within the gardens, holding an average of 1,500 fishes of 110 species; a quarter also showed invertebrates—about 700 individuals of 46 species. To house a collection of this sort a zoo needs up to 50 different buildings and space units of nearly 30 different kinds (as listed in the table on pages 162-4). Yet among the 60 zoos I have in mind the average space available was only 126 acres, or a little under one-fifth of a square mile.

The Roots of Modern Zoo Architecture

We saw in Chapter 2 (page 52) that only 30 existing zoos had passed their hundredth birthday by 1964. Nevertheless, the present complexity of zoos and zoo architecture has evolved over a period of about a thousand years.

The Benedictine monks of St. Gallen in Switzerland seem to have been the first true zoo architects of Europe. The ancient monastery, named after St. Gall, was founded by that Irish hermit in A.D. 610. By the ninth century it was a flourishing Benedictine community and one of the chief seats of learning in Europe. Attached to it was a study menagerie which included not only animals that were probably from the countryside around, such as badgers, marmots, bears, and herons; but also some exotics, such as silver pheasants from Asia. This menagerie differed from its medieval predecessors in having a quite modern layout—involving a cellular-division plan of animal houses, with carefully arranged

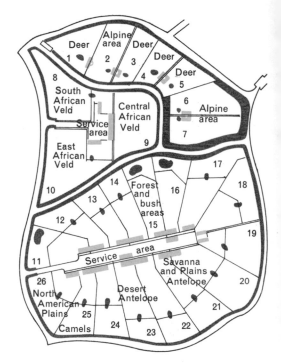

Top: The old moat at Bern, used for enclosing deer—an example of the simplest kind of animal enclosure. Contrast the complex modern ground-plan (above), which shows the ungulate enclosures at the Oklahoma City Zoo. A different effect is produced (right) by the "barless" system of moated pens at New York's Bronx Zoo.

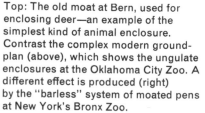

outdoor spaces and keepers' working spaces. As in a modern zoological garden, a plant collection was included: St. Gallen's botanic and herb garden was famous.

The St. Gallen plans were unsensational but eminently practical. As such, they were perhaps nearer the modern style than those of later European zoos, where practicality, although quite good, was often overwhelmed by noble and regal grandeur; for during the next nine centuries scientific zoos and great menageries were almost without exception on the estates of lords and monarchs. Outstanding among royal collections of the fourteenth century was that at the Hôtel de Saint Pol in Paris—first heard of in 1318 when Good King Wenceslas visited it to see the lions, and developed nearly half a century later by Charles V, while he was Dauphin of France. This was a truly lovely zoological garden, with beautiful flower beds, laid out with an eye for show. It was full of fowls, pigeons, turtledoves, large birds in great flights, many little aviaries and cages for singing birds, and gilded cages for "birds of Cyprus." It also had enclosures for boar, a house for lions, pools for seals, a great pond for fishes and—almost unbelievably—porpoises.

Several menageries of the fifteenth century, including one at the Palace of the Medici in Florence and another at Brussels, were distinguished as much for their architectural magnificence as for their zoological efficiency. But perhaps the finest early Renaissance zoo was that of René, Duke of Anjou, of Lorraine and Bar, Count of Provence and of Piedmont, King of Naples, Sicily, and Jerusalem. As far as we know, the zoo that flourished at his château of Angers, toward the end of the fifteenth century, had more of the "basic space units" of a modern zoo than any other of its time. They included a lion house, a small-mammal house, ruminant and ostrich enclosures, a great bird flight, cages for little singing birds, and a garden and pond for waterfowl.

The next zoo destined to influence modern mainstream zoo architecture was founded at the Château de Chantilly in 1530, by Anne de Montmorency. Chantilly was already a noble hunting park when Anne inspired its zoo; and many of her successors embellished and improved it. It had mammal houses, parakeet aviaries, a heronry, a falcon mews, fishponds, waterfowl pools, and paddocks for deer, sheep, cattle, and game-birds. By late in the seventeenth century this zoo-park had passed into the hands of those great patrons of zoology, the Condé family; and in 1673 the Condés brought in the first outstanding zoo architect, le Nôtre, to help in planning the new zoo at Vineuil based on the Chantilly plan, but with many imaginative improvements. By 1792, when Vineuil was sacked and destroyed by revolutionaries, it had doubtless shown a greater variety of animals in beautiful surround-

Above: A sixteenth century menagerie at the "Cour du Prince" at Ghent, Belgium. Lions were kept in the small square enclosure at bottom right. Below: The Vineuil menagerie in 1730.

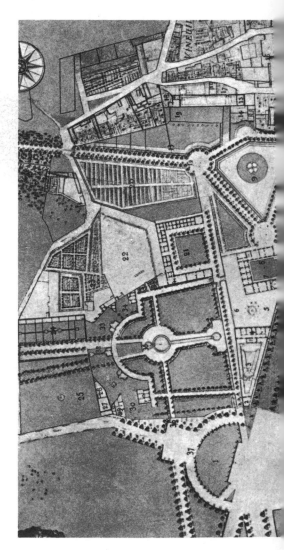

ings than any other menagerie save that at Versailles.

Throughout the eighteenth and nineteenth centuries, and in some cases well into the twentieth, the great zoos of the world built in an incredible mixture of styles. Vienna's Schönbrunn, oldest of surviving mainstream zoos, was, as we saw earlier, a paragon of regal delicacy; but like Chantilly, Vineuil, and Versailles, it was in the finest tradition of *human* architecture. It is true that most of today's centenarian zoos, and others nearly as old, tried to provide accommodations and access as suitable for their animals as they knew how. But more often than not the final frontage and architectural personality of a new house reflected the contemporary grand manner, or moved into the realms of what has been called the "atmosphere style." The botanic-zoological gardens of Stuttgart, for instance, were directly inspired by Eng-

Below: At Vineuil there was a hunting park as well as a menagerie. Both are shown on this drawing, which shows a hunt in progress (top), the duke of Bourbon (center), and a general view of the menagerie (bottom).

land's Moorish-style Brighton Pavilion. The old (West) Berlin zoo experimented with zebra houses in Arabian style, and a wild horse house in Persian style. Antwerp built a classic Egyptian temple, Rome built like Ancient Rome, Barcelona in the rococo Spanish fashion. London, for some obscure reason, built the predecessor of the present reptile house as a Swiss châlet. Stockholm, with more reason, built animal enclosures in Swedish farm style; while Lisbon made its zoo an exhibition of the native skill of the Portuguese in designing beautiful and durable tiles and tessellated pavements. Even quite lately, zoos have sought the atmosphere style in new buildings. Not much more than a decade ago Naples built its research and quarantine station in Pompeiian style. A small section of Chicago's great modern Brookfield Zoo was built only 30 years ago in the informal Italian farm style of the fifteenth century. However, if Brookfield here used a style oddly inappropriate for a middle western American zoo, at least it has also used the barless system, the one great architectural invention that belongs to zoos alone.

BASIC SPACE UNITS OF A MAINSTREAM ZOO

1. SMALL MAMMALS. A small-mammal house probably with satellite paddocks for kangaroos, wallabies, and wombats; and separate accommodations for larger rodents such as marmots, coypus, and porcupines.
2. PRIMATES. Monkey house and ape house (often combined), with various separate enclosures, such as hills or castles for baboons and macaques; and islands in ponds or lakes for spider monkeys and gibbons.
3. MAMMALS OF PREY. Usually a great-cat house, with separate enclosures for dog family, hyenas, raccoons, badgers, otters, and so on.
4. BEARS. Dens, pits, and enclosures, including a polar bear pool.
5. SEAL FAMILY. Large pools for seals, sea lions, elephant seals, and walruses.
6. VAST UNGULATES. Either separately, or in some combination, accommodations for elephants, tapirs, hippos, and rhinos.
7. LARGE UNGULATES. Houses and paddocks for horses and zebras; separate or variously combined accommodations for hyraxes, the pig family, camels, deer, giraffes, okapis, cattle, and antelopes.
8. SHEEP AND GOATS. Hills and rocky paddocks.
9. PENGUINS. Pool.
10. LARGE FLIGHTLESS BIRDS. Paddocks for ostriches, emus, cassowaries, and rheas.

Top: Frankfurt Zoo's bears are kept today in an open, Hagenbeck-style enclosure. Contrast the old bear-house of 1874 (above). Top right: The new camel and llama house at Frankfurt, contrasted with the old ones, which consisted of a big tent for the camels and another for the llamas.

11. BIRD HOUSE. This may have indoor "walk-through," or barless aviaries, and separate or satellite divisions for parrots, hummingbirds, pigeons, weavers, waxbills, and so on.

12. WATER BIRD ENCLOSURES. These often include ponds and islands for wildfowl and flamingos, aviaries and paddocks for long-legged marsh birds and waders, sea-bird flights, and pelican pools.

13. BIRDS OF PREY. Even today these are sometimes housed in comparatively small cages; but some modern flights for vultures, condors, and eagles are mercifully vast. Aviaries for day-flying birds of prey are often combined with owl aviaries.

14. GAME BIRDS AND BUSTARDS. Various combinations of pheasantries, crane paddocks, bustard runs, and so on.

15. REPTILE HOUSE. This needs to be heated and air-conditioned. Often it has a satellite outdoor reptiliary.

16. AQUARIUM. This is often combined with, or has as satellites, accommodations for manatees, small seals, and sometimes even dolphins.

17. INSECT HOUSE. This may have an apiary—an inspectable beehive—as satellite.

18. EXOTARIUM OR TROPICARIUM. This is a modern development, taking the form of a biggish climate-conditioned house in which carefully assorted animals (from 1, 2, 5, 9, 11, 12, 14, 15, 16, and 17 above) are shown in dioramic and ecological combinations.

19. CHILDREN'S ZOO.

20. EDUCATION BUILDING. Here there may be live and non-live zoological demonstrations, living displays of local fauna, and sometimes an animal art studio.

21. ANIMAL HOSPITAL. This is commonly combined with a research and autopsy laboratory and sometimes with an animal quarantine station, which is usually a satellite outside the gardens.

22. ANIMAL FOOD WAREHOUSE. This is often combined with central food-preparation kitchens.

23. WORKS AND MAINTENANCE DEPARTMENTS. Transportation units, fire engines, and similar equipment are housed here.

24. RESTAURANTS.

25. FIRST-AID POST. This often includes a lost-children depot.

26. ZOO SHOP.

27. ADMINISTRATIVE OFFICE BUILDING. This includes, or has as satellites, library, archives, lecture halls, meeting-rooms, accommodations for various societies, and research laboratories.

28. PARKING LOT. There is sometimes also a rail-
    road station or boat wharf.
29. FLOWER GARDENS. Interlacing all other space
    units are flower beds, arboreta, bowers, glades,
    shrubberies, and lawns with plenty of seats and
    public resting places.

The Hagenbeck Revolution

On May 7, 1907, Carl Hagenbeck's new zoo opened at
Stellingen, in the suburbs of Hamburg, to the amaze-
ment of the public and to the instruction of every contemporary and subsequent menagerie. Aided by the
Swiss sculptor and designer Urs Eggenschwiler, Hagenbeck had realized, ever since he bought the site in 1902,
that with deft architectural and earth-shifting touches
and the use of reinforced concrete and artificial rocks,
he could make an almost barless zoo. The same techniques, cleverly employed, also enabled him to imitate
the natural habitat of animals.

His landscaping devices have seldom been used better
by anybody since. Anyone who today visits the African
panorama at the Hamburg Zoo sees immediately in front
of him an elegant paddock containing gazelles and some
fine water birds, all of African origin—African flamingos, one or two species of African storks, and some very
delightful cranes. Behind them he sees rather large antelopes, and zebras; then behind these, appearing to be on
the same piece of African veld, with appropriate water-
holes, he sees lions. Behind the lions, the vista appears
to get very rocky and hilly; and on the rocks and hills
the visitor sees African wild sheep and ibexes.

Why are the zebras and ibexes not eaten by the lions?
The answer is that, not only between the visitor and the
gazelle paddock, but also between the gazelles and the
zebras, and between the zebras and the lions, and between the lions and the ibexes, there are unseen pits that
the animals cannot cross. From the normal public stand-
point, the whole vista looks as if it is continuous.

In 1907 preparing zoo vistas of this kind was not only
revolutionary but also laborious. There were, of course,
no bulldozers; and large-scale earth-shifting was largely
done by men with spades, buckets, and wheel-barrows,
aided here and there by mechanical steam shovels. The
use of reinforced concrete was not novel, but rare on
such a large scale, and then still expensive. Hagenbeck's
plans also involved copious use of water, not only in
some of the pit barriers but to embellish the landscape
with artificial lakes and ponds.

The Hagenbeck idea was not quickly followed, in spite
of its brilliance. The other zoos, in more competitive
days, would have reacted fast. In those pre-World War

Right: (top) The famous animal collector
and zoo pioneer Carl Hagenbeck looking
over the site he had chosen for his zoo,
at Stellingen, near Hamburg, Germany.
Middle: Building works in progress.
Hagenbeck, at great expense, built vistas,
"mountains," and moats to enrich his
animals' environment. Many modern zoos,
such as Chicago's Brookfield (bottom
right) have followed Hagenbeck's
initiative in landscaping.

days they did not. Alone before the first war London Zoo responded, with its fine Mappin Terraces (see page 175) of 1913. After that war, in 1919, the St. Louis Zoo built bear dens that were also inspired by Hagenbeck's work. Except for Mappin Terraces and bear dens, the zoos seemed curiously unwilling to adopt Hagenbeck's principle for about a quarter of a century.

Things eventually changed, however: today there is no mainstream zoo that fails to make use of the barless system, and few that are without artificial, or artificially carved, rock. The most spectacular example is the zoo at Vincennes (the Paris Parc Zoologique). There, in 1934, they were in the fortunate position of building a zoo from scratch, and they tried to out-Hagenbeck Hagenbeck. In fact, the French became so excited about the barless game that they made even more landscapes and vistas than Hagenbeck; and in my opinion made them rather too massive with artificial rock structures. Nevertheless, Vincennes is a noble zoo in which the animals do extremely well.

Carl Hagenbeck approached the whole pit system very scientifically before he felt that it could be safe. He made many experiments on the leaping and swimming powers of mammals—such as hanging stuffed pigeons at various heights to see how far the great cats would jump. (His lions and tigers could not reach seven feet, nor his leopards ten, though some lions and tigers in later experiments have reached just over twelve feet.) After studying their broad-jump talents, both standing and on the run, Hagenbeck made his lion and tiger trenches 28 feet wide. This was, it has now been proved, unnecessarily wide; even so, the Vincennes tigers were later given a 40-foot gap.

Since Hagenbeck's pioneer days of Stellingen, so universal has the barless system become, that it is now possible to make a diagram showing how broad and deep pit barriers should be for many kinds of animals. The diagram on page 167 is based on the safety measurements discovered by the experiments of a score of zoos. Barriers for some animals (especially Primates) normally contain water, although the depth of water is of no great importance. Pit barriers for lions and tigers can be reduced in breadth if they are water-filled; our diagram shows two distinct sets of measurements in this case.

I have said that no present zoo fails to make use of the barless system: but where space is severely restricted, vistas are not at all easy to contrive. London is certainly handicapped in this respect. It has one of the largest collections (in species numbers) of captive mammals and birds in the world and an area of only 36 acres. Most zoos with comparable collections are bigger—some much bigger. New York's Bronx Zoo has 252 acres,

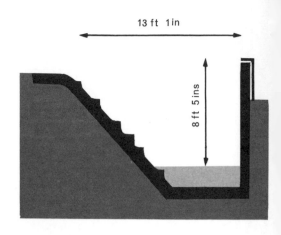

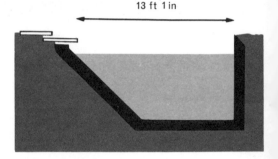

Different species of animals require moats of different shapes in order to prevent their escape. Above: Cross-sections of two moats at the Frankfurt Zoo. Upper: The rhesus monkey moat, containing 2 feet of water and a high wall-barrier. Lower: The spider monkey moat, in which the water, depth 6 feet, acts as the main barrier.

Top right: A graph showing the depth and breadth of moats required for various species. Moats containing water are shown in ochre; the rest are dry. Each shape or symbol shows the size or range of sizes of wet and/or dry moats required for a given species. In the key (below graph), shapes (left) and symbols (right) refer to similar shapes and symbols on the graph.

Right: The V-shaped, accessible moat in use at San Diego's Siberian tiger enclosure. The animals can enter the moat at will, and so cannot be trapped by falling into it.

BREADTH

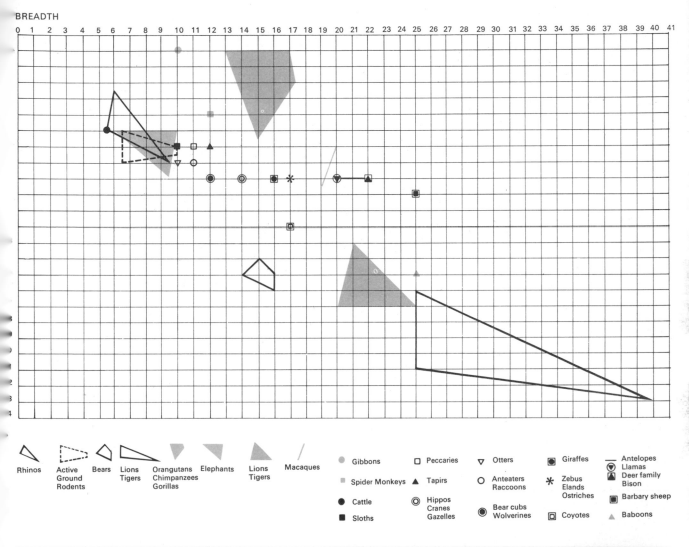

Rhinos	Active Ground Rodents	Bears	Lions Tigers	Orangutans Chimpanzees Gorillas	Elephants	Lions Tigers	Macaques

● Gibbons	□ Peccaries	▽ Otters	◉ Giraffes	— Antelopes
■ Spider Monkeys	▲ Tapirs	○ Anteaters Raccoons	✳ Zebus Elands Ostriches	▽ Llamas / ▲ Deer family Bison
● Cattle	◎ Hippos Cranes Gazelles	◉ Bear cubs Wolverines	▣ Coyotes	▣ Barbary sheep
■ Sloths				▲ Baboons

Above: An attractive "African Plains" exhibit at Barcelona Zoo. This is an excellent example of the use of a small moated area to house a number of species in natural surroundings. Left: The Antwerp Zoo combines the barless system for elephants with a series of animal houses built in the "Egyptian style."

Chicago-Brookfield 215, Munich 173, Washington 176, San Diego 91, West Berlin 74, Cologne 49, Frankfurt 49, and Rome 42. Among zoos with comparable collections only Barcelona with 30 acres, Amsterdam with 25, and Antwerp with 24 are smaller than London. The ideal size for a comprehensive zoo is at least 100 acres; and London suffers from its shortage of space. Amsterdam and Antwerp are both near the size below which it is impossible to house a truly comprehensive collection.

Zoos occupying an area of less than 20 acres are compelled to cut their coat according to their cloth, and decide that there are certain things they simply cannot try to do. This frees a certain amount of space, and often leaves them less cramped than the small comprehensive zoos. Bristol Zoo, for instance, occupies only 12 acres; but it is a very beautiful zoo, and here and there small Hagenbeckian vistas have been devised.

The benefits of the barless vista fall as much to the public as to the animals. The public feels free and feels that the animals feel freer than they might behind bars—whether they really do or not.

Great Park Zoos

One zoo was very fortunately placed to use the barless system. Quite high up in the Bavarian hills, Munich's Hellabrunn Zoo is copiously blessed with broad, swift streams of crystal running water; and the modern layout often uses these as safe paddock boundaries in preference to ditches.

Hellabrunn, founded in 1910 on 186 acres, is above the average extent for a mainstream zoo and has many of the qualities of a park zoo—one in which the enclosures, rather than the houses, create and dominate the landscape. Founded in 1927 by the Zoological Society of London, Whipsnade Zoological Park in Bedfordshire is the park zoo *par excellence*.

When the Society decided to start a park zoo to mark its centenary, Sir Peter Chalmers Mitchell, then the secretary, spent months searching for a wooded site within range of London in which beautiful vista paddocks (or panoramic enclosures) could be contrived, preferably not all on the same level. Finally he found an estate on the top of the Bedfordshire chalk downs, which some people said would be too draughty. It is indeed a bit windy at Whipsnade; but the park is perched at the edge of an escarpment, so that the cold winter air tends to flow down to the valley below and does not seem to worry the animals—or the people—at the top.

Whipsnade, on the whole, is not Hagenbeckish. The park is so big (567 acres) that there is no need to use rock constructions with artificial foreshortenings to make the vistas look bigger than they really are. As a matter of fact most of the vast paddocks at Whipsnade are enclosed not by pits and water but by fences. The technique has been to drop the fence in favor of a barless pit, so as to give an untrammelled view, only at the usual public vantage point. Around some of the paddocks the fence is really heavy; and around the rhino enclosure it is very heavy indeed, and has to be.

On the subject of fencing, I remember a spectacular mistake I once made in my inexperienced days as a zoo curator. In my second year with the London Zoo I was entrusted with the management of Whipsnade while the superintendent was away on vacation. At the time a shipment of warthogs arrived from Africa, the intention being to put them into a great paddock with gnus, various other antelopes, ostriches, and one or two zebras, to form an African fauna. Warthogs are powerful animals, and can be rather obstinate and restive on occasion; so I was advised to build a temporary sub-enclosure (within the paddock) of posts and wires, and to get the warthogs acclimatized and settled before letting them out into the full enclosure. When we uncrated the warthogs into this sub-enclosure they were through the fence in 30 seconds, simply because we had not calculated the strength of fence required to confine a lively 200-pound boar anxious to get a bit of fresh air and exercise after a long journey. If the story has a moral it is: if you are going to use fences they had better be strong enough. In the great park zoos they are.

One park zoo that is a particular favorite of mine was opened to the public only as late as 1952. It is very much of the Whipsnade type and exploits its 250-acre site in a most ingenious way. Its name is Skånes Djurpark (animal park of Skåne); and it is near the southern tip of Sweden, among the pine and spruce forests of a place called Höör, near Lund and Malmö. It has been developed by a Swedish nobleman, Count Björn Hamilton, and its object is to provide a miniature tour of the entire spectacular fauna of Sweden's forests and dales, alps and lakesides. As far as is possible everything is shown in its natural surroundings, with the use of very large enclosures, partly—but not entirely—on the barless principle. Where fences are used, they are the traditional wooden farm fences of southern Sweden; the buildings that house the animals are also built of wood in the traditional Swedish style. An example of Count Hamilton's ingenuity is the way in which he has solved the problem of giving the wolves a wide range while still allowing the public to get a good (and surprising) view of them. They are run in double paddocks on each side of the main public walk, with a connecting tunnel underneath, and they keep popping up at unexpected places.

Skanes Djurpark, in Sweden, exhibits its animals in large, open areas, not cages. The paddocks are separated from each other by fences that harmonize with the surrounding woodlands. Below: Fallow deer in front of three wooden fences, each enclosing a different species. Right: African dwarf goats, with a wooden winter shelter-house in the background.

Among exhibits of special interest at Skånes Djurpark are a paddock of breeding moose, breeding Swedish bears, fine Swedish wolverines, and the rare Swedish red deer, including the most magnificent known stag of that race. There are also many different birds, including the black stork and the white stork, which are now almost extinct in Sweden.

Whipsnade and Skånes Djurpark can fairly be described as specialized zoos, by virtue of being park zoos with abnormally wide animal ranges and deliberately limited collections. A specialist zoo that bears comparison with them is the Gardens of the Wildfowl Trust at Slimbridge, in Gloucestershire, England. I have already said something about the excellent work and fine breeding record of Slimbridge (in Chapters 3 and 4). Here I want to say a little about the choice and layout of the site.

Peter Scott chose the present site on the south bank of the River Severn estuary for three main reasons. First, it is the place where the largest flock of wild white-fronted geese winters in the British Isles—sometimes accompanied by several other kinds of geese.

Secondly, Slimbridge has had a working duck decoy ever since 1843. Berkeley New Decoy, originally used for trapping market ducks, consists of a small lake, entirely surrounded by woodland, from which tapering stretches of water radiate into the trees. These "pipes" are roofed with a funnel-like iron structure covered with netting, and ducks are decoyed into the funnels largely by encouraging them to follow a dog, which they will do out of natural curiosity. When the ducks are far enough down the pipes the operators disclose themselves from behind concealing wattled hurdles; and the ducks hurry into a bagnet at the end of the pipe. The decoy enabled the Wildfowl Trust to establish a duck banding station that it had long wanted in that area.

Thirdly, Scott found that Slimbridge had a whole group of fields in which he could easily add new lakes by bulldozing, plant new cover, open many ponds and channels, and make pleasant public paths and little hills. Soon, around a kernel area of 35 acres, the Trust had built the perfect reservoir for exotic wildfowl of every kind. Most, but by no means all, of these are wing-pinioned and cannot fly. As time has passed, more and more exotic species have been acclimatized to flying around free-winged.

Although Slimbridge opened in only a modest way to the public in 1946, it now houses the finest and most comprehensive collection of living wildfowl in the world.

The original buildings at Slimbridge were mainly oldish farm buildings and cottages. A range of new houses and scientific buildings has now been constructed under the architect Peter Bicknell.

171

Bringing an Old Zoo up to Date

One mainstream zoo particularly well placed to take full advantage of modern systems is San Diego. It has an extremely beautiful site, which is naturally carved into a complex of steep canyons, mesas (plateau hill-tops with steeply sloping sides), and spacious valley bottoms. Its topography makes the site a "natural" for vistas, and the canyons are so deep that some of them have been roofed over and made into gorgeous high cages for condors and other birds. One of San Diego's cages is 82 feet high, and 150 feet long, tapering in width from 75 feet at one end to 60 feet at the other. A public footpath enables zoo-goers to walk through the aviary itself.

San Diego Zoo is blessed in many ways. It has an excellent climate, with well over 300 days of sunshine a year; it has a low rainfall, yet enough water for irrigation; and it is very fertile, growing all kinds of trees and other cover in profusion. But perhaps one of its greatest blessings is that of comparative youth. It was founded in October 1916 by Dr. Harold M. Wegeforth and a small group of friends, and construction did not begin until 1922. By then many still-existing trends in zoo architecture and layout were already established, and San Diego

Above: Charles Faust, designer of the new gorilla enclosure at the San Diego Zoo, with a scale model of the pen. Above ground is the apes' rocky promenade deck; sleeping quarters are underneath. Below: The gorilla enclosure itself.

was able to plan and build progressively from the start.

Zoos founded in the nineteenth century are in a very different position. Their sites, often uncomfortably small, were chosen when the concept of zoo vistas still lay in the remote future, and their houses were originally built when ideas on animal comfort and hygiene were very different from those of today. To bring such zoos up to date means pulling down as well as building up, and an unsettling game of "musical chairs" while the work is in progress.

Before the London Zoological Society got its charter in 1829 it had already asked Decimus Burton, the man who designed the present layout of Hyde Park, to make a plan for its corner of Regent's Park. Burton's plan was never carried out; but at least he was appointed architect to the Society in 1830, and his wonderful giraffe house of 1837 is happily still in use, as are some of his bear pits of the early 1840s. The giraffe house, since reconstructed internally, was always a good one even by today's standards; and is now scheduled as a building of historical and architectural importance. The oldest building in the London Zoo is the Decimus Burton clock tower of 1830, which was bombed during World War II and later rebuilt brick by brick—the Society's way of

Above: London Zoo's old camel house, designed by Decimus Burton in the 1830s, is now used for storing deckchairs. The camels have been moved to the new Cotton Terraces. Below: The Burton camel house in its heyday.

London Zoo's large-cat house. Designed in 1876, it continues to be quite serviceable, because it was originally designed on a large enough scale. This view shows the interior; each pen leads to a spacious cage area out of doors.

taking its hat off to tradition. This building was originally a camel house, with two camel-shaped arches that the camels were supposed to stand under but could hardly turn around in. It is now used for storing deck chairs.

After Burton's time the rest of the nineteenth century went by with a good deal of higgledy-piggledy building, much of which is only being planned away as I write. Very little of it was distinguished, although the animals did well in some of the houses. Among the buildings that still remain, but will remain very little longer, are the great aviary (a pioneer very large bird flight of 1887, rebuilt in 1902); the lion house (1876), in its time the largest and certainly the best large-cat house in the world; and a tortoise house (1897), now partly occupied by small mammals.

No new general plan of any depth or merit was made until 1909, when the Society consulted the architect J. J. Joass. He made a rather good plan; but it was debated inconclusively for at least four years, shelved on the outbreak of war in 1914, and not as a whole implemented later. Nevertheless the Society did get some fine Joass buildings. It was Joass who designed the excellent offices and library, since changed only a little internally. Inspired by the Hagenbeck style, he also built the Mappin Terraces (1913), extraordinary artificial rock mountains for athletic ungulates such as sheep, ibexes, and goats. Under the Mappin Terraces is Joass's aquarium (1924), still among the world's best; complete with prodigious sea-water tanks and an ingenious circulation system. Finally Joass designed the Fellows' Restaurant (1929),

The Mappin Terraces at the London Zoo, built in 1913, are now used to house wild sheep and goats, which enjoy climbing on the steep, rocky surfaces. They were designed in direct imitation of Carl Hagenbeck's style (p. 165).

Above: London Zoo's penguin pool was originally built in 1934, with unique sloping concrete pathways. It has since been modified and the floor has been re-tiled.

Below: The old gorilla house at London Zoo, built at the same time as the penguin pool, currently houses a colony of chimpanzees. It contains poles and ropes.

only slightly modified since and universally admitted to be one of the finest in London.

The third attempt at a plan for the London Zoo came in the late 1930s, while Sir Julian Huxley was Secretary to the Society. It was then that the first modern concrete structures were introduced into the zoo in Regent's Park. They were the work of the revolutionary architect Tolek Lubetkin and his allied firm of engineers, Tecton. Only two buildings of that epoch survive—the gorilla house, now used for chimpanzees, and the penguin pool. A new elephant house, caught half built by the air-raid sirens on September 3, 1939, was never finished.

When World War II ended, things began to look quite good for the London Zoo, with the 1946 "gate" rising to 2¾ million and looking as if it would stay there. In 1947, therefore, the Society appointed F.A.P. Stengelhofen as permanent architect and entrusted him with working out a new rebuilding plan. At that time, at least a score of major houses and enclosures were over half a century old, and only a few of these were worth preserving. By 1951 (it takes time to do these things) Stengelhofen had produced a complete rebuilding scheme that combined forward-looking, new techniques of animal housing with a tender backward look at some of the old classics, which were to remain as pleasant fossils.

Just at this crucial moment the London Zoo ran out of money. It would be irrelevant here to explain in detail how this happened, but one very important reason was a drop in the gate numbers from the 2¾ million of 1946 to a little under 2 million in 1951. At any rate, the London Zoo was no longer as rich as it had expected to be, and Stengelhofen's plan was mostly shelved. By 1956 the only completed Stengelhofen buildings were two essentials—a sanatorium and a quarantine station.

Then came the appointment, as Honorary Secretary of the Zoological Society, of Sir Solly Zuckerman, not only a distinguished zoologist and anatomist but also a fertile begetter of projects and the means to finance them. The Society's council was so convinced that the money would somehow be raised that in 1957 it engaged Sir Hugh Casson as consultant architect. Casson was entrusted with producing yet another grand plan—London's fifth—in collaboration with Stengelhofen, who stayed on as staff architect. The new plan is related to the Stengelhofen plan much as Sir John Hunt's successful Everest expedition stood upon the shoulders of all previous expeditions; and in many opinions it is the most imaginative one ever contrived for a centenarian zoo.

Casson and Stengelhofen were joined by the landscape architect Peter Shepheard, and the three together got down to work. The whole plan was to be carried through in four defined stages; and essentials of course came

The "open-air ward" at London Zoo's new hospital, which was completed in 1956. Modern equipment and a highly qualified staff have led to a 90 per cent recovery rate for hospitalized animals.

first. Without good service buildings other improvements can scarcely proceed, so these were the subject of Stage 1. Stengelhofen's fine new Works Department building was finished in 1959, his Supplies building in 1960.

It was in May 1960 that Jack Cotton, the wealthy realtor, gave the London Zoo about $700,000, roughly equal to a whole year's gate receipts. This was immediately earmarked for Stage 2—the redevelopment of the Regent's Canal banks a section of the gardens.

First of all, Casson, with Frank Shaw and the engineer Stephen Revesz, designed a central bridge over the canal—a most beautiful thing of concrete, with canti-

Above: The old Decimus Burton giraffe house at the London Zoo. Its original (1836) design was excellent and it has fitted well into the new Cotton Terraces, built around it. Its interior (above right) has been modernized.

Below: Inside London Zoo's new zebra house, a feature of the display is that the animals are in brightly lit pens, while the public area is dark.

London Zoo's new Northern Aviary was opened to the public in 1965. It is built in the "walk-through style," and has a maximum height of 82 feet.

levered sides, a slung precast center section, and a two-level approach. This was built in 1962. In 1963 Stengelhofen saw the finishing of a project he had been working on for some years—his tribute to the first London Zoo architect, Decimus Burton. Revealed in its ancient external glory, but redesigned internally, was Burton's grand giraffe house. The wings that Burton had added had been half concealed by the follies of some later builder. Now they were again in full view, balancing the main building most agreeably. Outside, the bars have gone. Paddocks have replaced the old yards; and the only thing between the public and the giraffes, yaks, bison, zebras, and camels is a moated plant-walk.

Placed symmetrically on each side of the giraffe house are two new ungulate houses, designed, like the moated paddocks, by Peter Shepheard. Externally they are simple, and subordinate to the giraffe house; inside they are dramatic, with the public space dark and the animal dens lit from concealed upper windows. Below the giraffe house, on what was formerly a steep canal bank, Shepheard has laid out an almost level antelope enclosure below a balustraded artificial cliff. Snorkel-like structures project through the cliff-top; these are skylights to a range of antelope dens underneath.

Opposite the giraffe house, across the canal, is the Earl of Snowdon's grand new aviary, designed by him with Cedric Price and the engineer Frank Newby. Other zoos have large and splendidly designed aviaries, including Rome, Wassenaar in Holland, San Diego, and Chicago-Brookfield; but the Earl of Snowdon's Northern Aviary and Pergola in London is certainly one of the biggest, and from the architectural point of view by far the most original. It is about 185 feet long, 82 feet high, and 83 feet wide. Within it is a cliff on which suitable birds perch and may nest, a little lake, trees and bushes, and a wonderful cantilevered public walk that almost flies through the air. Commissioned in 1961, the new aviary was built and welcomed its first birds in 1965. It is the biggest aviary since St. Louis's great flying cage (227 feet long, 50 feet high, and 84 feet wide) was opened in 1904.

Stage 2 of the new plan ended with the completion of the giraffe house and its satellites. In a zoo of only 36 acres not all houses and space units can be moved or renewed at once. But once the antelopes had their new home next to the giraffes, the old antelope house of 1860 could go, and a new elephant-rhinoceros pavilion be erected on its site. This was Stage 3. The new elephant-rhino pavilion, designed by Casson, is now built; and is much the most controversial of the new buildings. The animals were being introduced only while this book was in final proof, so it is early yet to judge.

However, I find the new pavilion rather claustrophobic—although I do not know that the elephants necessarily will. It is a group of enormous inward-looking chambers arranged in a curious partial ring, designed for four elephants and four rhinos, in paired pens. Each of these pens connects to what we may call stand-by pens, or sick-bay pens, as well as to bathing pools and outside paddocks.

From the outside the public sees a galaxy of elephantine structures with jutting, snorkel-like lantern-lights sheathed in copper. The exterior walls are of rough-finished ferro-concrete. The London Zoo people describe this as a touch of Oriental fantasy. To me the houses look like African huts. Either way, the impression fits elephants and rhinos and the lands from which they come. Inside, the pens are approached along a winding public route that brings the visitor in front of each one of them separately and rather unexpectedly, owing to their informal arrangement. Two other features add to the dramatic effect: the animals stand at a high level, and the snorkels light them from above.

The opening of the elephant-rhino pavilion paves the way for the final stage of London Zoo's plan—a stage that will not be completed until the early 1970s. Most of the space where the elephants were previously kept, in the middle gardens, has now been freed; and there work has begun on a new small-mammal house, designed by Mischa Black, of the Royal College of Arts, and Kenneth Bayes. The design problem was a formidable one, for, among the mammals to be housed, some fly or glide, some burrow, some swim, some climb, and many are nocturnal. London Zoo's mammal curator, Dr. Desmond Morris, has been experimenting for years with new techniques of managing and showing a group of nocturnal animals under night conditions; and a whole section of this house will be nocturnalized. In other words, during our day the house will have night, and during our night it will have day.

When the new house is built, the old small-mammal house (the former tortoise house of 1897) can go, and so, I am glad to say, can the rather depressing birds-of-prey aviary (1866). Thus another corner of the main gardens will be cleared, ready for the next step in rebuilding and reshuffling. Altogether it will take about eight years to replace the last two dozen old space units with such new buildings and scenery as will make the London Zoo look nearly perfect.

New Ideas and New Approaches

Many innovations in zoo architecture stem from an increasingly humane approach to the management of captive animals. Only in the twentieth century did zoos

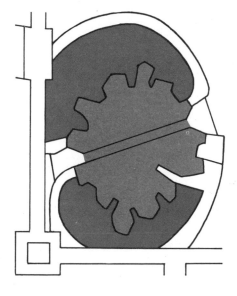

Above: Plan of London Zoo's new elephant and rhinoceros house. Paddocks are shown in gray, indoor accommodation in brown. Right: (top) A rhinoceros outside the new house, which has turrets providing light and ventilation for the interior. Architect Casson designed the house (below), using mainly ferro-concrete materials.

Above: A male Siberian tiger in the large-cat house at the Milwaukee Zoo. This enclosure is kept as cool as possible. It is open to the sky and so, in winter, the tigers can be seen in the snow. The public is behind three-quarters inch laminated glass (rear right). Visibility for the public is excellent, and viewing area is smell-free.

really face the fact that the care of animals involves financial, hygienic, nutritional and psychological obligations similar to those involved in the care of children. Today this is generally accepted; and progressive zoos often have a staff-animal ratio that, for the larger animals at least, is roughly the same as the staff-pupil ratio in a good boarding school.

Zoo architecture has expressed the new attitude in a variety of ways, including the design of superb hygienic kitchens for preparation of the animals' food. These are used with the same care and expense as the kitchen of a prosperous and popular hotel. In some zoos—notably Cleveland, Frankfurt, West Berlin, and Dudley (England)—the kitchens are on view to the public. The preparation of the meals is now a part of the show.

Increases in comfort that modern science and technology bring to humans are often quickly passed on to zoo animals. Air and humidity conditioning, for instance, reached some zoos as early as the 1920s. It came to the London Zoo with the great reptile house (1927), in which every den can have its temperature individually controlled, and to a large extent its humidity as well. Today air conditioning is common in zoos.

Zoo architecture must serve not only the physical needs of animals but also their psychological needs—particularly in the case of anthropoid apes. In the past ten years or so, brilliant residences have been built or remodeled for great apes at a number of zoos, including Chicago-Brookfield, Chester, Tokyo-Ueno, West Berlin, Antwerp, Zürich, Dallas, and Dudley (England). Antwerp has a cleverly designed series of indoor dens, spacious and full of furniture for apes to play on, because they need lots of entertainment to keep them happy. These dens are air-conditioned and separated from the public by glass to avoid the risk of respiratory infection. The inside dens communicate (by doors and flaps through which the animals can easily go) with marvelous outdoor dens equipped with playthings and occupational problems of various kinds. These are separated from the public only by a water ditch. Anthropoid apes cannot, or at least will not, swim. However, they can and will cross ice; so the outside dens of many modern ape houses have to be shut in freezing weather.

Devices such as these are features of the new animal combinations, or animal-plant combinations, that some progressive zoos are now experimenting with. These exhibits and space-units have been called vivaria, aquavivaria, tropicaria, exotaria, and all manner of names. Basically they are living developments of the old museum dioramas and exhibits showing ecology—the natural network of relationships involving living animals and plants and their environments.

If you go into the exotarium at Frankfurt-am-Main you have to pay a bit extra at the door. You can also hire a portable tape-recorder, with the aid of which the voice of Dr. Bernhard Grzimek, the Director, guides you around the whole series of living dioramas. When you go in, you are at once in Antarctica, among typical antarctic penguins—king penguins, Adélies, chinstraps, gentoos, and sometimes even emperor penguins. Real ice floes float in a great tank, with a large vista background. You can watch the penguins swim under the water and under the ice. The whole diorama is refrigerated throughout the year so that the penguins are at the temperature of their natural surroundings.

Just opposite, you are in the tropical Amazon, by the river edge. Piranhas—ferocious carnivorous fish—angel fish, and other elegant South American fish are swimming in what is, for their purposes, the Amazon River. The temperature and humidity are Amazonian, as are the small trees that grow by the water. Above, a tangled bank is adorned with Amazonian plants. Among the trees Amazonian butterflies flit about, and Amazonian birds disport themselves—tanagers, toucans, and the like. And there are other equally well-thought-out dioramas in Frankfurt's extensive and elaborate exotarium.

Frankfurt must be high on the list for the ingenuity prize among modern zoos. But all over the world such new ideas prevail. In Europe the London Zoo's new small-mammal house promises equal surprises; Cologne's new effects with combined seal and penguin pools, with watching places over and under water, are clever; other zoos have equally fascinating innovations.

The most successful American zoo buildings are characterized by the timelessness that natural façades give. Visit, for example, the superb antelope house at the St. Louis Zoo, completely hidden under lifelike rock formations and natural plantings. Detroit Zoo has similar artificial rock-covered buildings for various animals. A more conventional building, but worthy of note, is the St. Louis Zoo Bird House, one of the first to exhibit birds in open-fronted displays. Perhaps the most advanced displays in the United States now are those in the Bronx Zoo's new Aquatic Bird House. The Philadelphia and Denver zoos have exceptionally fine carnivore houses. By far the most ambitious of recent zoo structures in the United States is at the Milwaukee Zoo: one enormous building combines a series of great geographic displays showing predators and prey in their natural environment, separated by moats.

Such ideas work and proliferate only because the zoos of the world are at last beginning to stock up and share a vast know-how on humane animal management. This is the real point of zoo engineering and architecture.

Above: Two penguins in the Exotarium at the Frankfurt Zoo. This section of the Exotarium is known as the Polar Landscape, and is kept artificially cold, with ozone-enriched air. Underwater windows enable visitors to watch the penguins and aquatic birds (below) swimming and diving.

7 Zoo Risks and Research

Every kind of human enterprise carries its own special risks and offers its own special opportunities. Among special zoo risks are the danger that animals may spread disease and the possibility that they may escape. Among special zoo opportunities are those of research into comparative anatomy, comparative medicine, animal health and nutrition, and animal behavior.

I should like to place things in perspective by saying right away that the risks involved in keeping dangerous animals in zoos are very small; indeed, I suspect that a truck driver has a more dangerous job than a zoo keeper. Zoo keepers *have* been killed, of course, but only a few—

Lithograph (above), from a book published during the nineteenth century, shows escaped kangaroo putting visitors to flight at the London Zoo. Left: A more recent picture shows an empty corner of the Frankfurt Zoo after a bombing raid in the last war. Occasionally, escaped animals manage to establish themselves.

perhaps most of them by clumsy or nervous elephants or by poisonous snakes. It is also true that a few trespassing visitors, mad enough to climb into lions' dens after hats or on a bet, have never climbed out again. It is fair to say that dangerous animals confined in zoos present only a small occupational hazard to the zoo keeper, and virtually no risk at all to any but the lunatic fringe of the visiting public.

Dangerous animals are, of course, housed with the utmost security, and seldom get out. In the long history of the London Zoo I can find no events more serious than the escapes of: a famous golden eagle which lately escaped twice and on both occasions hit the headlines before it was caught; three polar bears (quickly persuaded back to their dens); an orangutan (which built a nest above the monkey house, producing more public interest than consternation); and a large zebra stallion that got out of the damaged zebra house during one of the night bombing raids of World War II. Sir Julian Huxley, then Secretary to the London Zoo, found the refugee zebra in the works yard and maneuvered it into a corner, whence it was boxed up by a couple of keepers on air-raid warden duty; they told Sir Julian he was lucky that the animal was a biter, not a kicker.

The bombing of World War II destroyed a fair number of London Zoo's animal houses; and it may seem remarkable that there were no escapes with worse consequences than that of the zebra. Yet London's experience was not unique. Several European zoos suffered worse damage than London; yet I know of no case where encounters with big escaped carnivores ended in a human fatality. When the war began, West Berlin had probably the most comprehensive collection of all classes of animals in the world. After the saturation raids of 1943-44, and the last days of April 1945, when the zoo became a battle ground, there were only 91 animals left alive. Also in Germany, on July 25, 1943, air raids destroyed 80 per cent of Hagenbeck's great zoo at Stellingen, killing eight people and 450 animals; for a time the famous Hagenbeck vistas (since replaced) looked like part of a moon landscape. The Frankfurt and Nuremberg zoos were also virtually destroyed. Yet through all this destruction, escaped animals, nervous though they were, gave relatively little trouble; and none of them, as far as I know, added to the wartime toll of human life. To sum up, dangerous animals in zoo captivity are not really very dangerous; they seldom escape except through some external cataclysm; and when they do they need not be as frightening as one might imagine. Most escapes, in fact, are birds.

Dangers to the Balance of Nature

Benign animals are usually housed less closely than dangerous ones. Indeed, the tendency today is to promote a state of semi-liberty for many of them. We have already mentioned examples of zoos that have free-flying "captive" birds. Several park zoos also have mammals (for instance, wallabies) at liberty in their grounds. The escape percentage of such animals can be, and often is, rather high. It is these escapes, rather than the escapes of dangerous animals, that are likely to cause damage, for they may seriously disturb the balance of nature in the country where they occur.

Introducing unnecessary exotics from one country to another is the greatest natural danger that the whole zoo movement presents. And by "the whole zoo movement" I mean not just zoos, but all other importers of exotic animals—including dealers, pet lovers, aviculturists, fur farmers, and acclimatizers. Altogether at least 125 species of birds have been "planted" by man in some country or countries outside their natural range; so have at least 96 species of mammals, including some of the world's most troublesome rodent pests. A few of these introductions have been made accidentally (as when rats have spread from one country to another as stowaways on ships), and a few others are the result of zoo escapes; but a large number have been deliberately made by acclimatizers.

Acclimatizers flourished more a hundred years ago than they do today. Few acclimatization societies are left now; but in their time they dedicated themselves to "improving" the fauna, particularly the game, of various parts of the world, by the deliberate introduction of deer, game birds, songbirds, rabbits, stoats, squirrels, and mongooses. Among the most active acclimatizers were colonists, bent on bringing to their settlements the wild familiars of their homeland; but they bungled the job badly, especially in island countries such as New Zealand and Hawaii. Continental homelands were less affected by acclimatizers; but in the course of their longer histories they have experienced the introduction of exotics in all kinds of ways.

Many animals have been introduced into the Americas at various times. Perhaps the most notable of the large ones are the horses brought by the early Spaniards, the ancestors of the wild mustangs that still survive in a few areas. Camels and zebras have been introduced at differ-

During the nineteenth century, some European aristocrats imported exotic species and tried to establish them. Above: The acclimatization farm of King Victor Emmanuel II of Italy near Pisa, in 1856, showing exotic cattle and dromedaries.

Another experiment in acclimatization,
this time in England. A herd of
American wapiti is here seen feeding
at Osmaston Manor, Derby, in 1894.

Mammal	When Introduced	Introduced by
Rabbit	Late 12th Century	Rabbit-Eaters
American Gray Squirrel	about 1876	Acclimatizers
House Mouse	Pre-Roman or Roman Times	Farmer-Traders
Black Rat	12th Century	Traders
Brown Rat	about 1728	Traders
* Fat Dormouse	1902	Private Zoo
* Coypu	about 1930	Fur Farms
* American Mink	1929	Fur Farms
* Indian Muntjac	1890 1929	Private Zoo Mainstream Zoo
* Chinese Muntjac	about 1900	Private Zoo
* Sika Deer	about 1870	Modern Animal Collectors
* Chinese Water Deer	about 1900	Private Zoo

ent times, but they did not prosper. Various exotic deer and antelopes, however, have been introduced and still survive; one of the most remarkable exotics introduced into the United States is the Barbary sheep, or aoudad, that now lives in New Mexico.

The effects of introduction have been most marked in islands. The table on page 188 lists a dozen exotic mammals that have been introduced into Britain (England, Wales, and Scotland), and that, with the sole exception of the muskrat, now breed ferally (that is, in the wild). Those marked with an asterisk have a limited distribution so far, the rest are more widespread.

Most of the mammals listed in the table are ones that Britain could well have done without—including some of the older introductions such as house mice, rabbits, rats, and the gray squirrel. The gray squirrels' acclimatizers were, among others, the Duke of Bedford at Woburn (then a private zoo), the administrators of the Royal Parks in London; an American with a private zoo at Richmond, Surrey; and the London Zoo. All these must share the responsibility for having brought this exotic to Britain where, over at least two-thirds of England and quite large areas of Wales and Scotland, it has

Above left: The gray squirrel, one of Britain's introduced animals. Above: A list of a dozen exotic mammals that have gone wild in Britain and succeeded in establishing themselves. Some of them have become widespread, while others (marked with asterisks) have not yet spread very far.

now entirely supplanted the native red squirrel. Wherever the gray squirrel has flourished, the red squirrel has ultimately disappeared. Besides this, the gray species is a crop and game robber. From 1953 until 1958 the British government actually put a price in its head (or rather, on its tail); but the measure did not seem to produce any large reduction on its numbers. If only people realized how edible it is, they would shoot more.

The fat, or edible, dormouse is also partly a zoo introduction, brought to England in 1902 by Walter Rothschild, later Lord Rothschild, for his private zoo at Tring in Hertfordshire. This small rodent has slowly colonized the whole of the heads of the chalk escarpment known as the Chilterns, over an area of about a hundred square miles. It is a very nice little animal and, as far as anybody can discover, is not much of an orchard pest, although it does some damage. However, many houses in the Chilterns now have little colonies of fat dormice in the attics—where they make noises like those of young elephants, as I have heard myself.

In some areas Britain's new exotic deer, introduced partly by the zoos at Woburn and Whipsnade, are now quite numerous. Despite the hard winter of 1962, which killed off quite a number of some species, there are probably 20 or 30 muntjacs within a few miles of where I am writing, in Northamptonshire. The Forestry Commission people, who administer most of their new range, do not think they do much harm to young trees, and of course they provide sport for those who legitimately shoot them. But this kind of introduction is not to be encouraged.

Zoos cannot be blamed for the introduction, in Britain and elsewhere, of a large number of animals that have escaped from fur farms. Mink have now escaped in many parts of Iceland and established themselves as wild animals. There they are certainly a menace to Iceland's really valuable stock of native waterfowl, preying on their eggs and young. They have also escaped, and are now breeding ferally, in other areas of Europe—notably Norway, Sweden, and Britain.

Around 1930 quite a lot of people in Britain, including some zoos and a number of circuses, began keeping nutrias, or coypus, in captivity. (Circuses often exhibited them as "giant rats caught in a London sewer.") There were escapes, mainly from fur breeding establishments; and eventually these big, aquatic South American rodents established two main colonies, one in the neighborhood of Slough, in Buckinghamshire, and the other on the banks of the River Bure in Norfolk, not far from Norwich. There was no big explosion of their numbers near Slough, though there are still a few there, near a sewage farm. The other colony, however, has spread

The house mouse (above), one of Britain's commonest mammals, is not native to that country; it was introduced about eight centuries ago (see table). A much more recent introduction is the small Chinese water deer, brought in at the beginning of this century.

through almost the whole of the Norfolk Broads and into East Suffolk. This area of East Anglia invites the coypu to succeed, for in its climate, and in its river system running through low-lying country, it is very like the coypu's native habitat in southern South America. The coypu was pre-adapted to life in the Norfolk Broads, and there it is now having to be controlled. It eats coarse grass and other weeds and steals no human food; but it burrows, and can cause erosion of river banks. Although the value of its fur is an incentive to trappers, its present population is still gradually spreading.

The American muskrat, whose valuable fur is well worth commercial exploitation, was introduced into Britain for that purpose between 1920 and 1940. Many of the early fur farmers had little know-how; around 1929 their muskrats escaped in southeast England, mid-Scotland, Ireland, and—most important—in the Severn Valley in Shropshire in west-central England. There they settled down to a life closely resembling that in their North American habitat. Fortunately a young ecologist, Tom Warwick, was able to point the way to the subsequent trap-out of the lot (aided perhaps by a disease outbreak) by a meticulous survey of their precise distribution and spread. Other parts of Europe have been less fortunate, and introduced muskrats have caused serious ecological disturbances over the whole of Finland, large parts of western Russia, most of Germany and the Danube Valley, and biggish areas of Belgium and France.

In the past 300 years Britain has also seen the introduction of quite a number of exotic birds that now breed there in the wild. Zoos introduced the Canada goose, the green pheasant, the little owl, Lady Amherst's pheasant, and the night heron; zoos and acclimatizers introduced the mandarin duck and the golden pheasant; sportsmen introduced the red-legged partridge. Britain's exotic introduced birds do not appear to be a threat to native wild life so far; even the little owl, for so many years hated by game sportsmen, has now been given a clean bill. Fossils show it belonged to our fauna in Ice Age times, anyway.

Birds, however, can bring great disturbances when "planted" in strange climes. Acclimatizers may be primarily responsible for the fact that no fewer than 14 species of indigenous native birds have become extinct in the Hawaiian Isles since 1837. Before the colonists came, Hawaii had about 64 species of breeding birds, including one family that was unique. The colonists have successfully planted 36 other species from the rest of the world; and at least some of the indigenes doubtless disappeared because of their competition. In New Zealand, in about the same period, European colonists planted 35

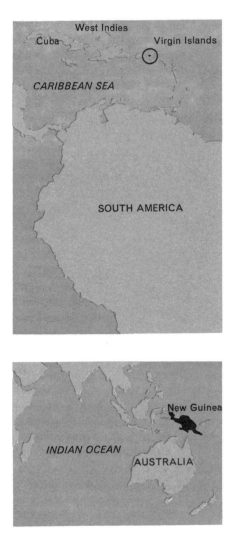

The greater bird-of-paradise (above right) is a native of New Guinea, shown black in the above map. It was introduced into Little Tobago, circled in map at top, by Sir William Ingram, in order to save it from possible extinction at the hands of ladies' hat designers.

Left: Thirty wild animal species that have been introduced into New Zealand by immigrants: 1. horse; 2. hedgehog; 3. blackbird; 4. sheep; 5. ferret; 6. sparrow; 7. skylark; 8. Australian swan; 9. black-tailed wallaby; 10. brown rat; 11. rook; 12. cat; 13. mallard; 14. turkey; 15. rabbit; 16. house mouse; 17. red deer; 18. flying phalanger; 19. little owl; 20. peacock; 21. moose; 22. cow; 23. hare; 24. wood pigeon; 25. chaffinch; 26. starling; 27. pheasant; 28. pig; 29. mynah; 30. chamois.

alien birds; at least six indigenes have already gone. But the acclimatizers have, perhaps, done their most spectacular work with the common starling and the house-sparrow, which they have taken from their homelands in Europe and Asia and now given an almost cosmopolitan range. Few people in the Americas, at least, feel too happy with all the "English" sparrows or the "European" starlings.

Yet there is another side to the story of planting exotic birds. There are birds-of-paradise in the West Indies, on just one island, called Little Tobago. This is the only place where they live wild outside the New Guinea area. Sir William Ingram bought Little Tobago (450 acres) as a second home for them in 1909, because of the terrible trade in bird-of-paradise plumes (for women's hats) that was then running from New Guinea to both North America and Europe. For a time there was a colossal slaughter of these birds in New Guinea and the surrounding islands. It was, in effect, stopped by bird protectionists in the United States and Britain who got laws passed in both their countries to make the import of bird plumage illegal. But meanwhile Sir William Ingram did his bit. He liked birds-of-paradise; he thought they might "do" on his little tropic island—and they did. More than half a century later a little colony still persists, now wardened, and the property of the British government, along with the island.

Most introductions of exotics, especially of exotic birds, are intentional. It is true that birds often escape from captivity, but few do so in an area where they will "take." The case of the budgerigar in the United States (see page 76) is one of the exceptions that prove a general rule; those that have established themselves in Florida derive entirely from escaped domestic stock. In most countries escaped budgies must get back home soon or die, but Florida has the ideal climate for them, and the little parrots may eventually spread to most of the southeastern United States, where the climate is equally favorable.

Health Risks

In the United States, where health standards are as high as any, there has been some public concern that the new stock of wild budgerigars might carry psittacosis, a disease named from *psittacos*, the Greek word for parrot; but this seems not to be so. In fact, at least twenty bird families have been found to harbor the virus of this disease, which has therefore now been given the more general name of ornithosis from *ornis*, the Greek word for bird. It is communicable to humans and gives them a serious form of pneumonia. The outbreak of psittacosis in Europe around 1929 *did* derive from parrots, and killed quite a few people, including a parrot-keeper at the London Zoo. It led at once to a ban on the importation of parrots that still persists, since South America, at least, still seems to be a reservoir for this disease.

The psittacosis regulations drew attention to the possibility that zoos might be spread-points for various diseases—particularly tropical diseases—of animals and men. The zoos have avoided becoming so by their own scientific security measures as well as by co-operation with government and port health authorities; and they are as safe as any comparable organization, such as a transit pool for domestic animals. They follow the same rules with all ungulates (hoofed mammals, including cattle) as agricultural organizations do. International regulations also apply to zoos as strongly as to anybody else. In Europe, for instance, no cloven-hoofed

One of the greatest risks involved in transporting animals is that they may take diseases with them. To prevent this, quarantine stations have been set up. Left: A giraffe being unloaded from a ship at Naples, for transfer to quarantine station. Below: At this station, a cow is tethered close to a wildebeest, to see whether the cow becomes infected.

ungulate can be moved from one country to another without a time in quarantine—because of the danger of foot-and-mouth disease, rinderpest, lung plague, bovine tuberculosis, anthrax, and other virus and bacterial diseases, some of which are communicable to humans.

Some European countries permit the import of ungulates only from other parts of Europe, and not from another continent. With such animals as African antelopes, therefore, some other country must act as import agents for them. In Italy the zoo at Naples runs a special quarantine station for African antelopes and other cattle on a nearby island. From there they pass, already acclimatized, to many of the zoos of Europe that cannot import directly from overseas. A few zoos of good standing have themselves been appointed as quarantine stations;

The elephant enclosure at the Chester Zoo, where in 1964 an outbreak of anthrax killed off the entire stock. The two African elephants seen here were obtained after the disease had been eliminated. Besides the big outdoor area, these elephants have an excellent, spacious house.

which shows that their veterinary service is first-rate and enjoys full government confidence. The London Zoo is one of them, and it accepts various "quarantine animals" direct from overseas.

Regulations controlling the import of many animals are even more strict in North America than in Europe; which is one reason why the American zoos have been concentrating so hard on breeding some species in captivity. The Catskill Game Farm in New York State is not only a very good and very beautiful zoo, but also an important ungulate-breeding center. United States and Canadian zoos like to take stock from there and a few other such stations and thus avoid the complexities of importing from overseas.

However meticulous zoos may be in their attention to health regulations, accidents can occasionally happen. In mid-March 1964, an outbreak of anthrax at England's Chester Zoo killed the finest stock in their\new elephant house—all three African elephants (including the only two bulls in England) and one Indian elephant. Eleven small carnivores also died. Anthrax, though much rarer than it once was, is a dangerous bacterial disease that cannot always be avoided by simple quarantining. It is communicable to many different kinds of animals and to humans; it is airborne, and outbreaks can be unpredictable. The Chester outbreak could have been due to the fact that animal skins from the Middle East are processed quite near Chester; and anthrax can persist in the ground, and on skins, for a considerable time. Zoos probably have little, if any, responsibility for the spread of this disease.

The Chester Zoo simply had bad luck. But the director knew how to save the rest of his stock by swift precautions. Anthrax corpses have to be destroyed by fire, even if they happen to be elephant corpses that must first be dismembered. At Chester this was done quickly enough to stop the outbreak getting out of control.

The Autopsy Laboratory and Anatomical Research

The animal mortality rate in zoos is lower now than ever before, because each new generation of zoo people has added to its predecessors' knowledge of the prevention and cure of animal ailments. Of course, zoos have always been anxious to keep their animals alive, but they have not always been particularly good at it; and in the early days there were plenty of people just waiting for the animals to die, so that they could dissect them and study their anatomy, or turn them into specimens for museums.

If all this sounds somewhat ghoulish, we have to remember two things. Nobody encouraged the animals to die; and there was no point in not making the fullest possible use of them once they *were* dead. It was, and still is, vital for the zoo man to study the dead zoo animal—not only to learn more about its anatomy but also to help ensure that other animals will die less soon.

The autopsy laboratory, or prosectorium, a crude place to start with, soon became an important and rather elaborate instrument of the successful zoo—a unit of dissecting rooms and research laboratories manned by a highly trained staff. In a modern prosectorium a professional laboratory assistant prepares the corpse for investigation; and an autopsist (himself a trained zoologist, pathologist, veterinarian, or combination of the three) makes tests of organs, diseased tissues, and so on—often sending material to specialist colleagues for

Not all zoos have a prosectorium—a well-equipped laboratory for the dissection and autopsy of dead animals. The Barcelona Zoo, however, has one (above), and is thus able to establish the cause of death of any animal, and take any necessary remedial measures.

further examination. Sometimes by establishing the cause of one animal's death the autopsy laboratory can be the means of prolonging other animals' lives.

The uniqueness of zoos as laboratories lies in the opportunities they can provide for study and research in many fields—including comparative medicine, pathology, animal behavior, physiology, and nutrition. Studies in comparative anatomy, naturally the earliest exploitations of zoo material, have always gone on; but with the rise of other studies this core science within zoology rather faded away for many decades. Only lately have a lot of bright young men and women come into comparative anatomy again, and it is now beginning to flourish once more. We have suddenly found that we do not know nearly as much about the general anatomy of animals as we thought we did. With the help of zoo material, new and even basic discoveries have lately been made about the structure of the brains, blood vessels, digestive system, and gland systems of common animals. For years these things had been overlooked, or were assumed to be known.

Among other things, the new generation of anatomists has carefully restudied the skeletons, skulls, and muscles of various birds. As a result they have thrown new light on the relationship of particular groups and on their position in the family tree. Indeed, revisions of the basic classification of all groups of animals continue to flow from the probings of the anatomist's scalpel and the slicings of his microtome. Zoos can sometimes provide necessary anatomical material more easily than can the gun or trap, and with less threat to the wild population. I have much respect for the circle of human vultures waiting for zoo animals to die and provide them with material for new discoveries. From the point of view of the progress of science it would be morally wrong not to make an animal available to serious students when it dies in a zoo.

Increasing Know-how on Animal Health

The rather grim autopsy laboratory of the nineteeth century was not only the starting-point for zoo studies in comparative anatomy, but also the starting-point for research into all kinds of problems concerning the health of animals. As the number of staff and part-time advisers increased, an improved diagnostic service evolved, that has now culminated in a preventive service. Such a service essentially involves an animal hospital. I could name nearly 50 zoos, including the London Zoo, that have built new animal hospitals or quarantine stations since the war; indeed, in the 1960s new zoo hospitals are being opened about twice as fast as new zoos.

The story of okapis in captivity provides a striking example of how zoos have increased their know-how on animal health. The okapi is the largest living land-mammal to have remained undescribed until the twentieth century. It shares a family with the giraffe, but unlike it lives in the dense forests of the Congo Basin. Okapis have numbers of parasitic worms, and are by no means easy to handle in captivity. The first one to leave Africa, in 1919, lived for less than two months in the Antwerp Zoo. Today they are isolated in quarantine quarters in the Congo before they go to zoos; there they

Above: At Epula, in the Congo, there is
a quarantine station that eliminates
parasitic infections in local species,
such as these okapis, before sending
them to zoos. Some 15 kinds of parasitic
roundworms, besides other parasites,
have been found in wild okapis.

are treated for worm infections with drugs. They thus reach zoos less heavily infected than they were, but usually have to go through a further period of isolation and treatment before they can become worm-free. At the zoos careful precautions are needed to prevent the

Feeding a large variety of animals is a complicated task. Left: Representative diets of a sample of animals, prepared by the Barcelona Zoo: 1. elephant; 2. deer; 3. giraffe; 4. crocodile; 5. ostrich; 6. penguin; 7. gorilla; 8. sea lion; 9. toucan; 10. macaw; 11. hummingbird; 12. bear; 13. pangolin; 14. lion. Some species require very specialized foods; the pangolin, for instance, needs four drops of formic acid in its daily food to replace part of its natural diet of ants. For hummingbirds, a mixture of honey, condensed milk, meat, meat extract, vitamins A, B, C, D, E, and water, is put in special bottles.

Above: Hand-rearing the baby gorilla Thomas at the Frankfurt Zoo. Baby gorillas need a milk diet very similar to the one for human babies, in contrast with the needs of adults.

spread of worms from one okapi to another. A few zoos, like Paris (Vincennes)—which bred its first second-generation okapis in 1961—have developed a captive breeding stock. As okapi worms are host-specific, a stock, once free, can stay so through the generations unless new infected animals are brought in.

Zoos had to learn much about drugs, and give intensive treatments, to save the lives of okapis and establish them as good doers in captivity. What they have learned, however, goes far beyond the culture of okapis. It is a contribution to the whole science of parasitology. A discovery about the parasites of one animal, whether they are specific to that animal or found also on others, can scarcely fail to improve parasitology as a whole. All such medicine is *comparative medicine.*

The science of comparative medicine compares the diseases of animals with those of other animals and of humans. In this field, all practical research may become pure research, and any pure research may become practical. Almost any study of the diseases of any animal may pay dividends—for instance, in the form of improvements in the health of domestic animals, or even man's own health. That is why the London Zoo, in 1962, started building the Nuffield Institute of Comparative Medicine, where the old studio of animal art formerly stood. I am in favor of animal art; but a mainstream zoo is quite right to spend its money first on an institute of comparative medicine. It is more important to keep animals alive and healthy than to have better pictures of them: it is ideal, needless to say, to do both.

Proper nutrition is, of course, essential to animal health, and it is a subject that zoos cannot forget, even if they would. Today zoos exchange much more information on animal diets than they did in the past. Even so, the task of feeding perhaps a thousand different species of higher vertebrates is complicated. The basic menu for many animals in mainstream zoos is still left, as it always has been, to the keepers' common sense, rule of thumb, and inspiration based very largely on trial and error. However, most zoos are well aware of what essential vitamins and trace elements their animals need; many of them have their own nutrition expert who checks the menus and diets regularly to see whether further improvements can be made.

Many advances in the art and science of feeding animals are made available to any zoo that wants to share them. Balanced diets for zoo animals were pioneered by Ratcliffe, in Philadelphia. These have since been modified by, for instance, the pharmaceutical company Hoffmann-La Roche of Switzerland, which works very closely with Hans Wackernagel, nutrition expert at the Basel Zoo. These workers have assembled very detailed analyses and breakdowns of ideal basic diets for herbivores, carnivores, omnivores, fish-eating mammals, and many important groups of birds. In addition, the *International Zoo Yearbook* has lately published a marvelously detailed survey of milk analyses and mammal hand-rearing techniques, the result of work done in nearly 50 zoos. Nevertheless it is only in the case of very delicate animals, or those that are really difficult to feed, such as koalas and pangolins, that zoos can and do find time to exchange *all* new discoveries on diet.

Not only is the food itself being more carefully studied than it used to be, but its preparation is also being more hygienically arranged. In a good zoo today each group of animals has its own food preparation room. Meals are usually distributed to animals as custom-designed units, suitable for one cageful or even one individual.

Suitability, of course, is paramount; but zoos must also count the cost. Feeding several thousand animals is an expensive operation by any standard. In 1963 it cost about $105,000 to feed the animals at London's Regent's Park Zoo, and about $64,000 to feed those at Whipsnade. With expenditure of this kind to face, every well-regulated zoo looks at its food bill at least once a year, breaks it down into its constituent elements, and sees what economies can be made. A cheap food may often be just as good for an animal as its more expensive natural food; it could even be better.

Zoos and Research in Animal Behavior

It has long been recognized that the proper care of animals demands more than a regard for their physical health and comfort; it also requires an understanding of their natural drives, habits, and behavior.

The strides in the study of animal behavior that have been made in the present century are formidable. What has happened is that two separate streams of thought have come together, and their protagonists are beginning to speak the same language. This was not the case two generations ago. The man who was interested in animal behavior was called, in a crude way, a behaviorist, and was believed (sometimes justifiably) to regard animals as if they were different kinds of machines, whose performance had to be described and measured. He used words such as "reflex" and "tropism" and tended to concentrate on laboratory experiments. On the other side were the psychologists, many of whom entered animal study from the study of the human mind. Often they tried, too quickly and too crudely, to compare animal drives and reactions to those of men, using an entirely different language to describe what they saw, or their interpretation of what they saw. They used words like

Right: At Ravenglass Bird Sanctuary, on the Cumberland coast, a group of research zoologists makes studies of the behavior of local species. The leader is Dr. Niko Tinbergen (right center) of Oxford University. Another well-known student of animal behavior is Professor Konrad Lorenz, seen in Bavaria with "imprinted" geese.

"complex" and "syndrome" derived from human psychology.

Since World War II, largely under the influence of Konrad Lorenz and Niko Tinbergen, the two streams have begun to codify an approach to the description of how animals behave in terms that both psychologists and behaviorists can use, and their students feel comfortable with. The extraordinary advances in our knowledge of animal behavior that have resulted (many of them published in the journal *Behaviour*, founded in

1947 and published in Leiden, Holland) have mostly come from people who have been studying animals in captivity, some of them in zoos.

Zoos with special facilities for research into animal behavior are numerous. Great animal studies are being made at the Max Planck Gesellschaft in Germany under Dr. Lorenz, who has always kept a zoo of his own for behavior study. There is a good zoo at Cambridge University for the observation of captive animals, mostly birds; and another, maintained largely for behavior studies, at Tel Aviv University in Israel. Yale has two important research zoos—a private establishment in its home state of Connecticut and another (for Primate studies in particular) in Florida. The University of California has an animal behavior zoo on its Berkeley campus; and there is also an animal behavior group working at Adelaide Zoo in Australia. In addition, students at many universities, when working for their doctorates on animal behavior projects, are assigned to the local zoo for their studies; the London Zoo, for instance, provides material for many such students, and now has its own ethology laboratory.

Some specialist zoos provide remarkably rich material for scientific behavior studies. One such is England's Slimbridge, with its incredible collection of flamingos, swans, geese, and ducks. G. V. T. Matthews, who has been working for over a decade on animal navigation, has done a great deal of his work on homing behavior with Slimbridge birds. A large number of ordinary wild mallards have become honorary members of the Slimbridge Zoo simply by having arrived there as squatters and built up a breeding colony. Matthews has been taking Slimbridge mallards away for considerable distances, releasing them, and watching what happens. He has discovered some funny things lately that do not altogether agree with his and others' demonstrations that most birds families "home" rather efficiently, navigating by the sun. He has found that mallards, whether liberated alone or in flocks, show a significant tendency to fly northwest; which means that they begin heading for home only if home happens to be northwest. Matthews has been working on this "nonsense navigation" of ducks for some years, and there is plenty of work still to be done.

Work at Slimbridge has also made many valuable new

Zoos can provide material for the study of animal behavior. The male brown bear (left) is showing stereotyped movements, walking round and round its cage along a loop-shaped track, which shows up clearly against the snow. It always walks in the same direction, sometimes pausing at one end of the loop (right of picture), where it is closest to a female bear in the neighboring cage. Stereotyped movements are a sure sign of wrong treatment. They generally indicate lack of anything definite to do at times of excitement— for instance, at feeding time. Such movements often lead to the animal rubbing itself sore and appearing pathetic to the onlookers. Zoos can counteract this by improving their feeding schedules and providing the animals with a more interesting environment.

Left: Some examples of the work being done under Niko Tinbergen. Far left and center left: Model heads of gulls used in experiments on mobbing behavior. Near left: A stuffed fox was also used to test the gulls' reactions.

contributions to the science of *comparative* behavior. Let us consider the behavior of an animal—a bird. If we watch its actions, and particularly its displays, we find that it uses its feathers in a certain way; that it bows in a certain way; that it raises its head in certain ways; that it flirts its wing in certain ways; and that it calls and uses its voice in certain ways. In courtship, or in showing aggression toward a rival, we find it goes through a stereotyped pattern of display, that can be sound-recorded, photographed, filmed; that is, it can be put on file for comparison, as if it were a museum specimen. The interesting thing is this: a bird's pattern of display is just as important as the length of its bill, the anatomy of its skull, the measurements of its leg bones, or the decorations on its breast in guiding researchers

Care must be taken in keeping together only those animals that will not fight. At Borasparken, in Sweden, elephant, zebra, and ostrich live in harmony (below). Experimental studies with lesser kudu and eland (top right) show that the head-up defense posture of the kudu gets no response from the eland. But in the case of oryx and gnu (lower four), threat behavior is the same for each species; as a result, they fight.

to a conclusion about its true relationship with other members of its family or group.

Every student of evolution longs to arrange the tree of descent (or ascent) of each family so beautifully that if forms a model of how the family really evolved. Students of the 146 known living species of Anatids (swans, ducks, and geese), and of the 93 or 94 known fossil or extinct species, have been puzzling for years about the shape of the wildfowl family tree. On comparing one group with another they have found it far from easy to decide whether the birds had a common ancestor lately or long ago; they have also puzzled about which species should belong to which subfamily or tribe, and which groups, indeed, should be given subfamily or tribal rank. These decisions used to be based purely on anatomy, from the study and comparison of specimens in museums. For the placing of fossil forms this is still the only way. But the students and archivists of behavior have found a powerful auxiliary method of improving the placing of living species.

A brilliant worker in this field is the American ethologist Paul Johnsgard, who has recently been working—for two years at Slimbridge and with other material in America—on the behavior of ducks. By marshalling his own behavior archives and comparing them with those of others, like the pioneer Lorenz, he has brought an entirely new order into the family of the ducks.

The eider ducks, of which there are several kinds, all look fairly alike, and their drakes are rather strikingly colored. The mergansers are strikingly colored too, but differently; they also have very different bills, long and serrated. On anatomical grounds only, few people have ever believed that there could be any close relationship between the eiders, mollusk-feeders at the bottom of the sea, and the mergansers, which catch fish with their saw bills. But if we study them as Johnsgard has, we find their basic behavior patterns so close that they are obviously very closely related, and must be put in the same tribe. Touring Slimbridge with a still camera or movie camera, recording day in and day out the behavior patterns of these beautiful birds, Johnsgard has come to know more about their true relationship in nature than if he had sat in a museum for a month of Sundays studying skins.

There is scarcely a mainstream zoo in the world where research work, of this kind of importance to systematics, is not taking place. All that is required (besides the trained student) is a fairly comprehensive collection of the members of particular families. As we shall later see, the trend in many progressive zoos today is to take special interest in particular families and groups. All this is grist to the mill of pure research.

8   Paths to Zoo Progress

Zoos and zoo techniques have come a long way since the early days; progress has been particularly rapid in the last three or four decades. The paths to further progress are of two kinds: those that are already well-traveled, and those along which the march has only recently started. It is the second kind that I want to emphasize in this chapter; but I should like first to take a quick look at the opportunities still presented by the old and well-tried paths.

The breeding of animals in zoo captivity is no new thing: yet among many difficult species, as we saw in Chapter 3, success has been achieved only in recent years. In a world where an explosion of human population puts ever-increasing pressure on animals in the wild, we may expect zoos to do all in their power to increase breeding successes, particularly with rare and endangered species. It is reasonable to hope that in the near future a few zoos will have built up breeding stocks of white rhinos and possibly mountain gorillas; and it is not impossible that zoos may yet save the California condor from extinction, as they saved the Hawaiian goose. At present, only something like 20 to 30 per cent of all zoo animals are born in captivity. By the end of the century the figure may well have risen above 50 per cent.

In architecture and layout, the present tendency of mainstream zoos is toward a barless, Hagenbeckian housing and display of animals. This, too, will doubtless continue as new zoos come into being and as old, overcrowded zoos solve the difficult problem of reorganizing their space and space units (pages 162-164). An experienced zoo man might tell us that there are certain animals to whom the size of cage is scarcely of consequence. If he did, he might add, without cynicism, that this was something he did not expect the public to appreciate. There is no doubt that the small, old-fashioned cage does make the public suffer, if it does not always make the animals suffer, and for this reason I believe the trend must continue to be against it.

In the medical care of animals I cannot foresee revolutions so much as improvements. After all, a basic hospital is now a standard part of every mainstream zoo. But of course there are animals that cannot be transferred to it. A female elephant in difficulty with a pregnancy cannot easily be moved to a hospital. Indeed, no zoo is ever likely to design hospitals which can cater for elephants; instead they are now designing elephant

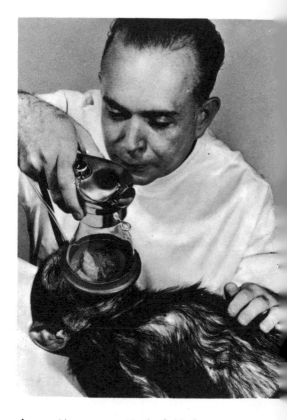

A recent improvement in the field of animal care is the Zoo Resuscitator (above), which can be used to provide artificial respiration for a wide variety of species. Right: Some species need spacious accommodation, others do not. Tigers are often content with barred cages and breed well in captivity.

houses with at least one available sick room on the premises. The new Casson elephant house in the London Zoo has two such rooms, to which any of its inmates (four elephants and four rhinos) can be moved if it falls sick. Peter Shepheard's new ungulate house in London also has a private sick den for every two public dens—perfect, for instance, for a recently-arrived okapi which is still being de-wormed, or for any new arrival that has to be kept quiet or looked after under sedation. Zoo hospitals, then, seem bound to evolve until they resemble a human hospital service, with its internal wards and its extramural care of patients who cannot be moved. Yet perhaps the most important development in this area will be the attachment of more scientific institutions to zoos—institutions like the Wellcome Institute of Comparative Physiology and the Nuffield Institute of Comparative Medicine (page 59).

A New Trend in Mainstream Zoos

A new line of progress is often started by a critical look at the past. Many mainstream zoos, when engaged in self-examination, could well criticize their own over-comprehensiveness. We have to recognize the existence of the "collector's instinct," or, as it might be more accurately put, the drive to amass an array of related objects as complete as possible. This is a way of celebrating the existence of order in the external world that is peculiarly appropriate to museums; indeed, museums deserve, and often get, manic collectors on their staffs. So, less fortunately, do zoos. As long as most living zoo men can remember, there has been an undeclared rivalry among certain mainstream zoos—including London, West Berlin, Antwerp, and New York (Bronx)—to have the largest living collection in the world; there are other zoos that want at least the largest collection they can house.

In 1927 London's 36-acre Regent's Park Zoo offloaded part of its collection to its 567-acre country estate at Whipsnade Park; in 1958 the 32-acre Ueno Zoological Garden in Tokyo offloaded part of its collection to the suburban Tama Zoological Park, with an area of 84 acres. Neither of these transactions seems to have released the societies concerned from the self-imposed duty of overcrowding their home zoos. This urge to be comprehensive seems to be at least partly inspired by collector's obsession rather than by the requirements of education and research. Alone among the great mainstream zoos, New York's Bronx Zoo has recently rejected total comprehensiveness and competitive collection as part of its policy, a move that will be widely appreciated.

One problem seldom faced by mainstream-zoo policy-makers is that the average zoo visitor cannot see a comprehensive collection in a comprehensive way. Merely

Three scenes from Tama Zoological Park, Japan. Above, a peacock, and below, an ibex—both in fine natural surroundings. Right: An unusual feature of the park is the moated lion area, in which the lions roam at liberty and visitors are confined to busses.

to get around such zoos as London, Bronx, Copenhagen, Frankfurt, Paris (Vincennes), Mexico City, or Barcelona, is exhausting. Many of my own zoo visits are for the purpose of making television programs. The producer and I may spend as long as ten hours looking around the gardens before we finally decide what we are going to do and where the cameras are going to be; by then we have probably concentrated on but one tenth of the total exhibits, and are already tired. When I visit a zoo purely for my own enjoyment I may need far longer. For instance, I remember going to the Copenhagen Zoo on a busman's holiday. I spent a whole day on the birds, with my friend Dr. Holger Poulsen, the bird curator; I came back the next day and "did" nothing but mammals, with some help from the Director, Svend Anderson; then I spent a third day at the Zoologisk Have with the brilliant young reptile man, Arne Schiøtz. And at the end of it all I had seen by no means all that the Copenhagen Zoo had to offer.

If a zoologist needs three days' hard labor to "get the feel" of a modern mainstream zoo, what does the average housewife, say, get out of a single visit? She goes to see the spectacular ones, the giraffes, and the hippos, and the big cats; she goes to the antelope house, and the monkey house, and she watches the sea lions being fed; she will see the giant panda, if there is one; and, if she has any energy left or if the children demand it, she will have a quick look around the aquarium.

In some ways, the mainstream zoos have *too* much to offer educationally. Yet many still seem to think they should try everything. Some have made gallant attempts, but all have been partial failures. I think zoos should accept the fact that it is no great virtue to have the most comprehensive collection of animals in the world—although some zoo must obviously have it. The best objective is to have a good cross-section of zoology, not to be all-embracing. No zoo could, or should, have a member of every family that has ever been shown; indeed some families are still so little known that they should not yet be kept anywhere except in some university zoo where they can be tended privately and quietly, under purely scientific management. The chief duty of a mainstream zoo is to show examples of all the important families of the animal kingdom *that really do well in captivity*. This means having representatives of thirty or more mammal families—from kangaroos to cats, from mice to giraffes; and representatives of forty or more bird families—from penguins to hummingbirds, from falcons to birds-of-paradise; to say nothing of certain fishes, reptiles, amphibians, and invertebrates. Beyond building up and maintaining such a collection of basics, any zoo does well to select certain families (or sub-

209

A group of penguins at Edinburgh Zoo, which exhibits and breeds several species, including king penguins and gentoo penguins. The king penguins are hand-fed every day, to ensure fair shares for the weaker ones.

families, or tribes) of animals and make a specialist hobby of them. Some are, in fact, beginning to do so, and I believe it inevitable that more and more mainstream zoos will turn to specialization of this sort.

Hobby zoos contribute more, not less, to science and education by concentrating on one or two groups; and the public certainly enjoy going to zoos with specialized hobbies. In Ireland and Britain people have got to know and appreciate Dublin's and Bristol's great cats, and most of them have heard of Edinburgh's penguins, which seem to breed more happily there in Scotland than in any other zoo in the world. Copenhagen is renowned for marvelous connoisseurs' animals like musk-oxen and other rare members of the ox-antelope family; Rome Zoo, too, is known especially for its fine show of antelopes, and Frankfurt concentrates particularly on the ecological presentation of tropical animals.

The hobbies of United States zoos well justify this trend; keen zoo-goers have been known to travel the continent to see the Bronx Zoo's flamingos and special waterbirds; San Diego's parrots and tortoises; Fort Worth's reptiles; Milwaukee's breeding herd of moose; Chicago-Brookfield's elephants, rhinos and other heavy mammals; and the small mammal collection in Washington's National Zoo. Specialties for which certain other zoos are famous are cited in the Appendix.

Visitors simply do not have the stamina to see all that there is to be seen in an over-comprehensive zoo. Unfortunately the same can be true even of a zoo that limits comprehensiveness to basics. Many mainstream zoos therefore, are now, giving increasing attention to taking leg-weariness out of a zoo visit. Even in a smallish zoo of 30 acres or so mechanical transport for the public is highly desirable; in a large-area zoo it is essential. San Diego Zoo, covering 91 acres, has a wonderful collection of busses of an open type, allowing panoramic vision. Not only can visitors to this lovely subtropical zoo go around it in great comfort on quiet rubber tires; they can also travel up and down the canyons on escalators. Some quite small zoos have also devised public transportation systems suited to their topography and their special needs. A good example is England's Dudley Zoo, near Birmingham, built on the hillside site of an old castle that is still there in the heart of the zoo. The polar bear pits and the penguin pools are in the ancient castle moat, which has been made suitable for them by ingenious zoo architecture. At Dudley they have recently built a chair-lift which takes people up the hill, so that they can walk the whole zoo downward.

In the near future, I believe, there will be some form of public transport in almost every zoo where it can be afforded and where it can be integrated into the land-

At the San Diego Zoo, with its canyons and mesas, progress around the zoo is made effortless by the provision of escalators. Such transport aids are useful in taking the hard work out of a trip around a large and hilly zoo.

scape. In a few zoos—London among them—this may be impossible, due to the difficulties of the site. Where this is so, it should be possible to provide more and better seating, and to arrange things in such a way that more animals can be seen with less expenditure of energy. When London's new plan is complete, there will be a new promenade, part of which will be elevated so that the public can get fine views of the animals from above. Additional seating and pleasant shaded nooks are also being provided, where visitors can stop and rest while they read their guidebooks and catch their breath.

Purely Specialist Zoos

We have seen that a number of mainstream zoos thrive by leavening their comprehensiveness with specialties. It is also true that many purely specialist zoos have become great, and the future promises many more of them.

The first wholly modern success of such specialization concerns the acclimatization of certain aquatic mammals—the dolphins and porpoises. Along with the whales and other related forms, they make up the Order of Cetaceans. Most of the truly gigantic whales are in a group known as the toothless, or baleen, whales. Their name comes from the fact that they have rows of baleen, or whalebone, hanging from their upper jaws through which their food is filtered from sea water. Dolphins and porpoises belong to a different group—the toothed whales. Within this group the dolphins and porpoises belong to different genera, although the animals are often confused and the names are commonly misapplied. Most dolphins have a beak-like snout and a streamlined body. Porpoises are generally smaller than dolphins and usually have blunt snouts and stouter bodies.

The smaller toothed whales were tried in captivity in the early years of existing centenarian zoos. London Zoo's first common porpoise arrived on December 4, 1862, and died the next day; and a common porpoise was stillborn in Brighton Aquarium in 1914. But no zoo group tackled the whales seriously until 1938, when the great new tanks of Marine Studios at Marineland, on the east coast of Florida, were first stocked with bottle-nosed dolphins.

With its greatest tank capacity of 540,000 gallons, Marine Studios pioneered both a revolution in zoo technique and a breakthrough in zoological science. From the work of this enterprising company stem new advances in our knowledge of the intelligence of dolphins and porpoises (as high as, or even higher than, that of anthropoid apes), their capacity for almost cultural play, and their refined powers of communication. Of the greatest interest was the confirmation of these small toothed whales' use of sonar (from *so*und *na*vigation *r*anging, the manmade apparatus that operates this way). The animals emit pulses of sound waves, both sonic (within human hearing range) and ultrasonic (beyond it) to detect the location of submerged objects. The waves are reflected back from the objects to the animals, which use the information for food-finding and navigation.

Florida's Marine Studios not only keeps toothed whales; it breeds them. The first recorded live birth to a captive whale occurred there on February 26, 1947, and very many have been born there since. Besides the common bottle-nosed dolphin of local inshore waters, the Florida Marine Studios successfully raises the rarer offshore spotted dolphin; and recently it has even succeeded in keeping the big pilot whale. These animals are trained by kindness and reward, and live with their

At Marineland of the Pacific, on the California coast, many new techniques for keeping marine mammals and fishes have been developed. Top: A bottle-nosed dolphin suffering from loss of appetite is given a vitamin injection. Above: Several thousand fish in the giant seawater tanks are fed by divers.

Above: Dolphins make a variety of sounds, including ultrasonic squeaks. Here a scientist at Marineland of the Pacific makes a tape recording of the vocalizations of a bottle-nosed dolphin. Left: Births of dolphins at Florida's Marineland have revealed the surprising fact that the young emerges tail first.

Besides their uses in research, the whales at Marineland of the Pacific provide entertainment for thousands of visitors each day. Left: Common Pacific white-sided and bottled-nosed dolphins leaping high on command. Lower left: In an illustration of confidence, a dolphin leaves the water (which it would never do in the wild) to greet its keeper. Below: Bimbo, the biggest whale in captivity, leaping high to take a fish from his keeper.

human keepers in a way comparable to a dog-man relationship. The gymnastic shows of these three marvelous animals must be seen to be believed.

In spite of the heavy capital expenditure involved, several enterprising groups invested in marine zoos after World War II, the second being Florida's Sea Zoo at South Daytona, not far from Marine Studios. The third, Marineland of the Pacific, was opened at Palos Verdes in California in 1954. It has the greatest aquarium tank on earth—640,000 gallons. Marineland of the Pacific specializes in Pacific white-sided dolphins and the big pilot whale. Bimbo, their performing pilot male, was 18 feet long and weighed 3400 pounds in 1962. Not long after the opening of the Palos Verdes establishment, Florida had two more marine zoos—the Miami Seaquarium, started in 1955; and a Theater-of-the Sea at Islamorada, on Upper Matecumbe Key, opened at about the same time. There is now another in Philadelphia.

The Russians had begun to study the common dolphin in captivity by the 1940s. But the first public marineland outside the United States was opened at Enoshima, Japan, in 1956. Enoshima has shown pilot whales and white-sided dolphins; but it specializes in bottle-nosed dolphins and Risso's grampus or dolphin.

At least nine species of toothed whales have now been acclimatized to life in zoos and most are responding well to rapidly developing techniques and proving good doers. The beluga, or white whale of the Arctic, has lately been in the New York Aquarium in Brooklyn; and that remarkable fresh water mammal, the Amazon dolphin, can be seen in the James R. Record Aquarium at Fort Worth, Texas.

Wherever they exist, marine zoos are proving a great draw. In 1962 Japan's Enoshima attracted some 2,400,000 visitors, Marineland of the Pacific over 1,300,000, the Miami Seaquarium about 700,000, and the New York Aquarium over 380,000. In the near future, people in several other countries will have the opportunity to see whaleries. In Spain a marineland was scheduled to open at Barcelona in 1965; and in Britain Blackpool's veteran Zoo-Aquarium, first opened in 1872, promises to go into the whale business. But greatest of all is the plan designed by that remarkable engineer and submarine naturalist, Jacques-Yves Cousteau, for Monaco.

Monaco's Oceanographical Museum, founded in 1910, is one of the greatest in the world. Every aspect of undersea exploration is exhibited there, including a unique collection of pioneer instruments. It also has a fine, traditional marine aquarium, fed by Mediterranean water, to which will soon be added a vast pool for big dolphins, and another for smaller dolphins, or porpoises. Cousteau's intention is to keep, and breed in captivity, any but the very largest toothed whales. Like all zoo men, he recognizes that it is at present impossible to keep whalebone whales in captivity, though it is theoretically possible in the long run. For the time being, at least, the multi-million-dollar cost of building a big enough whalery—and of providing toothless whales with an incessant supply of "krill" shrimps or other plankton (their natural diet)—is beyond all reason.

Our age is indeed an age of zoo specialization; and a specialist-minded group does not need to spend millions on a whale zoo before it can make new discoveries or attract and inform the public. The Wildfowl Trust collection at Slimbridge has already proved that concentration on one family of animals, which are basically good doers in captivity, can produce the most spectacular —and within its sphere the most informative—collection the world has ever seen. Slimbridge is, of course, an "organization" zoo, but it owes its inspiration and style to one man, Peter Scott. Individuals, if obsessed and enlightened enough, can make their personal mark on the progress of zoos, now as much as ever.

One such man is Peter W. Louwman, a busy and successful businessman with a keen and long-standing interest in ornithology. As opportunity permitted, he has developed at Wassenaar, near The Hague in the Netherlands, a private zoo in which birds are the stars. It was originally based on one enormous tropical house, with appropriate vegetation inside, and a plethora of tropical birds of many kinds. Recently he has added one of the finest outdoor flights ever designed—through which the public can walk, and in which he keeps approximately 400 birds of about 200 different species. Such large outdoor flights are found in only about half a dozen zoos in the world, and few, if any, are better than Louwman's. It is 150 feet long, very high, well wooded, and with plenty of cover. The public enter and leave through valved doors; few birds ever get out, and those that do always want to come back anyway.

Louwman concentrates on the songbirds of the world, and other small perching birds. He does not go in for many big birds or birds of prey; and of course he has none of these in his great aviary. As a result of concentrating on what he likes, he has produced a lovely, varied show of birds, with an extremely good breeding record; and he manages to keep a lot of rather rare species that people will come for miles to see.

Another specialist zoo, founded a few years ago by a dedicated individual, Philip Wayre, is that of The Ornamental Pheasant Trust, at Great Witchingham, in Norfolk, England. The pheasants, as we saw in Chapter 3, are good doers in captivity, just as wildfowl are. Wayre not only shows and breeds large numbers of exotic

The walk-through aviary at Wassenaar Zoo, near The Hague, in Holland. This 150-foot long outdoor flight shows how birds can, and should, be kept in captivity, with freedom to fly freely, and with hidden places in which to nest.

pheasants in wonderful surroundings and with great skill but also supplies private aviculturists and zoos all over Europe. No better collection of pheasants could be found anywhere in Europe, except possibly at Clères, in France, where Dr. Jean Delacour may have as many species in his excellent specialist gamebird and wildfowl zoo.

The Catskill Game Farm in New York, founded by Roland Lindemann, is another famous specialist establishment. It has the world's largest collection of captive wild ungulates, including the rare onager and the largest herd of Przewalski's wild horse.

One recent development in the zoo world that is not entirely a good thing is the proliferation of small roadside zoos. Many of them are operated without much

Scenes from Len Hill's fine aviary at Bourton-on-the-Water. Left (upper and lower): A few of the birds on show, including avocets, spotted bowi birds, and stilts. Above: A pair of Fischer's touracos. Below: A breeding pair of giant hornbills from India.

tenderness and with little regard for stock. Even orang-utans and other endangered species have found their way into stunt places angled to the progress of profits rather than of zoology. But I do not mean to say that every small zoo by a roadside is a racket. Far from it. One of the finest little zoos I know—it occupies only three acres—lies by the roadside in one of the prettiest villages in England.

Birdland, at Bourton-on-the-Water in Gloucestershire, is run by a building contractor Len Hill, and his family. Hill is a good gardener—indeed, a scholarly horticulturist—as well as a private aviculturist with a taste for keeping and breeding rare birds. He started his zoo as a hobby. When it had begun to flourish he suddenly realized that it was worth opening to the public. It costs only two shillings (less than thirty cents) to go into Birdland, and I think it is the best bargain in the business.

Recently, Hill has adapted a new greenhouse as a tropical bird house for hummingbirds and other small nectar-feeders. It is air conditioned and humidity conditioned, and he even produces artificial tropical rain in it. He may well be the first person in Britain to breed hummingbirds in captivity. He has a style with birds like that of a green-thumbed gardener with plants. He breeds difficult members of the parrot family, like Hahn's macaw, with apparent ease; and he has also bred the eclectus parrot. Many of his inmates fly around free-winged, including four species of big macaw, the African gray parrot, and several cockatoos. His tame glossy starlings from Africa come and take mealworms from visitors' fingers. He also keeps snakebirds, and some of the delicate jaçanas, or lily-trotters. The latter birds, also known as lotus birds, have extremely long claws, and can walk on floating vegetation on lakes; they do so on Hill's lily pond, which is a rare thing to see in any zoo.

Hill also has one of the finest collections of penguins in captivity. Indeed, I have never seen king penguins in such good condition as at Birdland—except perhaps in Edinburgh Zoo, where they also know how to keep them. Hill's breeding penguins have both an outdoor pool and an indoor pool in which he uses refrigeration to keep the temperatures right in summer. The indoor pool is designed so that it can be seen from above and from below; through glass the visitor can see the penguins swimming under water.

Zoos With Special Faunas

Many zoos, some of which are quite small, have found scientific and educational usefulness, together with considerable popularity, by concentrating on special or local faunas. A most unusual one is the Biblical zoo at Jeru-

salem. Its object is to have on show every kind of animal mentioned in the Bible. This is not so easy as it sounds, because no two scholars will ever agree as to what animals *are* mentioned in the Bible. For instance, the word *nesher* (Hebrew), or *nissr* (Arabic), can be variously translated as vulture or eagle; in our English versions of the Bible it gets translated as eagle, although in some contexts it almost certainly means the griffon vulture. The scholars in Jerusalem show both, of course.

Among zoos that specialize in local fauna, one of the best is Skånes Djurpark, in the south of Sweden. Several new zoos are being planned, and several older ones redeveloped, on these lines. The new zoo at Khartoum, in the Sudan, is being designed primarily to exhibit African fauna; an older zoo moving in the same direction is that at Pretoria, in South Africa. Under its new

Left: Part of a herd of fallow deer, the stags in velvet, in Sweden's Skånes Djurpark, which specializes in exhibiting the local fauna. Lower left: Swedish moose, rare in the wild, breed in the park. Below: A bobcat, or lynx, from Scandinavia.

A zoo that specializes in the local African fauna is at Khartoum, in the Sudan. By limiting its interests in this way, a zoo can concentrate on breeding rare local species.

director, Dr. D. J. Brand, Pretoria now deliberately concentrates on its own local fauna. It has the finest breeding record of antelopes in captivity, as far as I can trace. This, to my mind, gives Pretoria an entirely correct policy and purpose. The zoo is extremely popular with the public, very well managed, and is on a well-chosen area with 100 acres still to develop. Brand also has a fine staff. Almost all of them are African, including African teachers—Pretoria is very much an educational zoo—who make a full-time business of teaching Africans about their own fauna.

Some local-fauna zoos have to deal with a fauna so peculiar that few others have learned much about managing it. Often they enlist the help of university zoologists and other experts. Their work may sometimes help the very survival of endangered wild species and races. The small zoo at Tananarive is a good example. On its doorstep is the peculiar fauna of Madagascar. Peculiar is the right word. Madagascar—now Malagasy—has more special families of animals than any other landmass of its size; it has five families of birds found nowhere else, and many very queer mammals. It is only right and

Another zoo that specializes in exhibiting the local fauna is in Pretoria. Here, in a paddock, are three red hartebeests, not often seen in zoos outside South Africa.

proper that the Tananarive Zoo should concentrate on trying to breed and study some of these extraordinary animals in captivity; for any country lucky enough to have a peculiar fauna should ideally try to acclimatize it in zoos on the spot, before exporting unfamiliar material to other zoos. In Malagasy, where the general standard of education is not yet high, the work at Tananarive is educationally vital. It is also vital scientifically, and from the conservation point of view. In particular, the breeding of the purely Madagascan lemur families is as important as it is difficult—or *was* difficult, until Tananarive and some university laboratories and private people began to get good results in the last decade.

Australian zoos like Adelaide and Sydney are also concentrating on breeding their "difficult" indigenous mammals, the marsupials. South America is another great landmass with many animals unique to it. Here good zoos (including some veteran menageries) are developing—for example, in Rio de Janeiro and São Paulo in Brazil, Georgetown in British Guiana, Santiago in Chile, Caracas in Venezuela, and Port of Spain in Trinidad. All these zoos to a large extent concentrate on exhibiting their local fauna.

One zoo of local talent (or mainly local talent) is the largest in the world, at least in area. Askaniya-Nova in the Soviet Union, founded as early as 1880, is to be measured not in acres but in square miles. Here is a herd of European bison, another of Przewalski's wild horse, and several herds of native antelopes such as saiga (which are very rare in other zoos). But Askaniya-Nova is really an enormous state farm on which all kinds of animals are being tried in captivity, including certain African antelopes. The Askaniya-Nova people are still experimenting, for instance, with the domestication of the eland, an African antelope ox-like in its bodily form.

A superb example of the local zoo is the Arizona-Sonora Desert Museum at Tucson, Arizona, founded in 1952. A group of enthusiasts with a considerable knowledge of the desert ecology of North America has enclosed a large area of desert, keeping in it a community of desert fauna, with special apparatus for study. Visitors, for instance, can look through glass-fronted cutaways and see animals in their underground burrows. A substantial part of Walt Disney's fine film, *The Living Desert*, was made in the semi-captive conditions of the Desert Museum. This is a type of zoo enterprise that we may at least hope to see more of in the future.

Zoos of Sea and Seashore

Just as certain zoos specialize in showing local land fauna, so aquariums in many parts of the world specialize in showing the local seashore fauna, or the fishes

A major feature of the Arizona-Sonora Desert Museum is the reinforced concrete tunnel, from which visitors can see animals in their burrows, bats, and living tree roots. Right: Three diagrams show, from top to bottom, elevation, plan, and cross-section. The animals are viewed through glass screens in front of their dens; lighting is momentarily switched on by pressing on a rail in front of each den. Each den connects with an outdoor area, into which the animal can go at will.

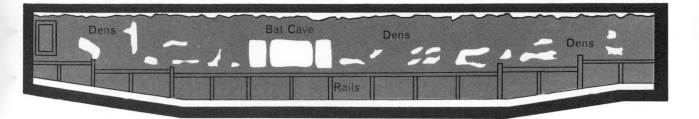

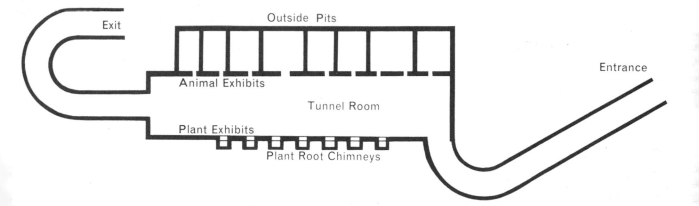

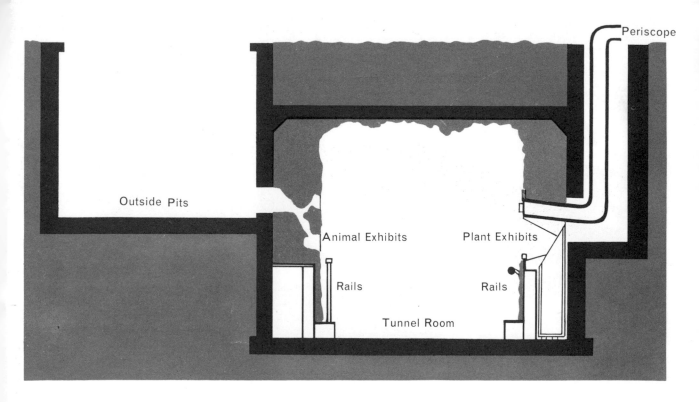

225

and invertebrates of the local shallow seas or coral reefs. Many of them are refined with highly natural surroundings, and even pools washed by artificial tides. The great Charlottenlund Aquarium at Copenhagen is very elegantly laid out in part to show that kind of fauna; so are the collections at Hamilton (Bermuda), Biarritz and Roscoff (France), Port Erin (Isle of Man), Foz-do-Douro and Lisbon (Portugal), Constantza (Romania), Vancouver (Canada), Honolulu (Hawaii), and others.

The brand new aquarium at Bergen (Norway), one of the most imaginative I have ever seen, deserves special mention. Most of it is at two levels. The top part has all sorts of tanks with rather specialized exhibits while the bottom part displays a representative cross-section of Norwegian fishes. The prime purpose of the aquarium

Left: General view of the Danish Charlottenlund Aquarium. Lower left: Rear view of the exhibition tanks, which are made of reinforced concrete with glass fronts. Fresh or salt water at any required temperature circulates through the tanks, making it possible to show many exotic species, such as the dwarf lion-fish (below).

is, of course, education for the Norwegians (whose prosperity depends largely on fishing) about their own fishes. But a visitor who goes down into the bowels of the Bergen aquarium can also see a more striking sight. On looking through one window he discovers that he is gazing, from the side, into an enormous open tank (which can also be seen from above, outside). In it are swimming various seals, some of which, as far as I know, have seldom or never been shown in any aquarium or zoo before. They include the bearded seal, the inner fjord seal (the miniature Arctic seal), the harp seal (also shown at the New York Aquarium), and the hooded seal, all brought down from northern Arctic waters by the Norwegian fishing industry.

Some thirty years ago, when I was on an Arctic ex-

pedition, I studied some of these seals in the wild; but I have never seen them so well as in Bergen—where, indeed, research students are now able to study their swimming motions in detail that they could never have observed in nature.

Considerably older than the Bergen Aquarium, but no less important, is that belonging to the Marine Biological Association at Plymouth, in England. Very well designed for a small aquarium, it is primarily for the purpose of study by members of the Association, but it is open to the public and well worth a visit. Doubtless the Association's attitude to the public can be expressed thus: "This is what we do, this is what we study; if you like to see it, too, you are welcome." And people come (over 80,000 a year), rather as they might come to look around an automobile assembly line. The classic aquarium at Naples is run in exactly the same way—primarily for study. Only at Naples can the public see some extremely interesting and beautiful Mediterranean species, including certain kinds of squids and several other connoisseurs' invertebrates.

At the Plymouth, England, aquarium, there is a good selection of fishes and invertebrates from local seas. Below: A spiny spider crab, the legs of which may span 15 inches. Top right: A flounder which lives in both fresh and salt water. Lower right: A dahlia anemone.

Four exhibits from the Naples aquarium, which specializes in local Mediterranean species. Top: Trigger fish, *Balistes carolinensis*. Above: *Xyrichthys novacula*, a relative of the wrasse group of fishes; it has not yet bred in captivity. Top right: A common octopus, *Octopus vulgaris*. Below right: A jellyfish, *Rhyzostoma palmo*.

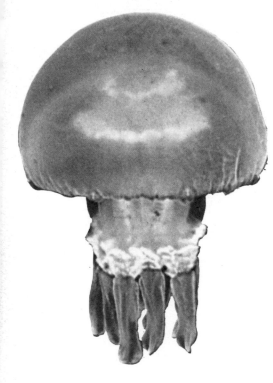

Zoos and Their Public

Relationships between the zoo world and the academic world has been close and deep for over a century. New York's Bronx Zoo, for instance, has a program in which Cornell University zoology students can get credit for work and research at the zoo. And for many years now the Bronx Zoo has given a course to teachers on how to make the best use of the zoo in school programs. But relationships with, and understanding of, the public have often stood in need of improvement. Most mainstream zoos, fortunately, are now doing something about this. Of course, many zoological societies already have arrangements by which the public can become members, friends, fellows or associates, and enter their gardens with special privileges. What I see coming is a considerable extension of such schemes, with special focus on young people. I have already mentioned London Zoo's youth club, the XYZ Club. Here I would only add that it already has a large membership and is a great success. In the United States the Bronx Zoo took the lead with its Reptile Club, originally started by a group of young herpetologists (as even young reptile lovers like to be called). More and more progressive zoos are now developing clubs and special courses for young people, and making arrangements by which schools can visit gardens on special terms. When such parties arrive, the zoo's education officer takes them on conducted tours to the limits of their (and his) stamina. Some zoos are also producing magazines and special guidebooks for young visitors. The Bronx Zoo has a special tour for blind people; they are allowed to touch the elephant's trunk as well as pat other animals to get the "feel" of them. And many zoos now send out vehicles that bring small collections of live animals to people in hospitals and others incapable of getting to the zoo.

Special guidebooks, conducted tours, and clubs for the young all recognize one rather important discovery of the present century: that the word "education" sounds stuffier than it really is, and that the word "entertainment" sounds more vulgar than it really is. This is certainly the view of all who write, broadcast, or make television programs for the public about zoos. Lately, in North America, Britain, and other parts of Western Europe, there has been a considerable change in the public's idea of zoos through the influence of radio, television, and popular magazines. Some of the animal magazines that have sprung up in recent years are extremely good, and have large circulations, especially in Germany. But perhaps the biggest change has come through television. Most mainstream zoos in the United States and in the capital cities of Europe have special links with their own television companies or authorities; and quite a number have television units and movie units attached to them permanently.

The great point about zoo television is that it refuses to recognize any sharp distinction between education and entertainment; it fuses them inextricably together. St. Louis Zoo has a program series widely televised. San Diego Zoo puts out weekly programs, some of which have been sent to Britain on film and used on the British Broadcasting Corporation's network; they are marked by the very highest interest quality and total zoological integrity. The same is true of Desmond Morris's programs on Britain's Granada Television's *Zoo Time*, from the London Zoo. There you are not getting a slick, entertaining journalist, who may love his subject without having sufficient background knowledge of it; you are getting a top animal behavior expert and zoologist, who is also the man in charge of the animals he is dealing with.

I have myself commentated on some 80 or 90 programs from about 50 different zoos. The B.B.C. has never told me to talk down, sideways, upwards, or in any particular direction to the public but has allowed me to play it straight. So I went around these zoos with some viewer friends of mine whom I assumed from the very start were as interested in animals as I was. To make this assumption creates a bridge between the commentator and his viewers.

In Britain four or five million viewers watch the regular television programs on zoos and other natural history subjects; many other countries have comparable audiences. Among the measurable consequences are increased visits to the zoos featured, *and visits with a more specific purpose.* For instance, after a program from a small-mammal house, the zoo featured gets a lot of people asking, say, to see "the angwantibo." Many of them, only a few days before, had never heard of an angwantibo (or golden potto, a small African Primate with a long snout and a stubby tail). But they had watched a television program about it, and now they had come to see exactly how it moves from one branch to another, and grips with its feet while hanging upside-down.

These are just the kind of visitors that all zoos want. No zoo can more than generally help the kind of person who, in all reasonableness, discovers that it is a fine day and there is no better way to amuse the children than to take them to the zoo. For the purposeful visitor zoos can do far more. It is primarily for such visitors that many zoos are now making labels on cages and enclosures more informative than ever before, with notes on the natural history and distribution of the animals concerned; it is for them, too, that zoos are designing more

Michael Boorer, education officer at the London Zoo, addressing a young audience in the zoo's lecture theater. The efforts of zoos and zoo-people to educate and entertain, as well as merely to exhibit, help to generate interest in zoology, and to create an understanding of the animal kingdom of which man himself is a member.

wall charts (such as family trees), more distribution maps, and more identification portraits, to supply useful background to the living exhibits.

The material of television, movies, tape recorder, and phonograph help not only the general public, but also the specialist and the research man. Many zoological societies and mainstream zoos now have their own movie units and staff photographers whose duty it is to document events of scientific importance and research value. Since 1889—when Ludwig Koch made his pioneer recording of the song of a common shama (an Indian thrush) on the wax cylinder of an Edison phonograph—the voices of nearly a quarter of all living species of mammals and birds have been recorded on phonograph record or tape. Many of them were first recorded in zoos.

Sound and vision are giving to zoo scholarship a new dimension of incalculable importance. As zoo archives pile up, zoo scholars multiply, and zoos themselves increase in number, the world will come more and more to see them as an essential part of its cultural structure. Zoos moved from being luxuries to being necessities over a century ago. They ceased around then to be exclusively the collections of royal and noble connoisseurs and became, instead, a public service. They have now also become vital to the conservation of many species whose existence is endangered by the increase in human population.

There is still an element, although not strong, of the public which is against zoos on principle. Pursued in full logic, this principle makes all animal captivity unacceptable. It is held by a minority of warm-hearted people, many of whom are highly educated and intelligent.

I have tried to show, in this book, that zoos are part of man's deepest strivings to understand the world around him; that without them he would have learned much less than the little he knows about the animals he shares the world with; that with them he has found vast scope for research, scholarship, architectural imagination, conservation, preservation, self-expression, tenderness, and a lot of innocent fun.

I would go so far as to say that the zoo phenomenon, more than any other movement, has changed man's thinking, in every human culture where it has become advanced, from the medieval notion that animals are objects of contempt, to the modern notion that they are objects of respect.

Without our zoos we should, in our thinking and philosophy of animals, be back in the Dark and Middle Ages. With zoos, in the style to which they have evolved, we can see ourselves as the servants, not masters and mockers, of moving life on earth.

Above: Ludwig Koch, the pioneer of bird recording, working in a field.

Above left: A group of London schoolgirls learning zoology at first hand—by direct observation of living animals at the zoo; they are on a conducted educational tour. Left: In the children's section of the London Zoo, a permanent display of instruction boards gives information about the animals.

Appendix: List of Zoos and Aquariums

This is a list of all the zoos and aquariums known to the author at the time of writing, in 1965. I have compiled this list from my own visits and notes, and from the excellent annual *International Zoo Yearbook*, published by the Zoological Society of London, to which I am much indebted. I have tried to make the list fully comprehensive, but it is possible that I may have missed a zoo or two. Countries are listed alphabetically, and zoos are listed alphabetically within each country. Figures for the number of species on show are conservative rather than high, and they refer to the year 1963. Of the 526 (or so) zoos and aquariums in the world, I have been able to give an extended notice of only 121. Many of the others have fine, often specialized, collections well worth a visit, as I have proved to myself.

ARGENTINA

Buenos Aires

1888. Jardin Zoologico de la Ciudad de Buenos Aires, Republica de la India, Buenos Aires. 44 acres; 250 species. The oldest zoo in South America.

Mendoza (c. 1908)

La Plata (1912 or before)

AUSTRALIA

Adelaide

1883. Adelaide Zoological Gardens, Frome Road, Adelaide. 19 acres; 350 species. Fine breeding record marsupials and birds.

Healesville

Melbourne

1857. Zoological Board of Victoria, Royal Park, Parkville, Melbourne. 55 acres; 200 species.

Perth (1898)

Sydney

1916. Taronga Zoological Park, Mosman, Sydney. 70 acres; big collection, imaginatively managed.

Sydney (Aquarium)

AUSTRIA

Innsbruck

Vienna

1752. Tiergarten Schönbrunn, Wien XIII. 16 acres; 750 species. The oldest mainstream zoo, and still with the architectural glory that the Emperor Franz Josef gave as a present to the Empress Maria Theresa. Animals nevertheless housed on modern lines, and good aquarium.

Vienna (Aquarium)

BELGIUM

Antwerp

1843. Société Royale de Zoologie d'Anvers, Place Reine Astrid 26, Anvers. 24 acres; 1,000 species. One of the great collections. Ingenious and excellent new housing, including barless aviaries; fine aquarium.

Heist an Zee

BERMUDA

Hamilton

1928. Bermuda Government Aquarium, Museum, and Zoo, The Flatts, Hamilton. 200 species. Good collection of local fishes and invertebrates.

BOLIVIA

Cochabamba

Oruro

BRAZIL

Belem (Para)

Porto Alegre

Rio de Janeiro

1945. Jardim Zoologico do Rio de Janeiro, Quinta Boa Vista, Rio de Janeiro. 25 acres; 350 species.

São Paulo

1958. Fundaçao Parque Zoologico de São Paulo, Av. da Agua Funda, São Paulo. 88 acres; 200 species.

BRITISH GUIANA

Georgetown (1907 or before)

BULGARIA

Sofia

Varna (Aquarium)

BURMA

Rangoon

1908. Rangoon Zoological Gardens, Kandawgalay, Rangoon. 69 acres; 150 species.

CANADA

Ardrossan

Calgary

1929. Calgary Zoological Gardens, St. George's Island, Calgary. 80 acres; 500 species. A fine free zoo with a comprehensive collection and a good mammal breeding record.

Calgary (Aquarium)

Edmonton (Children's Zoo)

Granby

Montreal

Moose Jaw (1928)

North Rustico

Quebec

1931. Le Jardin zoologique de Québec, Orsainville, Québec. 90 acres; 300 species.

St. Catherine's

St. Félicien

Toronto (1887)

Vancouver

1959 (or before). Vancouver Public Aquarium, Stanley Park, Vancouver. 250 species.

Vancouver (Stanley Park) (1888)

Winnipeg (1905)

CEYLON

Colombo

1908 (or before). Zoological Gardens of Ceylon, Allan Avenue, Dehiwala, Colombo. 42 acres; 450 species. One of the finest collections in Asia. Good breeding record.

CHILE

Chillan

Concepción

Santiago de Chile

Valdivia

Victoria

CHINA

Canton

Kunming

Nanking

Peking

1906. Peking Zoological Garden, Si Shih Men, Peking. 131 acres; 400 species. 3,850,000 visitors in 1963 made it the fourth most popular world zoo that year.

Pinkiang

Shanghai

Shensu

Tientsin

COLOMBIA

Bogotá

Medellín

CONGO REPUBLIC

Elizabethville

Leopoldville

CUBA

Havana

1959. Jardin Zoologico de la Habana. 58 acres; 300 species. A developing collection with 2,576,884 (free) visitors in 1963.

CZECHOSLOVAKIA

Bojnice

Bratislava

Brno

Decin

Dvur Kralove

Hluboka n. Vlt. (near Ceske Budejovice)

Jihlava

Lesna

Liberec

Olomouc

Ostrava

Plzen

Prague

Usti nad Labem

DENMARK

Aalborg

Charlottenlund

1939. Danmarks Akvarium, Charlottenlund, København. 200 species: a well-arranged, well-housed collection of tropical and native fishes.

Copenhagen
1859. Zoologisk Have, Roskildevej 32, København F. 25 acres; 800 species. The great Copenhagen zoo has many rarities—Sumatran rhino, musk-ox—and a very comprehensive bird collection.

DOMINICAN REPUBLIC
Santo Domingo

EL SALVADOR
San Salvador

ETHIOPIA
Addis Ababa
1866 (or before). Imperial collection of lions.
Menagesha
Zoo in planning stage.

FINLAND
Helsinki
1889. Korkeasaaren Elaintarha, Helsinki. 50 acres; 200 species. Has island (Högholmen, in Swedish) to itself, with splendid collection of native Finnish animals, among many others.

FRANCE
Arcachon (*Aquarium*)
Banyuls-sur-Mer (*Aquarium*)
Biarritz (*Aquarium*)
Clères
1919. Parc zoologique de Clères, Clères, near Rouen. 52 acres; 300 species. A lovely private zoo (but open to the public) in grounds of fine chateau. Internationally famous for its collection of waterfowl and pheasants.
Dinard (*Aquarium*)
Lyons
Marseilles
Mulhouse
Paris
1793. Ménagerie du Jardin des Plantes, 57 rue Cuvier, Paris 5ème. 9 acres; 450 species.
1934. Parc zoologique de Paris (Vincennes), 53 avenue de St. Maurice, Paris, 12ème. 40 acres; 250 species. Under same management. Has massive, barless Hagenbeck style and a fine breeding record—including second generation okapis.
Paris (*Aquarium*)
293 avenue Daumesnil.
Roscoff (*Aquarium*)

GERMANY
Augsburg
Berlin (East)
1954. Tierpark Berlin, Schlossstrasse, Friedrichsfelde, Berlin. 395 acres; 750 species. A spacious, brand-new, enterprising zoo with a good collection and fine housing.
Berlin (West)
1844. Aktien Verein des Zoologischen Gartens zu Berlin, Hardenbergplatz 8, Berlin 12. 74 acres; 2,100 species. Perhaps the most comprehensive collection the world has known. Totally rebuilt since the war, with vast modern houses.
Bochum
Bremen (*Aquarium*)
Bremerhaven (*Aquarium*)
Brunswick
Cologne
1860. Aktiengesellschaft Zoologischer Garten Köln, Riehlerstrasse 173, Köln. 49 acres; 550 species. Pleasant zoo park by Rhine, with fine new buildings, e.g. seal and penguin pools.
Cottbus
Dortmund
Dresden
Duisburg
Düsseldorf (*Aquarium*)
Eberswalde
Erfurt
Essen
Frankfurt-am-Main
1858. Zoologischer Garten Frankfurt/Main, Alfred-Brehm-Platz 16, Frankfurt-am-Main 1. 49 acres; 900 species. Splendid collection well housed, mostly in new imaginative buildings, e.g. revolutionary exotarium.
Freilassing
Gelsenkirchen
Göppingen
Halle (Saale)
Hamburg
1907. Carl Hagenbeck Tierpark, Stellingen, Hamburg. 67 acres; 300 species. The pioneer barless zoo, and after World War II rebuilding, still leads the style. Dramatic African panorama, and new tropicarium.
Hamm
Hanover
1865. Zoologischer Garten Hannover, Hindenburgstrasse 53, Hannover. 30 acres; 150 species. Another German zoo rebuilt since World War II with ingenuity and skill; rare animals, e.g. white (square-lipped) rhinos.
Heidelberg
Karlsruhe
Krefeld
Kronberg
Landau
Leipzig
Magdeburg
Munich
1910. Tierpark Hellabrunn, Siebenbrunnerstrasse 6, München 9. 173 acres; 650 species. Beautiful park with streams and woodland, and fine collection of ungulates, including living "reconstructions" of extinct aurochs and forest tarpan horse.
Münster
Neumünster
Neustadt (Pfalz)
Nordhorn (Westfalen)
Nuremberg
1912. Tiergarten Nürnberg, Am Tiergarten 30, Nürnberg. 148 acres; 250 species. Another spacious zoo with herds of rare ungulates in idyllic surroundings.
Osnabrück
Rostock
Saarbrücken
Stendal
Straubing
Stuttgart
1842. Wilhelma Botanisch-Zoologischer Garten, Bad Canstatt, Stuttgart. 30 acres; 450 species. Romantic Moorish architecture; very fine tropical houses.
Ulm (*Aquarium*)
Wuppertal

GHANA
Aburi
Kumasi

GREECE
Athens (in construction)
Rhodes (*Aquarium*)

GUATEMALA
Ciudad de Guatemala

HUNGARY
Budapest
1866. Budapest Fóváros Allat-Es Növénykertje, Budapest. 30 acres; 600 species. Fine collection of zebras and ungulates, also interesting domestic animals; fine breeding record; pretty gardens.
Pecs
Veszprem

HONDURAS
Tegucigalpa

INDIA

Ahmedabad

1952. Municipal Hill Garden Zoo, Kankaria, Ahmedabad. 31 acres; 250 species. Fine breeding record.

Amreli (Gujarat)

Baroda

Bombay

1866. Victoria Garden, Bombay 27. 48 acres; 150 species. Free; 2,000,000 visitors in 1963. Good mammal breeding record.

Calcutta

1875. Alipore Zoological Gardens, Calcutta 27. 50 acres: biggish collection.

Darjeeling

Delhi

1957. Delhi Zoological Park, New Delhi. 240 acres; 200 species. India's most modern zoo, planned by Carl-Heinrich Hagenbeck.

Dhrangadhra

1963 (or before). Indian Ornithological Garden, Dhrangadhra (Gujarat). 200 species. A new avicultural experiment with a good breeding record.

Hyderabad

Jaipur

Junagadh

Lahore

Lucknow

Madras

Mysore

Trichur

Trivandrum (1859)

INDONESIA

Bandung

Bukit Tinggi

Djakarta (1864)

Djakarta (*Aquarium*)

Jogjakarta

Semarang

Surabaja

IRAN

Tehran

ISRAEL

Eilat

Haifa

Jerusalem

1940. Jerusalem Biblical Zoological Garden, Romema, Jerusalem. 25 acres; over 100 species. A connoisseur's piece.

Petah Tiqva

Tel Aviv

1961 (or before). Tel Aviv University Zoo, Zoology Dept., Tel Aviv University. 1 acre; 250 species. Specializes in breeding rare birds and other small animals, with remarkable record. Open only to *bona fide* students.

Tel Aviv (public)

ITALY

Brescia

Como

Faenza

Milan

Naples

1950. Giardino zoologico di Napoli, Campi Flegrei, Napoli. 49 acres; 200 species. Fine site on vineyard hillside; good African collections, especially rare antelopes and monkeys.

Naples (*Aquarium*)

Oria

Pescasseroli

Rome

1911. Giardino zoologico e Museo di Zoologia, Comune di Roma, Viale Giardino 20, Roma. 42 acres; 800 species. Comprehensive collection, with fine antelopes and a great 100-ft. bird-flight of pioneer design.

Trieste (*Aquarium*)

Turin

1955. Giardino zoologico Città di Torino, Corso Casale, Torino. 10 acres; 200 species. Wooded park by banks of Po. Imaginative new tropical house.

IVORY COAST

Abidjan

JAMAICA

Kingston

JAPAN

Fujisawa

Enoshima Aquarium and Marineland, 2938 Katase, Fujisawa. 200 species. A modern, enterprising toothed-whale and general aquarium with a good breeding record.

Fukuoka

Hamamatsu

Himeji

Inuyama

Kagoshima

Kanazawa

Kitakyushy

Kobe

Suma Aquarium, Wakamiya-cho, Sumaku, Kobe. 300 species. A good fish collection.

Kobe

Kumamoto

239

Kyoto
   1903. Kyoto Municipal Zoo,
   Okazaki Hoshojicho Sakyoku,
   Kyoto. 10 acres; 250 species. A
   good small zoo.
Matusuyama
Nagoya
   1918. Nagoya Municipal Hi-
   gashiyama Zoo, Chijusa-Ku,
   Nagoya. 41 acres; 350 species.
Nara
Nishinomiya
Obihiro
Omuta
Osaka
Sapporo
Takamatsu
Takarazuka
Tokuyama
Tokyo
   1882. Ueno Zoological Gardens,
   Ueno Park, Daito-Ku, Tokyo.
   32 acres; 450 species. A main-
   stream big collection limited by
   space. Third most popular in
   1963; 3,880,186 visitors.
Tokyo
   1958. Tama Zoological Park,
   Hinomachi, Minamitama-gun,
   Tokyo. 84 acres; 150 species.
   Ueno Zoo's spacious, suburban
   park zoo.
Yokohama

KOREA
Seoul (S. Korea)
   1909. Chang Kyung Won Zoological Gardens. 49 acres; 100
   species.
Pyongyang (N. Korea)

KUWAIT
Salwa

MALAGASY REPUBLIC
Tananarive

MALAYSIA
Kuala Lumpur
Penang
Singapore
   1955. Van Kleef Aquarium,
   King George V Park, Singapore.
   400 species.

MEXICO
Culiacán
Mérida
Mexico City
   1926. Parque Zoologico de
   Chapultepec, Mexico City. 33
   acres; 250 species. The world's
   most popular zoo, with about
   5,000,000 (free) visitors in 1963.
   Good breeding record.

Mexico City (San Juan de
   Aragon)
Tuxtla Gutiérrez
Vera Cruz (Aquarium under con-
   struction)

MONACO
Monaco Ville
   1910. Musée océanographique
   de Monaco, Monaco Ville. 150
   species. A classic pioneer aquarium, with important development plans for "undersea park"
   and whale exhibits.

MOROCCO
Rabat

MOZAMBIQUE
Beira
Lourenço Marques

NEPAL
Katmandu (1933)

NETHERLANDS
Amersfoort
Amsterdam
   1838. Stichting Koninklijk Zoö-
   logisch Genootschap Natura
   Artis Magistra, Plantage Ker-
   klaan 40, Amsterdam. 25 acres;
   1,500 species. Zoo and aquarium with formidable collection;
   many rarities.
Arnhem
Rhenen
Rotterdam
   1857. Stichting Koninklijke Rot-
   terdamse Diergaarde. 37 acres;
   550 species. Fine deer, ox family, waterfowl; magnificent tropical house with orchids and exotic birds.
Wassenaar
   1937. Dierenpark Wassenaar
   667 Rijksstraatweg, Wassenaar.
   60 acres; 600 species. Specializes
   in birds of all the world, has fine
   tropical house and great new
   "walk-through" outdoor flight.

NEW CALEDONIA
Nouméa (Aquarium)

NEW ZEALAND
Auckland
   1931 (or before). Aukland
   Zoological Park, Grey Lynn,
   Auckland W.2. 42 acres (32
   open to public); 150 species.
Napier (Aquarium) (opened 1964)
Wellington
   1908. Wellington Zoological
   Gardens, Newtown Park, Well-
   ington. 154 acres (34 open to

public); 200 species. Fine breeding record.

NICARAGUA
Juigalpa (near Chontales)

NIGERIA
Ibadan
   Attached to the Department of
   Zoology, Ibadan University.
Jos

NORWAY
Bergen
   1961. Akvariet i Bergen, Nord-
   nas, Bergen. A brilliant piece of
   zoological architecture that exhibits principally the animals of
   Norway's great fishing industry;
   also arctic seals seldom shown
   in any zoo.

PAKISTAN
Karachi
   1886. Karachi Zoological Gardens, Garden Road, Karachi 3.
   33 acres; 150 species. New zoo
   now planned on 300-acre site.

PARAGUAY
Asunción

PERU
Lima (1913 or before)

PHILIPPINES
Manila
Quezon

POLAND
Gdansk
Katowice
Krakow
Lodz
Opole
Plock
Poznan
Warsaw
Wroclaw
Zamosc

PORTUGAL
Foz-do-Douro (Aquarium)
Funchal (Madeira) (Aquarium)
Lisbon
   1913. Jardim zoologico e de
   Aclimação em Portugal, Estrada
   de Benfica, Lisboa. 64 acres; 200
   species. Shady park with great
   paddocks for rare antelopes;
   huge lion and elephant enclosures, fine seal pools (rare monk
   seal).
Lisbon (Aquarium)

PUERTO RICO
Mayaguez (being rebuilt on new site)

RHODESIA
Salisbury *(Snake Park)*

RUMANIA
Bucharest
Constantza *(Aquarium)*

SAUDI ARABIA
Dhahran
Riyadh

SOUTH AFRICA
Bloemfontein
  1920. Bloemfontein Zoo, Bloemfontein. 35 acres; 350 species.
Cape Town (1897 or before)
Cape Town *(Aquarium)*
Durban
Durban *(Aquarium)*
East London
East London *(Aquarium)*
Johannesburg
  1909 (or before). Hermann Eckstein Park Zoological Gardens, Johannesburg. 103 acres; 250 species.
Lydenburg *(Aquarium)*
Port Elizabeth
Pretoria
  1898. National Zoological Gardens of South Africa, Boom Street, Pretoria. 120 acres; 500 species. A splendid collection with a fine record of breeding native African antelopes and other animals; it has a progressive educational policy.

SOUTH-WEST AFRICA
Okahandja

SPAIN
Barcelona
  1889. Parque zoologico de Barcelona, Parque de la Ciudadela, Barcelona. 30 acres; 350 species. Well-housed, well-shaded collection visited by over 4 million people a year—more than any other zoo in Europe.
Barcelona *(Aquarium)*
Jerez de la Frontera
Las Palmas (Canaries)
Madrid
Madrid *(Aquarium)*

SUDAN
Khartoum

SWEDEN
Borås

Eskilstuna
Frösö
Furuvik
Göteborg *(Aquarium)*
Höör
  1952. Skånes Djurpark, Höör, near Lund. 250 acres; 100 species (including wild breeding birds). A charming Swedish park zoo in conifer forest; breeds moose, red deer, wolves, and other native mammals.
Malmö *(Aquarium)*
Stockholm
  1891. Nordiska Museet och Skansen, Stockholm. 75 acres; 200 species. On a pretty island, a mixed ethnic muscum and zoo, with a fine breeding record of native Swedish animals.

SWITZERLAND
Basel
  1874. Zoologischer Garten Basel, Basel. 18 acres; 450 species. A superb zoo with a top breeding record; breeds gorillas (3 so far); rhinos, pigmy hippos, many rare birds. Fine new housing and exemplary management.
Berne (Bear pits from 1480)
Rapperswil
Zürich
  1929. Zoologischer Garten, Zürich 44. 22 acres; 350 species. Another example of the high Swiss standard of zoo management. Good ungulate collection; and interesting mixed tropical house with "walk-through" aviary.

THAILAND
Bangkok

TRINIDAD AND TOBAGO
Port of Spain (Trinidad)

TURKEY
Ankara
  1940. Ankara Zoo, Ataturk Orman, Ciftligi Hayvanat Bahcesi, Ankara. 16 acres; 150 species. Fine breeding record.
Izmir

UGANDA
Entebbe

U.S.S.R.
Alma Ata
Ashkabad
Askaniya-Nova
  1880. Askaniya-Nova Zoopark, Askaniya-Nova, Kahovka,

Ukraine. 4,053 acres; 100 species. The largest zoo in area in the world. Specializes in native ungulates, bison, acclimatization of antelopes.

Bakü

Dushanbe

Erevan

Grodno

Kaliningrad

Karaganda

Kaunas

Kazan

Kharkov

Kiev

Leningrad

Moscow

1864. Moskovskii Zoologicheskii Park, Bolshaya Gryzinskaya Ul., Moskva G-242. 49 acres; 550 species. A comprehensive collection shortly to be rehoused on a new site.

Nikolaev

Novosibirsk

Odessa

Perm

Riga

Rostov-nad-Don

Samarkand

Suchumi

Sverdlovsk

Tallin

Tashkent

Tbilisi

Termez

UNITED ARAB REPUBLIC (EGYPT)

Alexandria

1907. Alexandria Zoological Garden. 26 acres; 200 species. Good breeding record.

Cairo

1891. Giza Zoological Garden, Cairo. 52 acres; 400 species. A famous collection visited by 3,600,000 in 1963. Fine breeding record.

UNITED KINGDOM AND IRELAND

Andover (Weyhill)

Battersea (London) (Children's Zoo)

Belfast (Bellevue)

Birmingham (Edgbaston)

Blackpool (Tower)

Bourton-on-the-Water (Bird collection)

Brighton (Aquarium)

Braydon

Brighton (Devil's Dyke)

Bristol

1835. The Bristol, Clifton and West of England's Zoological Society's Gardens, Clifton, Bristol 8. 12 acres; 300 species. A gem of a modern small zoo, with exceptionally beautiful flowers, and a sound breeding record with black rhinos and other fine mammals.

Chessington

Chester

1930. The North of England Zoological Society's Zoological Gardens, Upton-by-Chester, Chester. 150 acres; 550 species. A progressive zoo with many new houses, including one of the finest elephant houses of all zoos; pretty gardens.

Chesterfield (Ashover)

Colwyn Bay (North Wales)

Crystal Palace (London) (Children's Zoo)

Dublin (Ireland)

1831. The Royal Zoological Society of Ireland's Zoo, Phoenix Park, Dublin. 32 acres; 250 species. Beautiful lake with waterfowl and gibbon islands; fine collection of breeding cats.

Dudley

1938. The Dudley Zoological Society's Gardens, Castle Hill, Dudley, Worcs. 48 acres; 400 species. A well-architectured general zoo built around a medieval castle, with much attention to care of animals and comfort of public.

Edinburgh

1913. The Royal Zoological Society of Scotland's Zoological Park and Carnegie Aquarium, Murrayfield, Edinburgh 12. 75 acres; 550 species. Good general collection on wooded hillside; fine collection of breeding penguins.

Exmouth

Exmouth (Aquarium)

Glasgow (Calderpark)

Great Witchingham (Pheasants)

Holt (Kelling Pines)

Ilfracombe

Jersey (Channel Islands)

1959. The Jersey Zoological Park and Wildlife Preservation Trust, Les Augres Manor, Jersey. 25 acres; 250 species. Specializes in breeding rare small mammals.

Kew Gardens (Bird collection)

Lilford Hall (Bird collection)

London

1828. The Zoological Society of London's Zoological Gardens, Regent's Park, London, N.W. 1.

36 acres; 1,400 species. One of the most comprehensive living collections in the world. Classic aquarium, and vast rebuilding program well ahead. The prototype of the mainstream zoo.

Longleat (Game reserve)

Malton (Kirby Misperton)

Manchester

1836. Belle Vue Zoological Gardens, Manchester 12. 70 acres; 250 species. General collection, with fine show of monkeys.

Morecambe (Aquarium)

A brand new "marineland" with dolphins.

Paignton

1923. The Herbert Whitley Trust's Paignton Zoological and Botanical Gardens, Paignton, Devon. 47 acres; 550 species. An excellent collection, with beautiful tropical houses and birds.

Paignton (Aquarium)

Peakirk (Bird collection)

Plymouth (Aquarium)

Poole

Port Erin (Isle of Man)

1892. The University of Liverpool's Marine Biological Station's Aquarium, Port Erin. 50 species.

Rode (Bird collection)

Sandown (Isle of Wight)

Slimbridge

1946. The Wildfowl Trust's Waterfowl Gardens, New Grounds, Slimbridge, Glos. 35 acres; 150 species, principally flamingos, swans, ducks, and geese. Many at liberty: the most comprehensive living collection of aquatic birds in the world. A wild bird sanctuary, too.

Southport

St. James's Park, London (Bird collection)

Torquay (Aquarium)

Tower of London (Bird collection)

Twycross

Wellingborough

Whipsnade

1927. The Zoological Society of London's Whipsnade Park, Whipsnade, Dunstable, Beds. 567 acres; 200 species. One of the finest park zoos in the world; fine animals in naturalistic surroundings on lovely wooded downland.

Woburn

1838. The Duke of Bedford's animal collection at Woburn Park, Bedfordshire, founded by the 6th Duke. A vast and stately park, with most of the world population of Père David's deer; also European bison, other great rarities, and ornamental birds in freedom.

UNITED STATES OF AMERICA

Albuquerque, New Mexico

Atlanta, Georgia

Baltimore, Maryland
1876. Baltimore Zoo, Druid Hill Park, Baltimore. 200 acres; 350 species. Good free municipal zoo.

Bear Mountain, New York

Birmingham, Alabama

Bismarck, North Dakota

Boston, Massachusetts (1912)

Boston, Mass. *(Aquarium)*

Bridgeport, Connecticut

Buffalo, New York
1870. Buffalo Zoological Gardens, Delaware Park, Buffalo 14. 23 acres; 350 species. A well-run free municipal zoo.

Catskill, New York
1933. Catskill Game Farm, Catskill. 920 acres (135 open to public); 200 species. Specializes in breeding ungulates (fine record) and supplying other zoos: America's "Whipsnade."

Chattanooga, Tennessee

Chicago, Illinois
1870. Lincoln Park Zoological Gardens, 100 W. Webster Avenue, Chicago. 25 acres; 550 species. Free municipal mainstream zoo associated with Lincoln Park Zoological Society. Tradition of comprehensiveness, good breeding record. 3,800,000 visitors in 1963.

Chicago, Illinois
1929. John G. Shedd Aquarium, 1200 S. Lake Shore Drive, Chicago 5. 350 species. Managed by Shedd Aquarium Society; excellent collection of fishes.

Chicago, Illinois
1934. Chicago Zoological Park, Brookfield, Chicago. 215 acres; 600 species. A mainstream collection, imaginatively housed, visited by 2,280,292 in 1963. Municipal zoo associated with Chicago Zoological Society.

Cincinnati, Ohio
1875. Cincinnati Zoological Society, 3400 Vine Street, Cincinnati. 54 acres; 450 species. A famous old zoo, with a comprehensive collection.

Cleveland, Ohio
1882. Cleveland Zoological Park, Cleveland. 110 acres; 400 species. Free municipal zoo managed by Cleveland Zoological Society, good breeding record.

Cleveland, Ohio *(Aquarium)*

Colorado Springs, Colorado

Columbus, Ohio
1927. Columbus Municipal Zoo and Arthur C. Johnson Aquarium, Powell, Columbus. 20 acres; 450 species. Municipal zoo run in conjunction with Columbus Zoological Society. Good breeding record; newest recruit to the Ohio State rivals, all verging on mainstream status.

Dallas, Texas (1904)

Dallas, Texas
1936. Dallas Aquarium, Fair Park, Dallas. 250 species. A popular and comprehensive (free) collection of fishes.

Denver, Colorado (1890 or before)

Detroit, Michigan
1928. Detroit Zoological Park, Royal Oak, near Detroit. 122 acres; 650 species. A mainstream collection with fine breeding record; free municipal zoo associated with Detroit Zoological Society.

Erie, Pennsylvania

Falmouth, Mass. (Woods Hole, 1904 or before) *(Aquarium)*

Fort Worth, Texas
1923. Fort Worth Zoological Park and James R. Record Aquarium, Forest Park, Fort Worth 10. 24 acres; 550 species. A comprehensive collection, mainstream.

Fresno, California

Garden City, Kansas

Grand Marsh, Wisconsin

Grand Rapids, Michigan

Great Bend, Kansas

Hattiesburg, Mississippi

Homer, Minnesota

Honolulu, Hawaii

Honolulu, Hawaii *(Aquarium)*

Houston, Texas
1959 (or before). Houston Zoological Garden, 509 City Hall, Houston 2. 42 acres; 400 species. A good (free) municipal collection.

Indianapolis, Indiana

Islamorada, Florida *(Aquarium)*

Jackson, Mississippi

Jacksonville, Florida

Kansas City, Missouri (1909)

Key West, Florida *(Aquarium)*

La Jolla, Calif. *(Aquarium)*

Lansing, Michigan

Libertyville, Illinois

Lincoln, Nebraska

Little Rock, Arkansas

Lodi, California

Los Angeles, California

1912. Griffith Park Zoo and Greater Los Angeles World Zoo, Los Angeles. 17 acres; 300 species.

Louisville, Kentucky

Madison, Wisconsin

Manhattan, Kansas

Marineland, Florida

1938. Marine Studios, near St. Augustine. 150 species. The pioneer toothed-whale and shark aquarium. Has bred dolphins in captivity since 1947.

Memphis, Tennessee

1908. Memphis Zoological Gardens and Aquarium, Overton Park, Memphis 12. 32 acres; 400 species. A fine (free) municipal collection, with good mammal breeding record.

Merced, California

Miami, Florida

1948. Crandon Park Zoo, Key Biscayne, Miami. 22 acres; 350 species. A good collection with a sound breeding record; associated with the Zoological Society of Florida.

Miami, Florida *(Reptiliary)*

Michigan City, Indiana

Middletown, Connecticut

Milwaukee, Wisconsin (1892)

Minot, North Dakota

New Orleans, Louisiana

New York City, New York

1864. Central Park Zoo and Prospect Park Zoo, 64th Street and Fifth Avenue, New York City 21. 7 acres; 100 species. The oldest surviving zoo in the Americas.

New York City (Brooklyn), N.Y.

1896. New York Aquarium, Coney Island, Brooklyn 24. 150 species, including toothed whales: modernized and impeccably run by N.Y. Zoological Society.

New York City (Bronx), N.Y.

1899. New York Zoological Park, 185th Street and Southern Boulevard, New York City 60. 252 acres; 1,050 species. One of the handful of really great mainstream zoos, and still actively developing under N.Y. Zool. Soc. (good breeding record).

New York City (Staten Is.), N.Y.

1936. Staten Island Zoo, 614 Broadway, Staten Island 10, New York City. 7 acres; 300 species. A good free show.

Norfolk, Virginia

Oakland, California

Oklahoma City, Oklahoma (1908)

Palos Verdes, California

1954. Marineland of the Pacific Oceanarium, Palos Verdes. 70 acres; 300 species. Toothed whales, in the world's largest aquarium tanks, are features of this fine marineland.

Peoria, Illinois

Philadelphia, Pennsylvania

1874. Philadelphia Zoological Garden, 34th Street and Girard Avenue, Philadelphia 4. 42 acres; 500 species. A splendid mainstream zoo managed by the Zoological Society of Philadelphia, with a fine breeding record, especially of apes and waterfowl.

Philadelphia, Pennsylvania

1962 (or before). Aquarama Theatre of the Sea, 3300 S. Broad Street, Philadelphia. 150 species. One of the latest ventures in displaying large sea mammals, including toothed whales, in giant tanks.

Philadelphia, Pennsylvania (Fairmount Park) *(Aquarium)*

Phoenix, Arizona

1962. Arizona Zoological Society, 60th and E. Van Buren Streets, Phoenix. 118 acres; 250 species. A new desert zoo that is successfully breeding most of the captive stock of the very rare Arabian oryx.

Pittsburgh, Pennsylvania

1895. Highland Park Zoological Gardens, Pittsburgh 6. 45 acres; 350 species. A fine free municipal zoo assisted by the Pittsburgh Zoological Society.

Pocatello, Idaho

Portland, Oregon

Providence, Rhode Island (1892)

Pueblo, Col. (1913 or before)

Racine, Wisconsin

Rapid City, South Dakota

Rochester, New York

Sacramento, California

St. Louis, Missouri

1903. St. Louis Zoological Garden, Forest Park, St. Louis 10. 83 acres; 600 species. A well-known free mainstream zoo, well-run by the municipality and the St. Louis Zoo Association.

St. Paul, Minnesota (1897)

St. Petersburg, Fla. *(Aquarium)*

Salt Lake City, Utah

San Antonio, Texas (1914)

San Diego, California

1922. San Diego Zoological Gardens, Balboa Park, San Diego. 91 acres; 1,200 species.

One of the youngest of the great mainstream zoos; with a perfect site and climate, and the good management of the San Diego Zoological Society, has a consistently exemplary breeding record throughout its collection.

San Francisco, Calif. (c. 1901)

San Francisco, California

1923. Steinhardt Aquarium, Golden Gate Park, San Francisco. 500 species. Magnificent (free) collection of fishes.

Scottsbluff, Nebraska

Scranton, Pennsylvania

Seattle, Washington

1900. Woodland Park Zoological Garden, 5400 Phinney Avenue N., Seattle 3. 90 acres; 350 species. Well-situated free municipal zoo.

Silver Springs, Fla. *(Reptiliary)*

Sioux Falls, South Dakota

South Bend, Indiana

Springfield, Massachusetts

Stoneham, Massachusetts

Stuart, Florida *(Reptiliary)*

Syracuse, New York

Tacoma, Wash. (1908 or before)

Tampa, Florida

1959. Busch Gardens, 3000 Temple Terrace Highway, Tampa. 200 acres; 350 species. Excellent free collection of birds (especially parrots) with good breeding record.

Tarpon Springs, Florida

Toledo, Ohio

1900. Toledo Zoological Gardens, 2700 Broadway, Toledo 9. 43 acres; 512 species. Another pioneer Ohio zoo, operated by city and Toledo Zoological Society: well-assorted collection.

Topeka, Kansas

Traverse City, Michigan

Trenton, New Jersey

Tucson, Arizona

1952. Arizona-Sonora Desert Museum, Tucson Mountain Park. 10 acres; 200 species. Specializes in the fauna of the American desert, with fine scientific, educational, and breeding record.

Tulsa, Oklahoma

Washington, D.C.

1886. National Aquarium, Bureau of Sport Fisheries and Wildlife, Department of Commerce Building, Washington. 150 species. A free display of fishes, especially of N. America.

Washington, D.C.

1890. National Zoological Park, Smithsonian Institution, Washington 9. 176 acres, 800 species.

The most comprehensive collection free to the public: a great mainstream zoo. Good breeding record.

Washington, D.C. (East Potomac Park)
A National Fisheries Center and Aquarium now in planning.

West Orange, New Jersey

Wichita, Kansas

Wilmington, Delaware

URUGUAY
Montevideo (1912 or before)

VENEZUELA
Caracas (El Pinar)
Caracas (Parque del Este)
Maracaibo
Maracay

VIETNAM
Hanoi (North Vietnam)
Saigon (South Vietnam, 1865)

YUGOSLAVIA
Belgrade
Brioni
Dubrovnik *(Aquarium)*
Ljubljana
Maribor *(Aquarium)*
Rovinj *(Aquarium)*
Sarajevo
Skopje
Split
Zagreb

Index

Page numbers in *italics* refer to illustrations or captions to illustrations.

A separate alphabetical listing of the zoos referred to in text begins on p. 250.

Abreu, Señora Rosalia, breeder of chimpanzees, 87, *87,* 88
Addax, 25, 127
Alexander the Great, 29, 30
Alligator, Mississippi, *154*
Amazon, simulated in Frankfurt/ Main exotarium, 183
America (North), map of, *108*
American Bison Society, 124
Amphibians, numbers in zoos, 158
Anaconda, *see* Snake
Anastasius, Emperor, *39*
Anatidae, 93, 94, 97; ancestry of, 205
Anderson, Svend, 209
Animals: "acclimatizers" of, 186, *186, 187,* 190, *190;* African, endangered, 126-9; behavior of, 200, *200,* 201, *201, 202,* 203-5, *203-4;* breeding in zoos, 72, 74-6, 78-100, 102, 103, 105-7, 206; caught for Roman Games, *36;* on circus posters, *31;* collection mortality of, 146-8, 195; confined in zoos, 68-9; dangerous, in zoos, 184-5; dealers, 135-40, 142-4, 146, 148-9, 153, 186; dealers' code, 149; Dionysian procession of, *30;* disease, 192; feeding in zoos, 182, *199;* food warehouses, 163; health, 184; hospitals, 163; housing in zoos, 74, *158, 160,* 162-4, *162-3, 165-8,* 166, 169-71, 174-5, 177, 179-80, 182-3; hunters, *see* dealers; medical care of, 206; navigation, 203; new importations of, in 16th century, 46; new species in zoos, 44; nomenclature, 44, 48; nutrition, 72, 184, *198,* 199, 200; occupational therapy for, 61-3, 66, 182; as pets, 80, *150,* 154; pictorial records of, 48; popularity poll, 67-8; prices of, 135-54, 156-7; quarantine, 150, 192 (*see also* Quarantine Stations); research on, 196-7, 199; trade of, between zoos, 152-3, *152-3;* transit, control of, 151; translocation of, 143; transport, 144, *144,* 145, *145,* 146, 148-9, 153, 186; transport (air), 145, *146-7;* transport, rules for, 149-50
Anjou, René, Duke of, 160
Anoa, 136
Anteaters, 46; great, 47; Marsupial banded, 103; *see also* Echidna
Antelope, 25, 97, 98, 224; breeding in captivity, 222; danger of extinction, 127; in Montezuma's zoo, 127; quarantine of, 150; Beira, 127; giant Sable, 127; mountain nyala, 127; royal, 127; Zanzibar, 127; *see also* Addax, Bontebok, Duiker, Eland, Gazelle, Gnu, Hartebeest, Oryx, Pronghorn, Saiga, Springbok
Anthrax, 192-4
Anthropoid apes, 84-5, 133; occupational therapy for, in zoos, 182-3; *see also* Gibbon, Chimpanzee, Gorilla, Orangutan, Siamang

Anthropoidea, 82
Antilocaprids, 97-8
Ape, 24, 29, *66,* 84; breeding in captivity, 80, 82, 84-5, 107
Ape house (at West Berlin zoo), *89*
Ape-men, 82
Aquariums, in modern zoos, 163; *see also* Zoos
Arabia, 25
Arena shows, 36-9
Aristotle, 28-30; *History of Animals,* 28
Arizona, 25
Armadillo, 46
Arpachiya civilization, 24
Ashurbanipal, King of Assyria, 27, *27*
Ass, 43; *see also* Wild ass
Attenborough, David, *140-1*
Audubon, John James, paintings, *109-10, 130*
Augustus I, Elector, 47
Augustus II, Elector, 47
Aurochs, 21, *25, 73*
Autopsy laboratory, 195-6, *195*
Aviary, architecture of, in modern zoos, *70,* 71, 163, 179; Greek, 28; of Lucullus, 34; of Montezuma, 43; of Varro, *32,* 34; 16th century, 46; *see also* Zoos
Avicultural Society, The (of Britain), 78
Avocet, *219*
Aye-aye, 81, *81*
Aztec codex, *43*

Babiroussa, 136
Baboon: breeding of, in zoos, 74, 82; transport of, *146-7*
Badger, 158
Baldwin, Paul H., 119
Bandicoot, in captivity, 105
Banks, Sir Joseph, 55, 61
Banteng, 98
Bartlett, Clarence, 145
Bat, by Leonardo da Vinci, *43*
Bayes, Kenneth, 180
Bear, 31, 40, 43, 47, 67, 158, *203;* fights, 38, *38,* 39, 47; games, *39;* housing in zoos, 162; nutrition of, 200; koala "bear," *see* Koala; Polar, *71;* escape of, 185; Syrian brown, 31
Bear house (in Frankfurt/Main zoo), *163*
Bear pits: at Barcelona, *157;* at Bern, *48*
Bedford, Dukes of: breeding of Père David's deer, 125; parrot aviary, of, 75, 79; *see also* Woburn Park (under Zoos)
Behavior, 201; *see also* Animals
Bicknell, Peter, design for Slimbridge, 171
Birds: "acclimatization" of, 25; ancestry of, 205; balance of, in nature, 186; behavior experiments, 204-5; breeding at San Diego, *94;* diets, 200; display of, in Egypt, 30; drawn by Leonardo da Vinci, 43; exhibition of, at Olympia, *148;* housing of, in zoos, 163; imported into Great Britain, 190; imported into United States, 136; numbers in zoos, 158; new species in Europe, 52; as pets, *149;* Pompeii, paintings at, 35; rare, on Madagascar, 224; recordings of,

235; research on, in zoos, 196; song, 216; survival of, 108, 112; transport of, 146-7, 148; "Ethiopian" bird, 30; game birds, 46
Bird of paradise, 46, 48; trade in, 191-2, *191*
Bison, 18, 123, *123;* Society for Protection of, 123; American, 124, *124;* European, 122, *122,* 124, 224; *B. priscus,* 18, 122; Bialowieza herd, 122, *122,* 124
Black, Mischa, 180
Blackbird, 28, 32, *34*
Blesbok, value of, 157
Bligh, Captain, 55
Boar, 43, 160; fighting, 47; wild, 34
Bobcat, *see* Lynx
Bonobo, *see* Chimpanzee
Bontebok, 127, *127;* breeding and survival of, 128
Boorer, Michael, *233*
Boos, Franz, 52
Bounty, H.M.S., 55
Bouton, Père, 78
Bovids, 97; breeding in zoos, 98, *99*
Bovine tuberculosis, 192
Bovoids, 97, *98-9,* 99; quarantine for, 192
Bowerbird, spotted, *219*
Brand, Dr. D. J., 221-2
Breeding of animals and birds, *see* Animals, Zoos, *also* names of specific species
Buck, Frank, animal dealer, 136-7, *137; Bring 'em Back Alive,* 136
Budgerigar, 112; breeding of, 76, *76, 77,* 192
Buffalo, Indian, 97
Bull: domesticated, 24, *25;* fighting, 38-9, 47; Ankole, *99*
Bunting, 34
Burrell, Harry, 100
Burton, Decimus: camel house at London zoo, *173;* designs for London zoo, 173-4, 179
Bush baby, 67; breeding of, 82

Caesar, Augustus, 38
California State Game Commission, 130
California, University of, animal behavior zoo, 203
Caligula, sacrifice of animals by, 39
Cambridge, University of, zoo for animal behavior study, 203
Camel, 40, 41, 43, 47, 50, 186; in Egypt and Mesopotamia, 31; Bactrian, 30; one-humped, 31
Capercaillie, 39
Cardinal, 46, 48; in Montezuma's zoo, 43
Carnivore, basic diet for, 200
Cassanova, Lorenzo, animal dealer, 138
Casson, Sir Hugh, consultant architect, London zoo, 177-80, *180-1;* elephant house, 208
Cassowary, 46
Cat: domestic in Greece, 28, *28-9;* big cats, 43, 72; wild in Egypt, 26; *see also* Lion, Tiger
Cattle, 26, 41, 97; quarantine of, 150; lyre-horned, *24;* short-horned, *24*
Cavagnole, cards for, *46*
Cayman: in Montezuma's zoo, 43; black, *140*
Ceboidea, bred in captivity, 84

Cercopithecine, bred in captivity, 82-3
Cercopithecoid, 83
Chachalacas, in Montezuma's zoo, 43
Charlemagne, Emperor, 40
Charles I of Naples and Sicily, 41
Charles V of France, 160
Charles IX of France, 47
Cheetah, 26, 31, 41; at London zoo, *155;* fights, 38; value of, 157; African, in danger of extinction, 127
Chicken, 28, 32; *see also* Fowl
Chimpanzee, 46, *66,* 67, 68, *68, 86, 87,* 112, *151;* breeding in captivity, 85, 87-8; discovery of, by Hanno, 86; early records of, 86; in space capsule, *112;* tea-party, at Bronx zoo, *65,* at London zoo, 61-2; therapeutic activities in zoos, *60, 61,* 61-3; value of, 157; pigmy chimpanzee (Bonobo), 85, *85;* in danger of extinction, 127
China, 27, *125-6*
Claudius, animal fights staged by, 39
Cobra, *see* Snake
Cock: in Greece, *28;* figurine of, 24
Cockatoo, 46, 78, 219
Colobine, breeding in captivity, 83
Columbus, Christopher, 43
Condé, Princes of, 47, 160
Condor, 46, 48, 172; Andean, breeding of, *70,* 106, *107,* 129; Californian, breeding in, 129, 130, *130,* 206
Constantinople: arena games at, 40; mosaic from, *39*
Cook, Captain, 119
Cortés, Hernando, 43
Cotinga, 46, 48, 148
Cotton, Jack, 178-9
Cousteau, Jacques-Yves, 214-5
Coypu, 189
Crab, *137;* spider, *228*
Crane, 28, 32
Crocodile, 67; killed in arena fights, 38; *see also* Cayman
Crow, 28
Curassow, 48, 51; *see also* Guan
Curlew, 47
Cuscus, *104*

Darwin, Charles, 55
Dasyuridae, breeding of, 103, *103*
Dasyurine, 103
David, Père, 124-6
Davy, Sir Humphry, 56
Deer, 22-3, 27, 43, *43,* 189; hybrid at Askaniya-Nova, *72-3;* in Montezuma's zoo, 43; moat enclosure for, at Bern, *158;* Chinese water, *189;* giant, 18; Irish, 18; Père David's, 124, *125;* red, 18
Delacour, Jean, 120, 152, 217; *Pheasants of the World,* 94
Derby, Earls of, 56, *118-9,* 120
Didelphidae family, *102*
Dik-Dik, 99
Dingo, 67
Disney, Walt, *The Living Desert,* 224
Dodo, 46, 110, 111, *111*
Dog, 21, 22, 67; breeds, distinct, 21; fight with cat, *28;* as domesticated animal, 21, 23; dung, fossilized, 21; skeleton, 21; quarantine of, 150; *see also* Greyhound, Hound

Dolphin, 212, *213;* Amazon, 215; bottled-nosed, 212, *212, 213, 214-5,* 215; common, studied in Russia, 215; spotted, 212; white-sided, 212, 215
Domestication of animals and birds, 22-5; *see also* Animal, Bird
Dormouse, 189
Dove, *25*
Dromedary, 41; pedigree value of, 157
Duck, 28, 32, 47, 203; breeding in captivity, 94; at Slimbridge, 171: American ring-billed, 97; American wood, 47, 96; Cape culture in, 99 shellduck, 96; Chinese mandarin, 47, 96; eider, 205; mallard, 97; Muscovy, 44, 47; red-crested captivity, 93-5; not bred in pochard, 97; scaup, 97; *see also* Merganser
Duiker, 99; banded duiker, 127, *127*
Dürer, Albrecht, animal drawings, *42,* 43
Durrell, Gerald, 139-40

Eagle, in Montezuma's zoo, 43
Echidna: of Australia, 100, *101;* of New Guinea, 100
Edwards, J. E., *154*
Eggenschwiler, Urs, designs zoo, 164
Egypt, 23, 25-6, 32, 80; early zoo
Eland, *204,* 224
Elephant, *16,* 30, 40-1, 43, 50, 67-8; in arena, 38-9; at London zoo, *63;* breeding in zoos, 106; housing at London zoo, 180; price of, 157; semi-domestication of, 24, *25;* sleeping habits of, *17;* trained, 32; African elephant, 138; killed by anthrax, 194
Emu, 46
Epulu (Congo), quarantine station, *156, 197*
Exceptional Young Zoologists' Club, *see* XYZ Club
Exotarium, in zoos, 163, 183, *183*

Falcon, 40, 46; in zoo of Kublai Khan, 43; in zoo of Montezuma, 43
Falconry, *40*
Fauna, 18, 21, 44; African, *222-3;* Hawaiian, 119; special, in zoos, 221, *221,* 222-4, 226
Faust, Charles, 172
Finch, 28
Fish, 27, 46, *212;* numbers in zoos, 158; at St. Pol, 160; *see also* Aquariums (listed under Zoos)
Flamingo, 28, 39
Fleay, David, 100
Flounder, *229*
La Fontaine, fables illustrated at Vineuil, 47
Foot-and-mouth disease, 192
Fossil, 21; dog dung, *see* Dog; records, 20
Fowl, 22, 160; breeding and hand-rearing, 106; domesticated, 93; wildfowl collections, 95-6; Light Sussex, 93; waterfowl, longest lived, 120; *see also* (under Zoos) St. James's Park, Slimbridge
France, 18, 39
Francis I, Holy Roman Emperor, builds Schönbrunn zoo, 50

Francolin, 28
Frederick II, Holy Roman Emperor, *41;* animal studies of, 41; traveling menagerie of, 41; zoos of, 41

Gallinule, 28, 51
Game reserves, *see under* Zoos
Gayal, 98
Gazelle, 25, 97, 127
Giant panda, *see* Panda
Gibbon, 84; breeding in captivity, 85; enclosure at Hanover zoo, *84*
Giraffe, *14,* 26, *26,* 31, 67-8, *138, 193;* breeding in zoos, 106, *106*
Glengall, Lady, 120
Glider, *see* Opossum
Gnu: white-tailed, 127, *127, 204;* value of, 157
Goat, 31, 98; housing in zoos, 163; wild, *see* Ibex
Goose, 23, *23,* 24, 32; behavior experiments with, 203; breeding in captivity, 93, 94; domestication of, 22, *22,* 23, 23; "imprinted," *201;* Canada, 190; Egyptian, 28; graylag, *23;* Hawaiian, survival of, *117-8,* 119-22, *120-1;* white, *23*
Gorilla, 67, 68, *150;* at Basel, *91;* breeding in captivity, 85, 88-92, *90,* 133, *199,* 206; danger of extinction, 127; discovery of, 86; with paraplegia, *197*
Gozzoli, *The Procession of the Magi, 42*
Gravettian culture, 21
Greece, 80; attitude to animals, 27-30
Greyhound, 26; *see also* Dog, Hound
Grieger, Wilhelm, animal dealer, 138
Grimwood, Ian, 148
Grzimek, Bernhard, 183; records of gorillas, 91
Guan, 48, 51; in Montezuma's zoo, 43; *see also* Curassow
Guan-Curassow family of birds, 46
Guenon, 82
Guereza, breeding in captivity, 83
Guglielmi, Gregor, 51
Guinea fowl, 24, 30, 33; sacrificed by Caligula, 39; African guinea fowl, 28
Guinea pig, 44, 46

Hagenbeck, Carl: founder of zoo, 138, *138-9;* architecture of zoo, 164, *164,* 166
Hamilton, Count Björn, 170
Hamster, 112
Hanno the Navigator, discovers "gorillas," 86
Harappa civilization, 24
Hare, in Egypt, 26
Haroun al Raschid, 40
Harrisson, Barbara, 114-6
Harrisson, Tom, 114,116
Hartebeest: Cape (Kaama), 51; Hunter's, 127; red, *223*
Hatshepsut, Queen, 26, *26,* 31, 41
Hawaiian Board of Agriculture and Forestry, 120-1
Hawk, 46; in zoo of Kublai Khan, 43; in zoo of Montezuma, 43
Heliogabalus, Emperor, 39
Hen, figurine of, 24
Henry I of England, menagerie at Woodstock, 40
Henry III of France, 47
Herbivore, basic diet for, 200

Heron, 158; night, 190
Hill, Len, Birdland, 219, *218-9*
Hippopotamus, 43, 67; in arena, 38; breeding in zoos, 106-7; value of, 157; pigmy hippopotamus, breeding in zoos, 160-7, *107;* in danger of extinction, 127, *127*
Hiram, King of Tyre, 24
Hodgson, B. H., 144
Hoefnagel, Georg, 48
Hoefnagel, Jacob, 48
Hoffmann-La Roche Co. of Switzerland, diet for animals studied by, 199
Hominoid, 84, 85, 91
Honeyeaters, 46-7
Hoopoe, 28
Hornbill, Indian, breeding, *219*
Horse, 20, 23-4, 43, 67, 186; wild, 20; forest, 20; Przewalski's, 20, *20,* 138, 224; *see also* Tarpan
Horsfield, Thomas, 56
Hound, 31; *see also* Dog, Greyhound
Hummingbirds, 46, 48, 219
Huxley, Sir Julian, 177, 185
Huxley, Thomas Henry, 55
Hyena, 25; brown, in danger of extinction, 127

Ibex, 25, *208*
Ibis, 51, 60
Ice Age, 18
Iguana, in Montezuma's zoo, 43
India, 24
Indri, 81
Infantando, Duke of, menagerie of, 46
Ingram, Sir William, helps preserve birds of paradise, 190-1
Insects, housing of, in zoos, 163
International Council for Bird Preservation, 151
International Union for the Conservation of Nature and Natural Resources, 112, 144; discourages sale of animals, 157; sponsors meeting on animal trade, 150-1; *see also* Survival Service Commission
International Union of Directors of Zoological Gardens, 151-2
International Zoo Yearbook, 60, 88, 116; survey of milk analyses in diets, 200
Invertebrates, numbers in zoos, 158
Iraq, 24

Jacamar, 46, 48
Jaçana (or lily-trotter), 219
Jackal, 22; puppies, 21
Jackdaw, 28
Jacquin, Nicolas, 51
Jaguar, in Montezuma's zoo, 43
Jamrach, William, animal dealer, 138
Jellyfish, *230*
Joas, J. J., plan for London zoo, 175, 177
Johnsgard, Paul, research on duck family, 205
Jones, Terry, 152
Joseph II of Austria, 51
Justinian, Emperor, menagerie of, 40

Kaama, *see* Hartebeest
Kangaroo, 46, 100, *185;* tree, *102;* breeding in zoos, 105
Karnak, temple garden, 25, *26*
Kea, *78*
Kirby, William, 56

Koala, 72, 105
Koch, Ludwig, 235, *235*
Komodo dragon, *see* Lizard
Kublai Khan, zoo of, 43

Lang, Dr. Ernst, 60, *91*
Langur, breeding of, in captivity, 83
Lansdowne, Marquis of, President of Zoological Society, 56
Lark, 34
Lascaux cave paintings, 18, *18, 19, 20, 20,* 21
Lear, Edward, 56
Lecomte, A. A., 145
Lemur, 46, 48; breeding of, 80-2, *80,* 224; *see also* Aye-Aye, Bush baby, Indri, Loris, Potto, Sifaka
Leopard, 26, 31, 41; fights, 38; height of jump, 166: clouded, value of, 157
Linnaeus, 48; *System of Nature,* 48
Linnean Society, 56
von Linné, Carl, *see* Linnaeus
Lion, 22, *27,* 40-1, 46-7, 67, 160; in arena fights, 38-9, 47; breeding in captivity, 72; drawn by Dürer, 43; height of jump, 166; pit barriers for, in zoos, 166
Lion-fish, *227*
Lizard: drawn by Leonardo da Vinci, 43; Komodo dragon, *140*
Llama, 46; in Montezuma's zoo, 43
Lorenz, Dr. Konrad, research into animal behavior, *200,* 201, 203, 205
Lorikeet, breeding in captivity, *78, 79, 79*
Loris, breeding of, 82
Lory, *see* Lorikeet
Louis XIII of France, 48; as zoologist, 47
Louwman, Peter W., 216
Lubetkin, Tolek, designs for London zoo, 177
Lucullus, 34; aviary of, 34
Lung plague, 192
Lutong, bred in captivity, 83
Lynx: in Egypt, 26, 41; bobcat, *221*

Macaque, 82, 112
Macaw, 44, 46, 51, *78-9, 111,* 219; breeding in captivity, 78-9; brought to Europe by Columbus, 43: *Ara chloroptera,* 78; *Ara martinicus,* 78
Macropodidae family, *102*
Macropus, 105
Madagascar, mammals of, 81-2
Maglemosian culture, 21
Magpie, 28
Mallard, *see* Duck
Mammals, 26, 44, 51; "acclimatization" of, 25, *189;* African, in danger of extinction, 127; balance of, in nature, 186; collection and transport of, 146-8; exotic, gone wild, *188;* fish-eating, diets for, 200; housing in zoos, 162, 180, 186, *212;* imported into U.S.A., 136; new species in Europe, 52; numbers in zoos, 158; recording of, 235; survival of, 108, 112
Mammoth, 18, 21
Manatee, West African, in danger of extinction, 127
Map: of European bison, *122;* of North America, *108;* of Saudi Arabia (oryx), *132;* of world's zoos, *52-3*
Maria Theresa of Austria, 50

Marine Biological Association, Plymouth, 228
Marmoset, 46, 47, 158; breeding in captivity, 83
Marsupials, 99; breeding and culture of, 100-5, *102-3;* nocturnal, *104*
Martius (explorer), in Brazilian rain forest, *44*
Matthews, G. V. T., work on animal navigation, 203
Max Planck Institute for the Physiology of Behavior, 203
Maximilian II, Holy Roman Emperor, zoos of, 48
Menageries: architecture of, 161; arena menageries and shows, 36-9; in ancient Egypt, 26-7, 30, 32; in France, 39; in ancient Greece, 27-30, 41; in ancient Rome, 32-3, 38-9, 43; of Charlemagne, 40; of Justinian, 40; of Medici, *42,* 43; of Montezuma, 43; of Ribeira (Portugal), 43; traveling menageries, in 14th-15th centuries, 43; in 16th-17th centuries, 44, 46-8; in 17th-18th centuries, 50, *68;* Polito's Royal Menagerie, *68;* Wombwell's Menagerie, England, keeps first gorilla in captivity, 89; *see also* Zoos
Menges, Joseph, animal dealer, 138
Merck's Rhinoceros, *see* Rhinoceros
Merganser, behavior pattern, 205
Mesolithic Age, *see* Stone Age (Middle)
Mink, 189
Mitchell, Sir Peter Chalmers, 169
Mohenjo-Daro civilization, 24, *25*
Mole, marsupial, 103
Mongoose, 25
Monkey, 25, 26, 28-9, 40-1, 47, 67; breeding in captivity, 80, 82-4; drawn by Leonardo da Vinci, 43; housing, *166;* transport by air, *146;* Allen's swamp monkey, breeding in captivity, 83; South American, 46; capuchin, breeding in captivity, 83-4; colobus, *83;* howler, breeding in captivity, 83; leaf, breeding in captivity, 83; patas, 83; proboscis, 136-7, breeding in zoos, 83; rhesus, 112; savanna, 112; mortality in transit, 148; snub-nosed, breeding in captivity, 83; spider, 83, *83;* squirrel, breeding in captivity, 83; *see also* Guenon, Guereza, Macaque, Titis, Uakari
Monotremes, 99-100
Montezuma, Mexican menagerie of, 43
Montmorency, Anne de, 160
Montmorency, Dukes of, *see* Condé
Moose, Swedish, *221*
Morris, Desmond, *59,* 63, 67, 180, 232
Mouse, 188, *189*
Muntjac, 189
Museums, *see* Zoos
Musk-ox, at Copenhagen zoo, 210
Muskrat, 190

Naples Research and Quarantine Station, 162, 193, *193*
Narbonne, bear fights at, *38*
National Game Reserves, *see* Zoos
National Parks, *see* Zoos
Nearchus, 30
Nebuchadnezzar, King of Babylonia,

as lion fancier, 27
Nenes, *see* Goose (Hawaiian)
Neolithic Age, *see* Stone Age (New)
New Zealand, animals imported into, *190*
Newby, Frank, 179
Nightingale, 28
Ninus, as lion fancier, 27
Nuffield Institute of Comparative Medicine, 59, 199, 208
Nutria, *see* Coypu

Occupational therapy for animals, 61-3, 66
Occlot, on Aztec codex, *43*
O'Connell, Pat, big-game trapper, 143
Octopus, *230*
Okapi: at Bristol zoo, *74;* at Epulu, *156;* worm infection of, 197, *197,* 199
Omnivore, diet for, 200
Opossum, *102,* 103; black flying opossum, *104;* flying opossum, 105
Orangutan, 30, 68, *92,* 112, 137; breeding in captivity, 85, 93, 133; escape of, in London zoo, 185; National Park for, at Bako, *115;* price of, 157; survival of, 113-7, *113-6*
Orang Utan Recovery Service (O.U.R.S.), 115, 116; Park at Bako, *115*
Orange, Frederick Henry, of Nassau, menagerie, 86
Orange, William V, Prince of, private zoo, 93
Ortolan, 32
Oryx, 25, 31, *204;* Arabian, 25, *132-3;* sale of forbidden, 157; scimitar-horned, 127
Ostrich, 27, 30; heads served at banquet, 39
Owl, little, 190
Ox, Ethiopian, 31; Indian, 31; wild ancestral, *see* Aurochs
Oyster-catchers, 47

Paca, 46
Paleolithic Age, *see* Stone Age (Old)
Paleolithic Art, *29*
Panda, giant, 67, 126, *126;* breeding of, in zoos, 126; discovered by Père David, 126; value of, 154, 156
Pangolin, diet of, 200
Panther and "pantheroi," 32; fights, 38
Parakeet, 30, 47; Australian grass, 76; Carolina, breeding and extinction of, 110, *110;* Indian ring-necked, *29;* Quaker, 79
Parasitology, 199
Parkinson, Anthony, game dealer, 142
Parrot, 24, 30; breeding in captivity, 74-6, 78-80; ban on importation, 192; distribution of parrot family today, *78;* eaten by men and lions, 39; psittacosis, 192; quarantine, 150: African gray, 24, 219; Amazon, 78; eclectus, 51, 219
Parrotlets, 46
Partridge, red-legged, 190
Peacock, 24, 30, 93, *208;* sacrificed by Caligula, 39; Congo, 94
Peafowl, 33, 93; Indian, 28
Penguin, 46, 219; housing in zoos, *210;* in exotarium at Frankfurt/ Main, 183, *183*

Phalanger, 105
Phasianini, 93
Pheasant, 28, 30, 216; sacrificed by Caligula, 39; eaten at banquet, 39; breeding in captivity, 93, 94; in Montezuma's zoo, 43; golden, 190; green, 190; Hume's bar-tailed, 94; Lady Amherst's, 190; Rothschild's peacock pheasant, 94; silver, 94; Swinhoe's, bred at San Diego, *94*
Pig, swallowed by snake, *137*
Pigeon, 24, 28, 32, 46; passenger, 108-10, *109*
Pigeon post, 32
Pigmy chimpanzee, *see* Chimpanzee
Pigmy hippopotamus, *see* Hippopotamus
Piranhas, in Frankfurt zoo, 183
Platypus, or duckbill, 99, 100, *100-1*
Pliny the Elder, 35-8
Pochard, Red Crested, *see* Duck
Polo, Marco, visits zoo of Kublai Khan, 43
Polynesians, in Hawaii, 119
Pompeii, Roman mosaic from, *29*
Porpoise, breeding in captivity, 212; at St. Pol, 160; transport of, *145*
Potto, breeding of, 82
Pouched mouse, breeding of, 103
Poulsen, Dr. Holger, 209
Prestwich, Arthur, 78
Price, Cedric, 179
Primates, breeding in zoos, 80-93; housing in zoos, 162, 166; management of, in zoos, 74; Yale studies on, in Florida, 203
Pronghorn, 97; breeding in captivity, 98, *98*
Protemnodon, 105
Przewalski's wild horse, *see* Horse
Psittacosis, 192
Ptolemy I, of Egypt, zoo of, 30
Ptolemy II, of Egypt, 30; display of birds, 30; value of animal collection, 32; zoo at Alexandria, 30, 38
Puma, in Montezuma's zoo, 43
Punt, Land of, *see* Somaliland
Python, *see* Snake

Quail, 28; day-old, *95;* in Montezuma's zoo, 43
Quarantine stations, *see* Epulu, London zoo, Naples Research and Quarantine Station
Quetzal, in Montezuma's zoo, 43; present zoo value, 157

Rabbit, *43,* 188
Raccoon, 46
Raffles, Sir Thomas Stamford, 55-6, *55,* 61
Ramesses II, 27; animal tribute paid to, *26*
Randall, Ken, big-game trapper, 143
Rat, 67, 188; American, 190; musk, 186
Ratcliffe of Philadelphia, diets for zoo animals, pioneered by, 199
Red rail, *111*
Red-shank, 47
Reptiles, housing in zoos, 163, 182; numbers in zoos, 158
Research station, *see* Naples Quarantine and Research Station
Revesz, Stephen, 179

Rhea, 46
Rhinoceros, *15,* 18, *25,* 31, 43, 67; in arena fights, 38; breeding in zoos, 106; horn, *128;* housing at London zoo, *63,* 180; trapping technique, 129, *129;* African black, *15,* 31; in danger of extinction, 127; price of, 157; hairy, 18; Indian, drawn by Dürer, 43; price of, 156; Javan, survival of, 131, *131;* sale forbidden, 157; in zoos, 132; Merck's, *19,* 20; Sumatran, *19,* 20; sale forbidden, 157; woolly, 18, 20; white (or square-lipped), breeding of, 129, 142; in danger of extinction, 127-9, *129;* distribution in zoos, 142-3; price of, 157; translocation of, 143
Rigge, J. S., private aviary of, 78
Rinderpest, 192
Roe, 34
Rome, zoology in, 32-6, 80; *see also* Menageries, Zoos
Rothschild, Walter, Lord, introduces dormouse to England, 188
Royal Society, London, 55-6
Royal Society for the Prevention of Cruelty to Animals, hostel at London Airport, 146
Rudolf II, Holy Roman Emperor, 48
Ruhe family of Alfeld, 138

Sahara, paintings from Tassili region, *21, 22*
Saiga, *124,* 224
St. Gallen, Benedictine monks of, 41, 158; botanic gardens, 160; zoo of, 158; zoo architecture, 160
Sakkarah, 25
Sanderson, Ivan, 139
Savery, Roelant, 48, 111, *111*
Savoy, Prince Eugène of, zoo at Belvédère, 48
Scaup, *see* Duck
Scharf, G., lithographs of London zoo, *56*
Schiøtz, Arne, 209
Schorger, A. W., 108
Scott, Peter, 97, 122, 152, 216; planning of Slimbridge, 171
Screamer, 46
Seago, John (animal dealer and hunter), 129, 142, 147; hunting technique, 143, *143;* translocation of rhinoceros, 143
Seal, 160; in Bergen aquarium, 227-8; fought by men, 39; housing of, in zoos, 162; transport of, *145;* bearded, 228; harp, 228; hooded, 228; inner fjord, 228
Sea lion, acts by, *62,* 63
Seleucus I, 30; elephants of, 31; silver coin of, *31*
Semiramis, as leopard fancier, 27
Shaw, Frank, 179
Sheep, 23, 98; housing in zoos, 163; Arabian, 31; Barbary, 46; Ethiopian, 31; Euboean, 31
Shepheard, Peter, 178-9, 208
Shipman, Harold C., 120-1
Shrew, tree: breeding in captivity, 80-1, *80*
Siamang, 84-5, 136
Sifaka, 81
Skunk, 67
Sloth, 46-7
Snake, 38, 67, 68; drawn by

Leonardo da Vinci, 43; in Montezuma's zoo, 43; anaconda, *135;* hamadryad, 38; python, 31, 38, after swallowing a pig, *137;* rattlesnake, 43
Snakebird, *183,* 219
Snowdon, Lord, aviary at London zoo, 179
Solomon, King, 23-4, 27
Somaliland, 26
Somerset, 11th Duke of, 56
Sparrow, 28, 190
Spider, 67-8
Spidercrab, *228-9*
Spix (explorer), in Brazilian rain forest, *44*
Springbok, *99*
Square-lipped rhinoceros (white rhinoceros), *see* Rhinoceros
Squirrel, gray, 188, *188;* red, 188
Starling, 28, 190; talking, 33
Stengelhofen, F. A. P., architect to London zoo, 177-9
Stilt, *219*
Stone Age, 122; Middle, 21-2; New, 21-2; neolithic pastoralists, 21; Old, 21-2
Stuart, Lady Arabella, 78
Stupicz, Matthias Leopold, 52
Sudan, 31
Sudan Game Preservation Dept., 142
Suke-Yim, 24
Survival Service Commission, 112-3, 115-6, 119, 125, 127-8, 132-3, 151; information files, 127; *Red Book,* 149; *see also* Orang Utan Recovery Service
Swan, behavior experiments with, 203; breeding in captivity, 93-4
Sweden, royal collections in, 48
Syria, 26

Tanager, 46, 48
Tanki, Empress, 27
Tapir, 46; American, 48; Malay, *156;* value of, 157
Tarpan, 20, *20, 73*
Tarsier, breeding in zoos, 82, *82*
Tasmanian Devil, breeding of, 103, *103*
Tavistock, Lord, *see* Bedford, Dukes of
Teal, 47
Thebes, animals brought to, *27;* murals on a tomb, *24-5*
Thomson, James, 145
Thomson, John, 145
Thrush, 32, *34*
Thylacine, becoming extinct, 103
Tiger, breeding in captivity, 72, *206;* height of jump, 166; killed in fights, 38-9, 47; pit barriers for, in zoos, 166; value of, 157; Indian, brought to Rome, 38; Siberian, *182;* white, *155*
Tinamou, 46
Tinbergen, Dr. Niko, research on animal behavior, *200,* 201, *203*
Titi, bred in captivity, 83
Topatopa Dam, 130
Tortoise, river, 38
Toucan, 46, 48
Touracos, 46; Fischer's touracos, *219*
Treus, Vladimir, *72-3*
Trigger fish, *230*
Tropicarium, in zoos, 163
Trumpeter, 46, 48

Tsalikis, Mike, captures anaconda, *134-5*
Tunisia, mosaic from, *30*
Turkey, 44, 46; in Montezuma's zoo, 43
Turtle, in Montezuma's zoo, 43
Tuthmose III, 26, *27*

Uakari, bred in captivity, 83
Ungulates, cloven-hoofed, quarantine of, 192; control of importation into America, 193; housing in zoos, 162-3

Varro, Marcus Terentius, aviary of, *32-3,* 34; diaries of, 34; zoo at Casinum, 34
Venne, Adrian van de, 111
Vertebrates, 44, 108; feeding of, in zoos, 199
Victor Emmanuel II, King: "acclimatization" farm of, *186*
Vicugna, in Montezuma's zoo, 43
Vigors, Nicholas Aylward, 56, 120
Vincent, Jack, Director of Wildlife Conservation, Natal, 142, *142,* 143
Vinci, Leonardo da, animal drawings of, 43
Vini, see Lorikeet
Vivisection, 196

Wackernagel, Hans, nutrition expert, 199
Wader, 47
Walker, Louis Wayne, 130
Wallaby, breeding of, 105
Wapiti, *187*
Warthog, housing of, at Whipsnade, 170
Warwick, Tom, survey of muskrat, 190
Waterfowl, 22, 46; menaced by mink, 189; ponds for, in Montezuma's zoo, 43
Wayre, Peter, 216
Wegeforth, Dr. Harold M., 172
Wellcome Institute for Comparative Physiology, 59, 208
Wenceslas, King, 160
Wen Wang, Emperor, zoological garden of, 27
Whale, breeding in zoos, 212; transport of, *144;* whalebone, 215; Beluga (white), 215; pilot, 212, *214,* 215; *see also* Dolphin, Porpoise
Whimbrel, 47
Wild ass, 31; Nubian, in danger of extinction, 127; Somali, in danger of extinction, 127
William the Conqueror, founder of menagerie at Woodstock, 41
William IV, King of England, grants royal charter to Zoological Society, 56
Wilson, Alexander, 108
Wolf, 21, 22; housing at Höör, 170-1; puppies, 21-2
Woodpecker, ivory-billed, survival of, 130

Xyrichthys novacula, 230
XYZ Club, London, 58, *59,* 231

Yak, 98
Yale Laboratories, *see* Yerkes Laboratories
Yale, University of, research zoos, 203

Yealland, John, 121, 152
Yerkes Laboratories of Primate Biology, Florida, 63, *87, 88*

Zebra, 50; in danger of extinction, 127; escape in London zoo, 185; transport of, *143;* African mountain, 51
Zebu, 31
Zeuner, F. E., 18, 20
Zoological Record, The, 59, 60
Zoological records, 25, 27, 43, 46, 48, 59, 157; at London zoo: documentation, 55, 59, 60; library, 15, 59, 60; records of other zoos held at London zoo, 59, 60; of Frederick II, 41; of Pliny, 34; of Varro, 34; at Versailles, 48
Zoological societies: of London, 56, 72, 169, 173, 177; publications of, 59-60, 151; Sec. (Hon.), Zuckerman, 74, 177; of New York, 151; Royal Zoological Society of Scotland, 151
Zoos, 10, 12-5, 17-8, 23-7; aims of, 56-8, 61; agriculture, help to, 60-1; animal and plant exhibits in modern zoos, 183; autopsy laboratory in, 195; basic space units in, 162-4; architecture and layout, 52, 157-64, 166, 169-71, 175, 177-80, 182, *235;* bombing of, 185; breeding in, 72, 74-6, 78, 100, 102-3, 105-7, 152, 206; children's zoos, layout of, 163; critics of, 68, 70-1, 148, 235; diets and food in, *198,* 199-200; education in, 163, *235;* emergency role as Zoo Bank, 133; flower exhibits at, *13;* hospitals, 206, 208; housing at, 74, 157, 174; layout, *see* Architecture; liaison with public, *10,* 231; management of, 24, 182; medical science, help to, 195; moats in, *166;* mortality rate in, 195 new trends in, 208-10; open zoos, 33, 162, 164, 166, 206; posters, *10;* rebuilding of, 173; research in, 195-7, 199, 200-1, *202,* 203-5; resuscitator, *206;* roadside zoos, 152-3; specialist zoos, 212, 215-7, 219, 221-4; staff, 12-7, 152, 182; supply of stock to, 134-50; survival in, 108, 110-33; television in, 231; trade between zoos, 152, 154; traveling zoos, *58;* valuation of animals in, 154, 156-7; veterinary science and work in, *14,* 61, 184-95; world's zoos, plan of, *53*
Zuckerman, Sir Solly, 74, 177

The following is a list of Zoos referred to in the text. This also includes Bird Sanctuaries, Game Reserves, Menageries, Museums, and National Parks. Aviaries and Aquariums are included under Zoos, unless they are separate institutions. The Appendix, pages 236-45, gives a complete list of present-day zoos.

Zoos: Alphabetical List

Adelaide: animal behavior research at, 203; breeding of monotremes

and marsupials, 99, 224; Javan rhinoceros in, 132
Amsterdam, 81; area of, 169; breeding at, 100, 105; Blaauw-Jan Menagerie, *50,* 51
Angers, menagerie at, 160
Antwerp, 208; architecture of, 162; area of, 169; breeding at, 94, 100, 105; Hawaiian goose at, 121; housing of apes at, 182; white rhinoceros at, 142
Argentine, 10
Arizona-Sonora Desert Museum, 224, *225*
Arnhem, pheasant breeding at, 94
Askaniya-Nova (Russia), 61, 224; experiments with deer, *72*
Australia: breeding in Australian zoos, 105

Baltimore, 54
Bako Orang Utan Park, *115*
Barcelona, 10; "African Plains" exhibit at, *169;* architecture of, 162; area of, 169; bear pits at, *157;* marineland at, 215; pheasant breeding at, 94; autopsy at, *195;* sample diets at, *199*
Basel, 40, 60, 68, 83; breeding of: gorilla, 91; Hawaiian goose, 121; pigmy hippopotamus, 106
Belvédère menagerie (Savoy), 48, *50;* stock given to Näugebäu, 48
Bergen, aquarium, 226-7
Berlin, *10,* 81; East Berlin, 105; West Berlin, 75, 83, 88, 208; architecture of, 161; area of, 169; breeding of: bovids, 98, echidna, 100, Hawaiian goose, 121, orang-utans, 117, first orangutan, 93; kitchens of, 182
Bern, bear-pits at, *48*
Blackpool Aquarium, 215
Bontebok National Park, South Africa, 128
Boråsparken, Sweden, *204*
Bourton-on-the-Water, Gloucestershire, 79, 219, *219*
Brighton Aquarium, 212
Bristol, *15,* 52, 72, 210; area of, 169; breeding at, *74,* 100; white tigers at, *155*
Bronx, *see* New York
Brookfield, *see* Chicago
Brooklyn, *see* New York
Buffalo, 54; breeding at, 105

Cairo, Giza Zoological Garden, 10; ancient menagerie at, 46
Caracas, 224
Cassinum, 32
Catskill Game Farm: breeding of: equines, 99, ungulates, 194, 217
Central Park, *see* New York
Chantilly-Vineuil, *44,* 46, *46,* 160-1, *160-1;* experiments in "acclimatization" at, 47
Charlottenlund Aquarium, 226, *227*
Chessington, macaw bred at, *79*
Chester: anthrax at, 195; elephant enclosure, *194*
Chicago: Brookfield, *16,* 210; architecture of, 162; area of, 169; aviary, 179; housing of apes at, 182; Lincoln Park, 19, 54
China, 27
Cincinnati, 54, 110

Clères (France), 120-1, 217
Cleveland, 54, 83
Cologne, area of, 169, 183
Colorado Springs, 83; breeding orangutans at, 117
Columbus, gorilla bred at, 91
Constantinople, menagerie at, 46
Copenhagen: Hawaiian goose at, 121; musk-ox at, 210; Sumatran rhinoceros at, *19*
Cuba, 10; Quinta Palatino chimpanzee colony, 87
Currumbin Bird Sanctuary, Australia, *79*
Cyprus, 41

Dallas, housing of apes, 182
Denver, 54
"Desert Ark" traveling zoo, *58*
Detroit, 183; breeding of orangutans at, 117
Dresden, menagerie at, 46, 48
Dublin, 52, 72, 210
Dudley, 210-1; housing of apes at, 182; kitchens, 182

Ebersdorf, menagerie at, 46, 48
Edinburgh, 210, *210*
Enoshima Aquarium, Japan, marineland, 215

Florida, Marineland, breeding of whales at, 212, *213*
Fontainebleau, menagerie at, 46
Fort Worth, James R. Record Aquarium, 215; reptiles, 210
Frankfurt-am-Main, 83, 85; area of, 169; after bombing, *185;* breeding of: chimpanzee, *85,* orangutan, 117, wallaby, 105; educational aids at, *12;* exotarium at, 183, *183;* hand-rearing a gorilla, *199;* housing at, *162-3, 166*

Garamba National Park, Congo, 144
Georgetown, 224
Ghent, 16th-century menagerie "Cour du Prince," *160*

Hague: private zoo of William IV of Orange houses first orangutan, 93
Hamburg: Hagenbeck Tierpark, 138, 151, 164, *165,* 166; African panorama at, 164; bombing of, 185; new architecture of, 164; Municipal zoo, bison in, 122
Hanover, gibbon enclosure, *84*
Healesville (Australia), 100; platypusary, *100*
Honsholredijk menagerie, earliest record of chimpanzee in zoo, 86
de Hoop Game Farm, South Africa, 128

Islamorada Aquarium, Florida, 215

Jerusalem Biblical Zoo, 219-21

Kansas City, 10
Karlsburg, menagerie at, 46-7
Kew Gardens bird menagerie, 52
Khartoum, fauna in, 221, *222*
Knowsley Park (England), 56, 108, *118-9;* Hawaiian goose at, 120
Kruger National Park, white rhinoceros in, 143

Kyle Game Reserve (S. Rhodesia), white rhinoceros in, 143

Leckford (England), 121, 152; pheasant breeding at, 94
Lincoln Park, *see* Chicago
Lisbon, architecture of, 162
London, Regent's Park, 12, *55,* 61, 71, 94, 144-5, 150, 166, 208, 211-2; aims of, 55; animals in: bison, *122,* chimpanzee, 86, 88, echidna, 100, elephant "Jumbo," *152-3,* gray squirrel, 188, Hawaiian goose, 120-1, orangutan, 93, panda, 126, 154, passenger pigeon, 108, thylacine,`103, white rhinoceros, 142; aquarium, 175, 177; area of, 166-7; architecture of, 162, 173, *173;* aviary at, *56,* 174, 179, *179,* 180, 182; bombing of, 185; cat house, *174;* education at, *233, 235;* elephant house, 63, *180;* Ethology Station, 193, 196; expenditure, 17 (on food), 200; Fellows' restaurant, 177; finances of, 177, 179; foundation of, 56; gardens, *16;* giraffe house, *178;* hospital and sick-bay, *14, 177,* 208; lion house, *174;* Mappin Terraces, 166, 175, *175;* monkey house, *56;* parrot house, 75, *75;* penguin pool, *176;* quarantine station at, 193, 196; rebuilding of, 174-5, *176,* 177-80, *178-9,* 182, 183; reptile house, 182; royal charter granted, 56; stock, 134: purchase of, 135, valuation of, 154, 156-7; television from, 232; tortoise house, 175
Lsokop Dam Reserve, Transvaal, white rhinoceros in, 143

Madrid, 52
Manchester, 63
Manila, 82
Marineland of the Pacific, *see* Palos Verdes
Matopos National Park, Southern Rhodesia, 143
Melbourne, breeding of monotremes and marsupials, 99
Memphis, 10
Mexico City, 10
Miami Seaquarium, 215
Milwaukee, 183, 210; cat house, *182*
Morecombe, Marineland, 215
Morocco, 50
Moscow, 10, 122; expenditure, 17; panda in, 126
Munich, *73,* 151; area and layout, 169; breeding of bovids at, 98
Murchison Falls National Park, white rhinoceros translocated to, 143
Museums: El-Djem Museum of Antiquities, *30;* Monaco Oceanographical Museum, 215; Naples, National Museum, *29;* Sarawak Museum, *114;* Singapore, Raffles Museum, 55; Tucson, Arizona-Sonora Desert Museum, 224, *225*

Naples: Aquarium, 228-31, *230;* Research and Quarantine Station, 192, *192-3;* architecture of, 162; zoo, 83, 99

Näugebäu, menagerie, 46, 48
New York City: Bronx, 148, *158*,
183, 208, 231; area of, 169;
breeding of guerezas at, 83;
feeding time at, *64;* orangutan at,
116; platypusary, 100; purchase
of stock, 135; special programs,
231-2; waterbirds, 210; Brooklyn,
215, 228; Central Park, 10, 54, *54*
Nuremberg: bombing of, 185;
orangutan at, 93

Oklahoma City Zoo, ungulate
enclosure, *158*
Ornamental Pheasant Trust,
Norfolk, England, 94, *95,* 216
Osmaston Manor, Derby, wapiti at,
187

Paignton, 94
Palos Verdes, Marineland of the
Pacific, *144,* 212, *212-3, 215*
Paris: Jardin des Plantes, 52, *53,* 55;
Parc Zoologique, Vincennes, 166,
199; The Louvre, menagerie at,
46-7; St. Pol menagerie, 169; the
Tuileries, menagerie, 46; Versailles,
menagerie, documentation at, 48,
49, 161
Peakirk, 211
Peking, 10, 125-6
Philadelphia, 54, *54,* 82, *82,* 152;
Carolina parakeet at, 110; echidna
at, 100; gorilla at *90;* opossum at,
102; orangutan at , 93
Phoenix, Arizona, oryx at, 133
Plymouth Aquarium, *228*
Pohakuloa, Hawaii, Goose Farm,
117, 121
Port of Spain, 224
Prague: menagerie at, 46, 48, 94, 200;
dodo at, 110; Przewalski's horses
at, *20*
Pretoria, 98, 142, *142,* 221-2, *223*

Quinta Palatino chimpanzee
colony, *see* Cuba

Ravenglass Bird Sanctuary,
Cumberland, *200*
Rio de Janeiro, 224
Rome: antelopes at, 210;
architecture of, 162; area of,
169; aviary, 179
Rotterdam, breeding at: Hawaiian
goose, 121, orangutan, *116,* 117,
pheasant, 94

St. Gallen, menagerie, 158
St. Germain, menagerie, 46
St. James's Park, 52, 96, *96*
St. Louis, 19, 54, 142; aviary, 179;
TV programs, 232
San Diego, 10, 54, 63, 210; area of,
169; aviary at, 71, 179; Scripp's
aviary, *70;* bird incubators, 94;
breeding at, 100, 105; breeding
of: chimpanzees, 88, condor,
106, *107,* 130, 172, guereza, 83,
koalas, 72, proboscis monkey,
83; bus tour of, *58;* echidna at,
100; escalators at, *211;* expenditure
of, 17; foundation of, 172 gorilla
enclosure at, *172;* layout of, 172;
monkeys at *83;* polar bear
enclosure, *71;* python at, *66;* sea
lion pool, *62;* Tasmanian devil at,

103; tiger enclosure at, *166;*
TV programs, 232; waterfowl
pools, *97*
San Francisco, 10, 72
Santiago, 224
São Paulo, 224
Saudi Arabia, 143
Savoy-Belvédère, *see* Belvédère
Schönbrunn, *see* Vienna
Skånes Djurpark, *see* Stockholm
Slimbridge, Gloucestershire, 97,
120, 152, 216; behavior studies at,
203-5; duck banding station, 171;
duck decoy at, *171;*
Hawaiian goose at, 121; layout
and site, 171
Sophia, 94
South Daytona Sea Zoo, 215
Stockholm: architecture of, 162;
bison in, 123; Skånes Djurpark,
Höör, 170-1, *170,* 221, *221*
Strasbourg, 105
Stuttgart, 63; architecture of, 161
Surabaja, breeding of proboscis
monkey, 83
Sweden, menagerie in, 46
Sydney: breeding of: monotremes
and marsupials, 100, 224,
orangutans, 117

Tama, Japan, *208;* breeding of
pheasants at, 94
Tananarive, 81, 223-4
Tel Aviv University, 60, 78, 203
Tokyo, 10, 208; housing of apes at,
182
Toledo, Ohio, 14
Tower of London, menagerie, in
1820, *41*
Tring Park, private zoo, 188

Udjing Kulong Reserve (Java), *131*
Umfolozi Game Reserve
(Zululand), white rhinoceros in,
128-9, *142;* translocated from, 143

Vienna, Schönbrunn, 48, 50, 51, *51,*
52, 161
Vietnam (South), 10
Vineuil, *see* Chantilly

Washington: National Aquarium,
54; National Zoological Park,
10, 54, 210; area of, 169; gorilla
bred at, 91; pigmy hippopotamus
at, 106; white rhinoceros at, 142
Wassenaar, aviary at, 179, *217*
Wellington, 100
West Nile Reserve, translocation
of rhinoceros from, 143
Whipsnade, 79; breeding of:
deer, 189, Hawaiian goose, 121,
wallabies, 105; cost of food at,
200; layout of, 169-71
Wildfowl Trust, *see* Slimbridge
Woburn Park: bison at, *123-5;*
breeding of: deer, 189, Père
David's deer, 124, pheasants,
94; wallabies, 105; gray squirrel at,
188; parrot aviary, 75
Woodstock (Oxfordshire),
menagerie of Henry I at, 40-1;
moved to London by Henry III, 41

Yellowstone National Park, 52

Zürich: ape housing at, 182;
gibbon house, *71*

Credits